THE LIMITED HERO

IN

THE NOVELS OF FORD MADOX FORD

The Limited Hero
in The Novels of
Ford Madox Ford

by
NORMAN LEER

MICHIGAN STATE UNIVERSITY PRESS
1966

Copyright © 1966

Michigan State University Press

Library of Congress Catalog Card Number: 66-23084

Manufactured in the United States of America

For

Dad, Lil and Ron

Contents

Preface ix

1. The Importance and Direction of Heroism in Ford's Thought 1
    Recent Interest in Ford
    The Uniqueness of Ford
    Three Biographical Factors
    The Artist and the "Small Producer"
    The Pre-War World

2. The Early Novels and the Ineffectual Hero 25
    The Hero and Ford's Technique
    The Significance of the Early Novels
    Past and Present: The Historical Novels
    The Early Heroes and the Pre-War World
    The Hero Satirized

3. Heroism and Responsibility in *The Good Soldier*: The End of a Phase 68
    The Significance of the Novel
    The Question of Genre
    Structure and Technique
    The Major Figures and the Double View
    The Novel's Climax: Passion and Convention

4. Heroism and Responsibility in the Tietjens Novels: A New Beginning 105
    The Hero and the First World War
    The Politician as Hero
    The Marsden Case: The Victorian Politician and the War
    The Purpose of the Tietjens Novels
    Parade's End and the Critics
    Some Do Not
    No More Parades
    A Man Could Stand Up
    The Last Post

5. The Late Work and the Limited Hero 160
   Dichotomy and Intention in Ford's Late Work
   The Shift in Ford's Role
   No Enemy: A Momentary Calm
   The Final Novels
   The Answer of the "Travel" Books

6. A Concluding Estimate 211

   A Working Bibliography 220
   1. Books by Ford 220
   2. Writings in Periodicals by Ford 226
   3. Books with Contributions by Ford 230
   4. Translations by Ford 231
   5. Periodicals Edited by Ford 231
   6. Books about Ford 231
   7. Writings about Ford in Periodicals 233

Preface

This study is an attempt to isolate an important factor in the work of a novelist who has only recently begun to receive his due critical attention. As a writer, Ford Madox Ford was extremely prolific, noticeably uneven, and in his own way centrally involved in the historical currents of his time. His development of the "public hero" and of the "limited hero" as a private alternative was a reaction, at least in part, to the conditions of the post-Victorian period and the first four decades of the twentieth century, albeit a reaction very much shaped by his own particular point of view. An examination of this development and of the techniques through which it evolved—particularly the use of the double perspective by which the public hero was to be both admired and condemned—will reveal a unity and pattern in all of Ford's work that has not yet been perceived.

Although it is hoped that this study will be self-explanatory, one small technical matter requires comment. One of the means used by Ford to gain the desired tone of personal impression in his autobiographies, late "travel" books, and some of the novels was the use of ellipses. In order to distinguish Ford's use of this device from my own as an indication of textual omission, I have enclosed those ellipses which are his in parentheses.

Whatever success this study has achieved owes much to the help and interest of many people. I have received invaluable information and commentary from T. Barton Akeley and Joseph Brewer, both of whom knew Ford personally, David D. Harvey of the University of Washington, Joseph Pequigney of the State University of New York at Stony Brook, and Richard M. Ludwig of Princeton. Useful material and additional information have been given me by Robert W. Mitchner, Donald J. Gray and William R. Cagle, all of Indiana University. Mrs. Janice Biala Brüstlein, a close acquaintance of Ford during his last years, has generously answered my queries about Ford's late political views and also sent a description of his last, unfinished novel. Without the secretarial help of Marion Stein, Cecelia Grimm, Carol Schneider and Agnes Elpers and the expert editorial help of the Michigan State University Press staff, this work could never have taken its final shape. And above all, for his direction, commentary, and encouragement, both intellectual and emotional, I should like to express my warmest thanks to my good friend, Professor Alan M. Hollingsworth of Indiana University, without whom this work would never have been at all.

N. L.

THE LIMITED HERO

IN

THE NOVELS OF FORD MADOX FORD

1.

The Importance and Direction of Heroism in Ford's Thought

EVER SINCE 1950, when the Tietjens tetralogy under the title of *Parade's End* received its first one-volume publication, there has been a marked upsurge of interest in the writings of Ford Madox Ford. In England, Graham Greene is directing a project to reissue all of Ford's works, and Ford scholarship has been given fresh impetus by the recent publication of important critical works along with David Harvey's very complete descriptive bibliography. Other studies have been promised, and some have already appeared in partial form. Such an increased interest in Ford indicates that he is now being taken seriously in his own right, and is no longer dismissed as the writer who collaborated with Joseph Conrad and who, on his own, produced a vast number of uneven novels and reminiscences. The growth of Ford scholarship is testimony to his uniqueness as a writer, and at the same time a sign that the provocative nature of his ideas is gaining greater recognition.

As a thinker, Ford was acutely conscious of the collapse of the Victorian world as well as of the violent and unstable years which followed. He viewed the Victorian period and its aftermath in terms of figures, such as Ruskin or Carlyle, whom he saw as public heroes and whom he blamed for their tendency toward verbal abstractions at the expense of effectiveness in countering the breakdown of their world. Partly because of his preoccupation with the failure of the Great Victorians, Ford came to see not only the Victorian era but the world during his lifetime in terms of the heroic figure. In his eyes, the Victorian idealists were supplanted—in the years before the First World War—by leaders who were without values and who themselves reflected the corruption of their society. These nominal aristocrats, in turn, gave way to the politicians, who were equally cynical and without values, but who were also a far greater threat to society by virtue of the power at their disposal. Finally, during the nineteen-thirties the emerging political dictators gave this power a new and especially violent expression. All of these heroic figures were characterized by Ford by their evasion of actual problems, by their veiling of this evasion in heroic rhetoric, and by their increasing reflection of the corrupt society which they were supposed to lead. The sense of a world that was falling apart under the burden of a misdirected and evasive

heroism became one of the dominant motifs in Ford's work, but it was a motif that was given complexity by the author's proposal of an alternative and by the dual nature of his response, to at least the idealistic hero.

All the while that he condemned the existing public figure, Ford also acknowledged and even emphasized the need of his society for moral leadership. And it was the recognition of this need that caused him to take a noticeably double attitude toward the hero. Even as he drew the paralysis of his verbal idealists, Ford acknowledged their superiority to the world around them; and he condemned the more corrupt heroes just because they had renounced their function of significant leadership. The portrayal of such complex figures required that Ford develop a technique which would register his double attitude, and which would render the simultaneous dignity and ineffectiveness of his major characters. Concentration on these public heroes, along with the use of the double perspective, and the gradual movement toward the alternative of private heroism became the distinctive features of Ford's work, and a study of these features should help to clarify his special place in the world of late nineteenth and twentieth-century letters.

Despite their importance, the thematic development of the hero in Ford's work, his underlying double attitude, and his gradual movement toward a private ideal have received almost no critical attention. Even those critics who have acknowledged the hero as a central element in his novels have simplified Ford's position, and have seen his work as a regretful portrayal of a waning aristocracy in its final phase. Such an interpretation, as we shall see, has often led critics to praise certain Ford heroes to a degree that is out of proportion to their characteristics as presented in the novels themselves. Moreover, it has left the impression of a narrow social and political partisanship that does little justice to Ford's complexity as a thinker.

Richard Cassell, a representative critic, contends that Ford "discovered the true focus for his picture of life in the trials of the gentleman of honor," and that "The early novels like those that follow them, offer various portraits of the chivalric ideal. Usually the gentlemen who possess the soul of honor are contrasted with those who do not and with those who fall somewhat between the two extremes." This aristocratic hero, Cassell goes on, "is a determined but not stodgy defender of the fine traditions of his class, his party, and his nation, for he realizes they give him the assurance of knowing where he stands when moral decisions face him." Cassell grants that Ford's heroic protagonists are sometimes "out of tune with their times," but he feels that this merely results in their seeming somewhat quixotic.[1] Cassell does not recognize the degree of blame that Ford placed on his gentlemen of honor for the very social breakdown that left them figuratively tilting windmills.

IMPORTANCE OF HEROISM IN FORD'S THOUGHT

Writing in a similar vein, Walter Allen argues that "In the midst of tribulation Ford can only put forward a code of conduct: the facade of civilized life must be preserved at all costs." This "facade" was actually, in novels such as *The Good Soldier*, one of Ford's major targets; but Allen goes on to assert that characters such as George Moffat of *The Benefactor* or Edward Ashburnham, the "good soldier" himself, "define the essential Ford character and also, one suspects from the evidence of his non-fictional works, his own conception of himself: The English gentleman—Ford sometimes called him the Tory—for whom money exists only in order that others may be helped, who neither explains his actions nor apologizes for them, who follows his code without question and in full knowledge of the consequences, which are inevitably that his motives will be misunderstood and that he will be betrayed by those whom he had befriended. He suffers, but he suffers in silence." Allen also sees Christopher Tietjens, who by the end of the *Parade's End* tetralogy grows into a limited hero, as a simple duplication of Moffat and Ashburnham, and thus fails to perceive the distinction between the conventional public hero and Ford's later private counterpart.[2] Another critic, Frank Macshane, finds a "pattern" that remains "much the same in all" of Ford's novels: the typical Fordian hero is an altruist, and he is pitted against "a world run on the principles of dog-eat-dog. And if this selfish world carries on as it is accustomed to, there will be more and more chaos and eventually, one final Armageddon."[3]

If Cassell, Allen and Macshane give a one-sided picture of the Fordian hero, two other critics who see Ford as the spokesman for a dying Tory faction over-simplify not only his view of the hero, but his ideas on politics and society as well. They suggest a partisan affiliation not to be found in the works themselves. R. P. Blackmur suggests that "If there is an image upon which Hueffer's [Ford's] sensibility can be seen to declare its own force it is an image of devotion to lost causes known to be lost . . . which is why he had to be facile, and why he could not supply his novels with the materials for judgement."[4] Another variation of this same critical approach is advanced by Morton Dauwen Zabel when he contends that there is a basic "uncertainty of motive" in Ford's work as a whole and that this uncertainty "may be traced at least partly to his inability to resolve and localize his aesthetic and civil morals." Zabel goes on to argue that while Ford "was hospitable to revolt and insurgence in the creative order," he remained in his social views " 'a sentimental Tory,' " and this conflict, Zabel adds, resulted in an "irresolution that denied his work conviction and a center."[5]

By far the best writing on Ford to date is that of John A. Meixner, a critic highly sensitive to the qualities of anguish and complexity in the novelist's work. But Meixner, for all his acute perceptiveness, fails to provide a detailed discussion of *Parade's End*, which he dismisses rather

superficially. Like Blackmur and Zabel, Meixner also regards Ford himself as "emotionally committed to the values of a life he recognized to be dying—a life feudal, agrarian, local, scaled to human size," and directly antithetical to "the industrialized, giant, impersonal society which was emerging to take its place."[6] Meixner's sense of Ford's commitment to the old values is so strong that it leads him to dismiss the last three Tietjens novels, in which the protagonist changes from a public to a private hero, as unnecessary.

It is evident, then, that critical interpretation of Ford has been very favorably inclined toward his aristocratic protagonists. But such an attitude presents a partial and distorted picture of the author's work; for while the conventional hero is definitely a key figure, and even receives partial assent, he is modified by a complexity of attitude and a development of alternatives that are central to Ford's thought throughout his life.

The presentation of a declining aristocracy and the theme of social decay are hardly limited to Ford's work. In varying forms, they are a preoccupation of much of the literature of the nineteenth and twentieth centuries. What is peculiar to Ford is the consistent recurrence of this preoccupation throughout his work and the complex perspective with which it is handled. In retrospect, Ford's life and writing can be divided into three periods: the years before the First World War, years which marked the breakdown of the Victorian world; the actual War, which was the culmination of this breakdown; and finally, the period from the end of the First World War to the beginning of the Second, a span of time which saw the emergence of the political dictator and the full development of Ford's alternative, the limited hero. Artistically, the period before the First World War received its strongest rendering in *The Good Soldier*, a novel which brought to fruition the sense of breakdown that had dominated Ford's earlier work, but which also displayed for the first time with any fullness, the complexities of the double perspective, and achieved thereby a dimension that was only suggested in the earlier novels. The mood of the War experience itself and its effect on the conventional hero was caught most intensively by Ford in the Tietjens tetralogy, which also embodied the first comprehensive development of his notion of the limited hero. Finally, in the years following the War, this private hero came more and more to dominate Ford's thought.

During each of these major periods, Ford tended to define the world around him in terms of the hero. The ineffectual idealist, who was too detached from society, and the corrupt and often cynical hero, who was too immersed in it, became for Ford embodiments of the central problems of the post-Victorian world, in which he found both a growing corruption and an absence of really relevant ideals. Similarly, the politician and the dictator, both of whom Ford regarded as extensions of the corrupt

hero, received the brunt of the novelist's blame for the horrors of the First World War and its aftermath. All of these heroes were marked by their blindness to the real problems around them. Instead of providing a consistent leadership by which these problems might be solved, they retreated behind a cloud of rhetoric and either stepped back into their small and private worlds, or else set up an illusory world, built on their own power (which of course made the illusion real) and marked by an increase of cynicism, corruption, evasion of central issues, and even violence.

Finding the public hero hopeless, Ford felt that he had to propose an alternative, and this was the basis for his increasingly open advocacy of the limited hero. If the public hero was identifiable by his evasive rhetoric, Ford's private figure was noticeable for his strict avoidance of the rhetorical mode and of all moral tendentiousness. If the politician and the dictator were marked by the increasingly large public domain in which they acted, Ford's hero was characterized by a carefully restricted range of operation. The limited hero was thus intentionally circumscribed in two respects: first, he did not attempt to formulate and verbalize a general morality, but hoped rather to teach by his own example; and secondly, his direct sphere of influence was confined to his own immediate life. In both these respects the limited hero came to epitomize a subdued and private response to the world that was in direct contrast to the brassy exterior of his more conventional public counterpart.

The emergence and development of the limited hero in Ford's writing involved an aspect of technique that has never been given attention by his critics. This technique—that of the double perspective—was Ford's way of registering his complex response to the public hero, and later became a way of differentiating this conventional figure from the "limited" counterpart. The double perspective, by which the heroic figure was shown in all his aspects, both good and bad, arose from Ford's interpretation of the Victorian period, and it became in his greatest novels a means of achieving psychological dimension, and even a tragic point of view. At the same time that Ford condemned a figure such as Edward Ashburnham in *The Good Soldier*, he was able to suggest a mute and perverted dignity which imparted depth to his hero and placed him in a position of relative superiority to a world that was even more corrupt than himself. This double perspective, although partly evident in the novels preceding *The Good Soldier*, received its strongest expression in that novel and in the Tietjens tetralogy, where through a skillful manipulation and diminishing of this perspective, Ford was able to suggest Tietjens' change from a conventional to a limited hero. During the nineteen-thirties, Ford's sense of the world around him grew so pessimistic, and his desire to offer the limited hero as a solution grew so intense, that the double attitude split in two; and while the late novels became almost wholly critical pictures of their

society, the author's non-fiction assumed a markedly didactic tone through which the limited hero was given a full and urgent affirmation.

Except during this final decade of his life, however, and particularly in the years up to and including the writing of the Tietjens tetralogy, Ford's response to the conventional hero remained complex, and the double perspective remained intact as an expression of this complexity. As the conditions he found so undesirable continued, however, to grow, Ford's response, compounded of profound regret and sometimes strong aversion, finally led him to propose the alternative of limited heroism as an answer to a crumbling world.

Ford's ultimate advocacy of the limited hero can be traced in part to three factors in his life: first, his strong aversion to the Great Victorians; second, his growing conviction that the life of the artist and the "Small Producer" offered a meaningful alternative to the ineffectiveness of these public heroes; and third, his sense of the breakdown and corruption of pre-War society. To fully understand the development of Ford's fiction and to grasp the importance of his pre-War novels, it is necessary to isolate these factors, to fix them briefly in his life, and then to examine each in detail. His non-fiction, and especially his autobiographical works provide considerable insight into the development of all three of these strains in his thought, and are therefore significant in clarifying the ideas expressed in his novels.

The facts of Ford's life are well known, and can be readily summarized. He was born in London in 1873, the son of Doctor Franz Hueffer and Catherine Brown. His father was a music critic of German birth, and was also a student of medieval Provençal culture, an interest which he passed on to his son. His mother was the daughter of the pre-Raphaelite painter, Ford Madox Brown, who took in and supported Ford after the elder Hueffer's death in 1889. The boy's father had been a great friend of William Morris, and Ford himself was a nephew of William Rossetti. Thus, his connection with the intellectual leaders of the late Victorian period was from the first intimate and personal. Schooling and the years before the War were outwardly uneventful, save for a few key episodes. One was Ford's entry into the Catholic Church in 1891, at the age of eighteen, an entry made under family pressure and toward which Ford's attitude remained ambivalent throughout his life. Another was his marriage to Elsie Martindale in 1894, a premature elopement brought on by interference from both families. This marriage, faltering from the start, collapsed in 1910. In that year, Ford met Violet Hunt, an active social figure in London's intellectual world. He tried to obtain a divorce and marry her in Germany, by claiming German citizenship from his father's side, but was unsuccessful. He consequently moved into Miss Hunt's home, South Lodge, as an ostensible lodger, and stayed officially until 1919. Actually, the couple had pretty much fallen apart by the outbreak

of the War; and towards the end Miss Hunt even began to slander him among her friends by starting rumors of his German sympathies. Scandal came when his wife sued for libel those papers which printed Miss Hunt's references to herself as Mrs. Ford, and the ensuing uproar made complete Ford's separation from conventional society.

Actually, all through his early years Ford had already placed himself apart by his growing identification with the arts. Central to this identification were his acquaintanceship with Joseph Conrad, begun in 1897, with Henry James, Stephen Crane, Ezra Pound, and other leading figures of the literary world; his editorship of the *English Review* from 1909 to 1911; and his growing rejection of English society. The War, in which he served as an officer from 1915 to 1918, seemed to him simply the culmination of a long social collapse, and soon after it was over, he became first a physical and then a national expatriate from English life.

From 1919 to 1922 he placed himself apart as a small farmer in Sussex. He had met, and now lived with Stella Bowen, a young Australian artist. But his sense of isolation from his native country and his growing attraction to France led the pair in 1922 to leave England forever. In 1923 they were in Paris, where Ford edited the short-lived but important *transatlantic review*. The years immediately following were creatively fruitful and saw the production of the Tietjens books. In 1928 Ford and Stella Bowen parted with no regrets, neither desiring a permanent union; and the final decade of his life was spent with another painter, Janice Biala. This last decade was marked by a growing sense of despair on Ford's part over the political world, which he saw as clearly careening toward a second war, and an increasing urgency in his advocacy of the "Small Producer" as an alternative. These final years were spent in Provence, with the exception of a few financially-necessary lecture tours. Death came in June, 1939, just before the outbreak of the second European conflagration, which he so feared and which he saw clearly in its coming.

Ford's own recollections, particularly of his early years, give more insight than the mere biographical facts.

As can be seen from his family connections, he was from early childhood surrounded by the awesome figures who daily passed through his grandfather's house. Urged to strive to their heights, he was, instead, terrified by them. In an essay on the Great Victorians, Ford related how his early encounters with these men had been recalled in the fear which he felt of being captured by the Germans during the War. He doubted that his "imagined Germans would have taken just that gigantic miching and mowing shape if it hadn't been for the nature of my childhood ambience. I was then horribly imbued by those people with a sense of my Original Sin so that I used to have innumerable fears when the candle was put out (....)" As a boy he feared that "Mr. Ruskin or Mr. Carlyle or Mr. Holman Hunt—or even Herr Richard Wagner! should with their

dreadful eyes come into a room when I was alone and where there was no other exit (. . .)."[7] The constant exposure to the talents of the Great Victorians, the awe in which they were held by his parents, their self-declared genius and morality alongside of his father's reference to him as a "donkey," all these combined to impress upon Ford a constant feeling of inferiority, and a constant resentment toward the dominant Victorians who forced upon him this sense of guilt.[8]

But while Ford derived from his father's invectives a strong sense of his own unworthiness, he also acquired through Dr. Hueffer the first inklings of the glories of Provençal culture. The Doctor had published at the age of twenty-four a critical edition of the works of Guillem de Cabestanh, a twelfth-century troubadour. Nine years later, in 1878, he published a more ambitious work, *The Troubadours; A History of Provencal Life and Literature in the Middle Ages*. In 1880 he lectured on troubadours at the Royal Institution, and in 1887 he produced, in conjunction with A. C. Mackenzie an opera, *The Troubadours*, which had de Cabestanh as its hero. Douglas Goldring suggests, and Ford himself also acknowledges, that the elder Hueffer "undoubtedly passed on his passion for Provence to his eldest son." This interest led Ford to translate, at the age of "eleven or twelve," poems by de Cabestanh as well as by the German Minnesinger, Walther von der Vogelweide.[9]

His childhood dislike of the Victorians remained with Ford, into the war years, and affected more than his fear of being taken prisoner by the Germans. He served as an officer in the British Army from 1915 through 1918, and this experience only increased his sense of the disintegration of the old order. In particular he felt, and was to convey in the Tietjens novels, a lack of communications between the civilian leaders and the soldiers at the front. Most of the decisions emanating from Whitehall bore little relation to the reality of the battle-lines, and this gap only added to Ford's dislike of the politician and helped to toughen his sense of independence. After the War, and before leaving England for good, he returned briefly and took up the life of the "Small Producer." In 1919 he wrote to one of his few political friends, the Liberal Minister, C. F. G. Masterman that he had taken "a labourer's cottage in the country where I am still." He added that he had just changed his surname to Ford, as he did not wish "to be put up with the inconvenience that a Teutonic patronymic causes," and he also noted that he had "made a rather beautiful garden with the work of my own unaided hands, and I subsist rather largely on its products."[10] A combination of unfortunate personal circumstances and the disillusioning experience of the War had led him now to assume the self-sufficient life of the "Small Producer." But while the limited hero became for Ford both a personal way of life and a controlling idea in his later work, this development was anticipated not only by the earlier circumstances of his own life; such as his first taste of country

life in 1897, but also by his rejection of the Victorian public hero in most of his work up to the outbreak of the War.

Throughout his life, Ford consistently saw the Victorian period in terms of the Great Man; and his numerous autobiographical works, in which he could speak more directly than in his fiction, provided a constant verification of the attitudes expressed in the novels. Ford's chronicle of himself was begun in 1911 with *Ancient Lights*, resumed in 1921 with *Thus to Revisit*, and again in 1932 with *Return to Yesterday*. It was also continued in *It Was the Nightingale* in 1933, and in the 1937 volume, *Portraits From Life;* and fragments of autobiography appear as well in the volumes of criticism and "travel."[11] In any examination of Ford's memoirs it is necessary to keep in mind Ford's tendency to color and exaggerate details. Herbert Gorman in a personal reminiscence recalls that Ford "fabricated and elaborated his life as assiduously as he fabricated and elaborated his books. Both were almost the same to him."[12] And Richard Aldington recalls how Ford once told Aldington's father of a meeting with Lord Byron,[13] who had died almost fifty years before Ford's birth. Goldring remembers his visiting Ford in Paris in 1927, when the latter was fabricating for himself a past that included schooling at Eton as well as the Sorbonne.[14]

Yet Ford's "assumed personal and dramatized selves," may have been, as Richard Cassell suggests, part of his "life-long search in both art and life for serenity."[15] Relevant here are Ford's strong sense of inferiority, inherited from his childhood, as well as his feeling of a lack of values in the world. It may even be that despite his denigration of the public hero, Ford felt the need to create for himself a strong personality, which could claim an Eton education and acquaintance with Lord Byron, in order to create for himself a private hero who would offset the seeming impotence of the public one. Stella Bowen, who lived with Ford during the nineteen-twenties, comments on the sense of disproportion between his complex personality and its external frame:

> The stiff, rather alarming exterior and the conventional omniscient manner, concealed a highly complicated emotional machinery . . . it produced an effect of tragic vulnerability; tragic because the scope of his understanding and the breadth of his imagination had produced a great edifice which was plainly in need of more support than was inherent in the structure itself. A walking temptation to any woman, had I but known it.[16]

And Douglas Goldring suggests that Ford's fabrication of an Eton background was an attempt to emulate the type of the country gentleman epitomized for him by Arthur Marwood, whom he greatly admired, and who served as the model for Christopher Tietjens.[17] All questions of attempted heroism aside, Ford himself admitted quite frequently the fac-

tual inaccuracy of his memoirs. He claimed, that he wished to capture not the facts but the proper "impression" of an incident or person. The limited and subjective truth of the particular artist was to him more important than any attempt at objective truth, and in examining Ford's autobiographical writings, we shall therefore take his impressions at face value as embodiments of the attitudes he wanted to convey.

In *Ancient Lights* (significantly called in its American edition *Memories and Impressions*) Ford gave his fullest and most nearly contemporary picture of the Great Victorians. In the dedication to his two daughters, Christina and Katherine, he declared his intent to compare his impressions of the world of the Victorians and those of the present day. The present world, he said, "is not the world of twenty-five years ago, but it is a very good world. It is not so full of the lights of individualities, but it is not so full of shadows for the obscure."[18]

Thus Ford established the sense of guilt and inferiority which the presence of the Great Victorians had engendered in him as a child. *Ancient Lights* was pervaded by a sense of the great figures referred to in the title, and Ford saw these men in terms of their predominant trait—their moralizing:

> And it must be remembered that the great figure flourished and expanded not so much on account of his technical qualities as on account of his moral worth. The great figure was, as a rule a long-bearded person of a wind-blown aspect. He commanded respect—he insisted upon it—not because he was going to give pleasure by the beauty of his words or the music of his periods, but because he was a sort of moral alchemist. He cared relatively little whether he gave our fathers pleasure: he was going to solve the riddle of the universe. Upon the whole he was a rather disagreeable man, and if we are glad that we came into contact with such in some numbers during our early years, we are quite certain that we are much more glad that they no longer exist.[19]

It is interesting to see Ford here, as early as 1911, counterposing the role of the public hero against the idea of giving pleasure, a function which he reserved for the artist, and which was to become a central motif of his books during the nineteen-thirties. The tendency of the Victorian idealist to see everything in terms of a "higher morality" had cast a cloud of words over reality, thereby frequently reducing the moral to mere rhetoric. It was the rhetoric of Victorian morality, Ford believed, that had made a compromise with Victorian corruption and had done so by evading it. And the loss of this "higher morality" forced the individual to re-examine his own specific moral commitment: "We have not any longer our Ruskins, Carlyles, George Eliots, and the rest. We have in consequence very much more to work out our special cases for ourselves,

and we are probably a great deal more honest in consequence."[20] With the idea of a desirable individual responsibility, Ford was already beginning to shift the sphere of morality from the public to the private, and thereby to limit the nature of the heroic response.

Ford's most direct encounter with the Great Victorians had been through his childhood acquaintance with the Pre-Raphaelite Brotherhood. On the one hand, Ford strongly admired the members of this group, for he saw them as artists, held together by their strong "devotion to their art . . . against a world which very much did not want them."[21] Moreover, he saw the inner group of Pre-Raphaelites as serious practicing artists, too busy to bother with the aesthetic pose that was picked up by some of the outer circle of followers.[22] But for Ford the Pre-Raphaelites also combined the new aestheticism with vestiges of an older didacticism. They valued paintings as objects of beauty in themselves, but tried at the same time to give their paintings moral significance by frequently deriving a moral from an older, model work of art. In his critical study of the Pre-Raphaelites, Ford accorded the group recognition as serious artists by suggesting that they looked to the painters before Raphael out of an interest in rendering specific details as opposed to ideal types. This interest in rendering detail, according to Ford, made Pre-Raphaelism a forebearer of Impressionism, and placed it in opposition to the ideal-centered classicism of Sir Joshua Reynolds. But the Pre-Raphaelites, he concluded, differed from the Impressionists in their interest in didactic painting, and he pointed out that the attempt to impart a moral to their pictures often conflicted with their stated aims.[23] It was this didactic element that most disturbed Ford in their work, and that led him to place the Pre-Raphaelites among the ranks of the Victorian moralizers.

The form of exaggeration of which Pre-Raphaelism was most guilty was its idealization of the Middle Ages. The tendency of these artists to think "in terms of Florentine Art or Arthurian Romance" often led to a rendering of literature rather than real life.[24] Love was the sentiment most idealized by Rossetti and his group; and Ford contrasted the Pre-Raphaelite notion of love with the more specific medieval and modern varieties. He asserted that for the Pre-Raphaelites and romantics in general love was "a great but rather sloppy passion." It was something that "you swooned about on broad, general lines, your eyes closed, your arms outstretched. It excused all sins, it sanctified all purposes, and if you went to hell over it you still drifted about among snowflakes of fire with your eyes closed and in the arms of the object of your passion." By contrast, "Mediaeval people took their own individual cases on their own individual merits, and guilty love extracted some kind of retribution, very frequently painful, as often as not grotesque. Or sometimes there was not any retribution at all—a successful intrigue 'came off,' and became mate-

rial for a joyous *conte*. It was a matter of individual idiosyncrasies then as it is today."[25] Pre-Raphaelite love by contrast was an over-idealized and fuzzy passion, one that shielded its adherents from all sorts of imaginary surroundings, even Paolo and Francesca from the fires of hell. The lovers in Rossetti's picture are protected from the flames by their passion, which forms, "as it were, a moral and very efficient mackintosh over them." Ford concluded that "the Pre-Raphaelite view of mediaeval love was a very different thing from real mediaevalism. That was a state of things much more like our own."[26]

The greatest fault of the Brotherhood in its treatment of love was one which Ford attributed to idealists in general—an inability to take account of the nature of specific reality. Love, under this approach, was deified rather than observed. By way of contrast to these romantic generalizations, Ford found the poetry of Christina Rossetti, in its attention to little things, much closer to both the medieval and modern temperaments: "We have no longer any time to look out for the ultimate design. We have to face such an infinite number of little things that we cannot stay to arrange them in our minds, or to consider them as anything but accidents, happenings, the mere events of the day." Because, he said, "we can perceive no design," we are "thrown more and more in upon ourselves for comprehension of that which is not understandable," and "in this way we seem again to be returning to the empiricism of the middle ages."[27] In his view of Christina Rossetti, Ford expressed two themes which recur constantly in his work—the sense of the baffling complexity of the modern world, and his preference for coping with this reality on specific and empirical terms.

Much of the blame for the didacticism and exaggeration of the Pre-Raphaelites Ford placed upon Ruskin, the one Great Victorian who championed the group. He saw both Ruskin and Rossetti as romantics, "Rossetti with perhaps an over-sweetening of sensualism; Ruskin with undoubtedly a Puritanic over-strenuousness of moral purpose in his aesthetic teaching." Ruskin came to represent for Ford the Victorian moralizer, and as Ford drew him he was "an almost dangerously one-sided Old Man of the Sea of Art," who exercised a "continual falsification of aesthetic standards to give body to his ethical doctrine."[28] Ruskin, of course, regarded art as moral just because it depicted nature, which in itself had moral qualities. Ford and Ruskin differed in their basic ideas of where the morality of an object was to be found, in the rendering or in the thing rendered—but an additional reason for Ford's special dislike of the author of *Modern Painters* can be inferred when he speaks of Ruskin's neglect of his grandfather, Ford Madox Brown: "And this was at a time when Ruskin must have known that a word from him was sufficient to make the fortune of any painter."[29] While Ford seems to have harbored a personal resentment toward Ruskin, the latter also came to sym-

bolize for him the artist who subordinated his own art and that of others to a morality of cloudy rhetoric.

Another moral dogmatism more typical of the late Victorian period in its attempt to specify the ideal in a program of action, was the socialism developed by such figures as William Morris and the Webbs. In his caustic portrayal of Morris and his followers at Kelmscott House, Ford saw them as extentions of the Pre-Raphaelite tradition. He presented them as rather child-like and ridiculous, but all the same a threat because of their fervent attempts at social reform. Their mannerisms and ideas became an implied extension of earlier forms of Victorian morality. Ford remembered the Sunday afternoon meetings at Kelmscott House as rather quaint, almost make-believe gatherings:

> William Morris would stride up and down between the aisles, pushing his hands with a perpetual, irate movement through his splendid hair. And we, the young men with long necks, long, fair hair, protruding blue eyes, and red ties, or the young maidens in our blue curtain serge with our round shoulders, our necks made long as possible to resemble Rossetti drawings, uttered with rapt expressions long sentences about the Social Revolution that was just around the corner. We thought we were beautiful, we thought we were very beautiful; but Pre-Raphaelism is dead, aestheticism is dead. . . . It is dead, all dead, and that beautiful vision, the Social Revolution, has vanished along with the 'bus that used to run from the Langham hotel . . . to Charing Cross.[30]

Apart from being a mannerism, the socialist movement was also, in Ford's view, an attempt by the Pre-Raphaelite Brotherhood to institutionalize its standards of art: "They were convinced that once the world saw a Philip Webb-designed room filled with the mediaevally inspired furnishings from William Morris & Co., with a copy of the Kelmscott Press's Chaucer open on a reading pulpit. . . . Then man should stand in his doorway gazing out over great fields of golden-growing wheat and rejoice in the coming of the mediaeval social reform."[31]

The impression of childlike simplicity was repeated in Ford's picture of his grandfather and Morris, "under the shadow of a social revolution that I am sure my grandfather did not in the least understand, and that William Morris probably understood still less."[32] Thus, on the one hand, the socialist movement was seen by Ford as something of a plaything for artists, totally detached from reality, but at the same time as an attempt by these artists to make real their ideal way of life as a possible alternative to the world around them. Ford confessed that one day, while sitting in a French restaurant in Soho, he came to fear "that a temporal tyranny might be a bad thing, but that the intellectual tyranny that my young friends would set up when their social revolution came round the corner

... that this intellectual tyranny would be infinitely worse than anything that Ivan the Terrible could ever have devised."[33] And in the same vein, he amusingly related how once he "was approached by a deputation of Fabian members" and informed that the cloth cap he was wearing " 'stuck out' on their countryside. I was requested to abandon it."[34] Even after the First World War, Ford humorously pictured himself as plagued by Fabians, who "as has always been the case on hilltops, drifted about and seemed to regard me as a brand to be snatched from the forces of militarism and Teutophobia and to be turned into a whitened fingerpost on the roads toward Guild Socialism."[35] Ford's attitude toward these persistent groups of roving socialists was often expressed with humor, but beneath the tone one senses that while he may have seen them as childish, he nonetheless viewed their dogmatism with grave concern.

Clearly, Ford's disapproval of the Great Victorians was strong, and yet even his early writings reveal the double attitude toward the hero that was to characterize a work such as *The Good Soldier*. As Ford saw it, the Great Victorians, in spite of their rhetorical dogmatism, had nevertheless provided some standard of values, however mistaken these values might have been. But their world had simply bypassed their pronouncements, and was soon left without any standards at all. This decline was referred to again and again in Ford's discussions of England before the War. There was a noticeable ambivalence in his attitude which remained unresolved until he began to explore new types of heroism. In spite of his rejection of the Great Victorians, Ford himself decried the lack of a moral center in the world around him. Admittedly, in place of the Victorians there could now be seen the "prize-fighters, aviators, and performers for the cinema. But these scarcely fill in the departments of public morals and ethical codes the places that used to be occupied by Pericles, Cicero, and Lucius Junius Brutus."[36] The new popular heroes scarcely provided any reasons for the adulation they received.

Ironically, as Ford saw it, it was the Great Victorians themselves who were responsible for the collapse of their own world. They had removed themselves from the real conflicts of Victorian society, and thus became incapable of resolving them. Darwinism, for example, shook "severely all the traditional standards," and although the Victorian heroes of Darwin's time "functioned along the lines of those traditions, their priestly glamour vanished with the passing of themselves and their contemporaries." In the shadow of their retreat, they left only chaos.[37] True, the general population had extinguished the spirit of altruism; for "when, fairly effectively, they slew priestcraft and revealed religion, they scotched also several of the things for which priestcraft and revealed religion seemed to stand."[38] But the Victorian heroes, the Carlyles and Ruskins, were especially at fault through their loss of touch with Victorian reality and their ex-

pounding of their own tendentious ideals, to which few of the contemporaries of Darwin bothered to listen.

Ford went so far as to blame the Great Victorians for the First World War. Their dogmatism combined with an evasion of the encroaching materialism and self-interest of their age brought about a climate in which poison gas could be used to assert the self-interests of nations and individuals:

> Wouldn't, I mean, Poison Gas be just the sort of thing that, could they have invented it, the Ruskins and Carlyles and Wilberforces and Holman Hunts would have employed on their enemies or their blood brothers become rivals? So their Germanic disciples used it when their Day came. Inevitably! Because the dreadful thing about nineteenth-century Anglo-Saxondom was that it accepted with its bitter comfort-plus-opulence mania not merely itself but the entire, earnest, listening world. What effect could a serious and continued reading of those fellows have had but 1914? (. . .) And 193(. . . .)[39]

The linking of Ruskin and his group with the German users of poison gas was the climactic and most vehement point in Ford's indictment of the Victorian public hero. Poison gas was seen as a weapon of the hero, but of a highly corrupted one; and as Ford pointed out, the corrupted hero was part of a more corrupt society, which in turn corrupted the entire world. In this respect, it is interesting to note that in the same statement Ford referred to the Germans of the World War I period as "disciples" of the Great Victorians. He might have spoken in a historically loose and figurative manner, but the link is indicative of his attitude toward the Great Victorians and their legacy of large and ineffective words.

As an antidote to the empty rhetoric of the hero, Ford proposed the close and honest rendering of the concrete and the particular given by the artist, and especially by the novelist. Our civilization, as he saw it, had little solace left but the arts, and even the most materialistic of societies had to develop art if it was to sustain itself. Art was necessary because it could take man outside himself, to a detached vantage point from which he could gain some perspective of his own life and that of his fellows.[40] The function of the arts was then to educate, but not to preach a direct moral. Rather the artist placed before his audience, for observation, the possibilities of life: "the artist today is the only man who is concerned with the values of life; he is the only man who in a world grown very complicated through the limitless freedom of expression for all creeds and all moralities, can place before us how these creeds work out when applied to human contact, and to what goal of human happiness these moralities will lead us."[41] Art thus allowed both the artist and his audience to become aware of the complexities inherent in a given situation. This

orientation toward complexities and particulars was clearly opposed to the generalizing tendencies of the Great Victorians. Virtue was derived from art in the sense that the awareness of complexities allowed a moral choice that was based on the full sense of a concrete situation, and that remained aware of a partial sense of disillusionment, desirable for the very caution it imposed. The artist performed his service by showing "that Heaven on Earth is to be found only in the kind hearts of kindly men who have known disillusionment."[42] It was their distrust of abstract morality that caused the writers of Ford's circle—James, Conrad, Crane, and Hudson—to appear in Ford's eyes as "amoral" writers, interested in no other moral than the one Ford ascribed to Crane, "that if you jumped blind baggages to Hot Pan or got sunk in the Caribbean and had to swim ashore, you would one day come to be able to swat flies with the foresight of your gun—supposing your gun to have a foresight."[43]

In contrast to the Impressionist writers, whose goal of "amoral" rendering Ford strongly admired, there were the writers such as H. G. Wells, who often used their work to advance didactic programs, and who, as Ford saw them, accepted and glorified the new society of science and the machine. The factor in Wells's writing that most disturbed Ford, however, was not so much the advocacy of scientific progress, but the generally didactic tone—the moral rhetoric which Ford associated with the hero. Ford summarized his view in an amusing, if unfair, caricature of Wells's decision to write utopian novels, in which Wells appears to himself as a prophet of the future in military dress:

> By the quality of your writing and your quick brilliant touches you would make that imagined Future look so attractive that mankind would call on its statesmen and politicians to give them that sort of world and no other (. . . .) If you could do that you would indeed become the General Officer commanding the Forces of the Universe. You would shout to the world: 'Humanity will Advance by the Right! Move to the Right in Fours! Form F-O-U-R-S! (. . .) RIGHT!' (. . .) And humanity would do it.[44]

Ford's dismissal of Wells is inaccurate and cursory, but in a study of Ford's own attitudes what is important is that he viewed Wells as an heir to the Great Victorians. Like the Great Victorians, Wells met life with a rush of rhetoric; but unlike Ruskin and his contemporaries, he no longer paid verbal allegiance to the old moralities. His rhetoric was used to proselytize for the new scientific world. Wells and his group became for Ford the intellectual parents of the second type of public hero, the type that was to rule after the War. This sort of hero would be most often found among the bungling politicians, and would later achieve his most frightening embodiment in the totalitarian dictator. The politician was to become for Ford a figure of increasing stupidity, and in the works of the

nineteen-thirties he was finally depicted with something approaching blunt horror.

In 1897 Ford himself took up residence at Pent Farm, the house which he was later to lease to the Conrads. Even at this early stage in his career, the country came to represent for him a more specific, circumscribed, and self-sufficient way of life than he had found in the commercial cities; and the life of the "Small Producer" along with the artistic response, became basic antecedents of limited heroism. In 1906 Ford published *The Heart of the Country, A Survey of Modern Land*, a description of rural life, and part of a trilogy describing English life in general. Here he began to sketch out the virtues of the independent farmer: his persistence, his strong sense of liberty; his dominant individuality built on much suffering and achievement.[45] Here, too, he began to draw his admiring portraits of the pragmatic and stoic peasants, such as Meary Walker, whom he sketched again in 1932 in the autobiographical *Return to Yesterday*. Meary, Ford wrote, "kept on going all through life. She was always cheerful; she had always on her tongue some fragment of peasant wisdom."[46] There was even in these early writings a strong tone of respect for the country and its people, which contrasted with the ironic tone in which Ford presented their contemporaries, such as the followers of Ruskin and Morris. That this respect for the peasant persisted through Ford's life is clearly indicated by the passage on Meary Walker, and stronger evidence can be found in Ford's later development of the "Small Producer."

In the early *The Heart of the Country*, almost as a fore-shadowing of his later works, the author proposed a utopia, built around a society of small independent field-laborers who were "the basis, the bed-rock upon which the social fabric of our country must rest." In this ideal society, noticeably unorganized for a utopia, all the inhabitants of a certain acreage would be in the position of landholders. There would be a chance to rise to higher positions through savings, industry, and aid from banks. Ford was not wholly averse to state ownership of the land. But he felt strongly that a man should be able to purchase the right of private occupancy of a certain amount of land, much as he now buys postage stamps.[47] These early writings on the country indicate that Ford's advocacy of the limited hero after the War was not a wholly new direction in his thought. During the period up to this climactic breakdown, however, he was more aware of the increasing ineffectiveness of the older standards of virtue and responsibility than of any possible solutions, and any solutions remained implied rather than directly developed in his work.

In contrast to the country, one of the most noticeable characteristics of pre-War urban society was its size, a massiveness that let London cast "oblivion upon her dead and" cloud "out the individualities of her liv-

ing." The largest city in England had become nothing but an oversize "graveyard."⁴⁸ Along with the great size, there was an increasing standardization, one which made London look like anywhere else in the world, and thus by its lack of distinction seem even larger. An influx of mass-produced merchandise, and of the canned goods which were such anathema to Ford was noticeable everywhere.⁴⁹ Modern life had grown more and more to want values and definition. When the Great Victorians lost their hold, there had been no one to take their place. It was virtually impossible for a man to inspire himself, much less anyone else, in the gray London world. The Great Victorians had left behind only this emptiness. One of the problems that the limited hero would face would be the establishment of his own identity in the context of this giant void.

The inertia of the Victorian hero, and the standardized commercialization of English society had produced a mass of people homogeneous in their daily lives, bombarded by all sorts of heterodox ideas, and consequently without a clear line of personal commitment:

> For modern life has left behind old faiths, old illusions, old chivalries and old heroisms. But at times, and spasmodically, it chafes after these old and impracticable virtues. Individuals continue to strive to assert themselves against the pressure of the body politic: individuals attempt at times to hold up torches in the general greyness. And inasmuch as it becomes daily more difficult to emerge, so the friction of the struggle induces irritability.⁵⁰

The absence of any faith as a clear basis for ethics developed simultaneously with a blatant opportunism, of which the commercial spirit was the everyday manifestation, and of which the Boer War was, for Ford during the pre-World War years, the culmination. This imperial war "appears to me," Ford remarked in *Ancient Lights*, "like a chasm separating the new world from the old. Since that period the whole tone of England appears to me to have entirely changed. Principles have died out of politics, even as the spirit of artistry has died out among the practitioners of the arts."⁵¹ Moreover, the Boer War was part of a general military climate that was engulfing the world. This climate also produced the Spanish-American War, the Russo-Japanese conflict, and the Greek-Italian campaigns against Turkey. "And all the while, in every state of the globe, went on the sabre-rattling that ended in the late Armegeddon. It was universal."⁵²

It was this increasing recognition of the abyss that had been left by the irrelevance and withdrawal of the Victorian moralists that gave rise in Ford's writings to the double view of the hero. Though he did not want to return to the world of the Great Victorians, he was, at the same time, painfully distressed by the lack of commitment and the increasing medi-

IMPORTANCE OF HEROISM IN FORD'S THOUGHT

ocrity that he found in English society. "We don't care," he wrote in *Ancient Lights*. "We don't care enough about anything to risk hurting each others feelings." He found this lack of agitation a practical sort of *modus vivendi*, but added that "it is impossible to be practical in the things both of heaven and earth. There is no way to do it."[53] The uninvolved, "unimaginative" Englishman would be, moreover, "the type of the future."[54] This was because the English, rather than facing the almost constant disillusion of life, had made existence bearable by overlooking tragedy, and relegating their relationships to the level of "Good Conduct." Their high degree of propriety made England "a place to which to return," but a place without passion.[55] Their lack of passion and inability to cope with it evoked two of Ford's most persistent criticisms of English society, criticisms which appeared again and again throughout his novels, and which underlay much of his condemnation of the conventional hero.

The confusion of the pre-War period was further heightened for Ford by the adverse conditions of a growing industrialism. In *Return to Yesterday* Ford commented that "the hideousness of the poverty in the early nineties the world over would now be incredible," if similar conditions were not still visible. "And it is not merely that hunger, cold and squalor beset the actually destitute. It was the terrible anxiety that forever harnessed the minds of those who were just above the starvation line." The threat of unemployment was constant, and being jobless meant a slow "sinking away from all the light. . . . It was a day of nightmares universal, showing no sign of coming to an end. Nothing could happen but what did—a world-wide flood of disorder ending in Anarchism. That was inevitable."[56] In this condition of potential anarchy, Ford told his countrymen, "if we have consciences, we must seek to perceive order in this disorder, beauty in what shocks us, and premonitions of immortality in that which sweeps us into forgotten graves."[57] But in accord with his insistence that the ideal had to have its basis in the particular, this order could not be imposed from outside. Instead, it had to come from direct observation and rendering of the society, of both its chaos and possible order. Only through such a rendering could the order penetrate deeply enough to bring about the "change of heart in the whole population of the globe" that was necessary if we were "To have a living civilization." The only person who could achieve this direct observation and render it effectively was the artist; "And every real artist in words who deserts the occupation of pure imaginative writing to immerse himself in the public affairs that have ruined our world, takes away a little of our chance of coming alive through these lugubrious times."[58] The artist, in other words, because of his roots in the particular and his ability to evoke the "change of heart," became Ford's first limited hero; and if he deserted his

role, Ford cautioned that he would be guilty of a betrayal as strong as that of the Great Victorians who had preceded him.

Ford took his role as artist seriously, for his work was the means by which he could try to render objectively his impressions of the world. The techniques which he developed were, as might be expected, reflections of this world which seemed to him so lacking in meaningful heroism, as well as of his double attitude toward the heroic figures themselves. In his novels these ostensible leaders remained, at least until Christopher Tietjens, embedded in their own abstractions, to all purposes in a state of impasse with the world. For society as a whole, they provided neither direction nor example, and in a world without accepted standards, life often had a sense of inconclusiveness. Without values, it was often difficult to know how to resolve situations. And two or more conflicting values could only confuse the issue. The novel, if it was to render the world as Ford saw it, would have to be built upon this feeling of inconclusiveness. It would often lack a real ending to a series of events, and it might not have a strict beginning, middle, or end. Means other than the straight narrative line would have to be worked out for moving the plot along. One of the methods Ford devised for this purpose was *progression d'effet*. To achieve this technique, events leaving a particular type of impression—let us say incidents indicating a marriage without communication between the partners—are piled one on top of the other, until their effect is cumulative and induces the end that Ford desires. *Progression d'effet* is thus a building up of a succession of similar events and, as Kenneth Young points out, the story if it progresses will move faster and faster, and with an ever greater intensity.[59] Another device for breaking the conventional narrative line was the use of time-shifts. With this device, a situation could be constructed around points of emphasis or a shift in observers, and a less purely chronological pattern could thus be drawn. These, like many of the other devices used by Ford, were attempts to alter the strict sequence pattern of purely narrative writing. Robie Macauley recalls a talk given by Ford in 1938, in which the novelist explained that his method of making conversation seem more natural, and more in accord with the continual breaks and unfinished thoughts of ordinary speech, was to use the ellipsis, and thereby avoid an exchange of careful sentences suggesting nothing so much as the hand of the author.[60] Through the use of ellipses, conversation could become a series of sometimes connected thoughts, rather than a contrived dialogue with a careful beginning and end.

All of the various technical devices used by Ford were brought together, in their purpose, by the larger organizing device of the "affair," the inconclusive interaction of a small group around which most of Ford's novels were built. The author himself saw life as a succession of "affairs:"

IMPORTANCE OF HEROISM IN FORD'S THOUGHT

And no one will deny that his life is really a matter of 'affairs'; of minute hourly embarrassments; of sympathetic or unsympathetic personal contacts; of little marked successes and failures, of queer jealousies, of muted termination—a tenuous fluttering, and engrossing fabric. And intangible![61]

Life for Ford was, in other words, a series of small and unheroic encounters without endings. Paul Wiley comments on the appropriateness of the "affair" as a device for registering this particular aspect of modern life. Wiley sees the "affair" as "a tense balance between artistic scrupulosity and historic skepticism," and also notes that it is a means of indicating how far removed contemporary life is from heroic suffering, and therefore from tragedy. "To Ford, the universe doesn't offer . . . ready signs of intent. Even if life contained design and one were able to discern it, we would actually experience this design as a series of unforeseen accidents. . . . Thus the Affair ironically represents the incompatibility of high tragedy and the temper of modern life, and minimizes the role of positive fate."[62]

Thus the "affair" became a structural device by which the writer could focus on the muted tensions of personal encounters without clear beginnings or ends. It enabled the author to render a situation, and yet it is interesting to note that this seemingly impersonal rendering could in itself convey an attitude toward modern life. In this sense, it shared an important characteristic with many of Ford's stylistic and structural devices: an attitude was often conveyed by the nature of the device itself, and further attitudes could be embodied in the author's arrangement of his material. From this characteristic we can observe that impersonality in art became for Ford a method rather than a point of view. The attitudes of the author might be central to the work, yet the author as omniscient manipulator never intruded. Ford's use of his own technique is, as we shall see, somewhat uneven. In some of the minor novels the intrusion is obvious and the control of characters and events is weak. But at its best, Ford's technique allowed him to comment on his world, and yet to remain ostensibly outside it, allowing the details to work for themselves and avoiding the distortion caused by the author as all-knowing hero.

In addition to rendering the unheroic and inconclusive nature of the world around him, Ford also developed a singularly important technique to register his increasingly complex perceptions of this world. This technique, as already mentioned, was that of the double perspective, and the psychological shadings which Ford was able to evoke through its use gave his work a dimension that placed it far above any merely surface picture of social decay. The tortured doubts and confusions of his major characters suggest that same inward-turning spiral of the twentieth-century consciousness that intrigued such writers as Dostoevsky and the early T. S. Eliot. But Ford, by granting his characters a relative social dignity

along with their actual ineffectiveness, was able to convey a complexity and a representative sense of the everyday world that might have been lost under a more purely critical or pathological focus.

Turning now to Ford's pre-War novels, many of them largely critical and even satiric in tone, we will see that they were both germinal to the development of his more sophisticated work and significant in their own right. These novels were essentially condemnations of the early public hero and of a society in which he was growing progressively ineffectual and by which he was sometimes corrupted. But they already hinted at the development of the double perspective—the tempering of condemnation by a perception of mitigating qualities—that was to reach its climax in *The Good Soldier* in 1915. Once Ford had attained the sense of complex tragedy so evident in this first major novel, he had to move in a new direction. The simple stance of condemnation of the conventional hero was no longer adequate; and the double perspective, if carried much further, might have led to a dead end. An alternative, even perhaps an affirmation had to be found; and Ford found both, at least to his own satisfaction, in the development of a limited hero, whose answer to a disintegrating and morally corrupt world lay in the assertion of his own private mode of life.

NOTES

[1] Richard Cassell, *Ford Madox Ford: A Study of His Novels* (Baltimore, 1961), pp. 114–117, 140.
[2] Walter Allen, *The English Novel* (New York, 1955), pp. 315–317.
[3] Frank Macshane, "Pattern of Ford Madox Ford," *New Republic*, CXXXII (April 4, 1955), 16–17.
[4] R. P. Blackmur, "The King Over the Water: Notes on the Novels of Ford Madox Hueffer," *Princeton University Library Chronicle*, IX (April, 1948), 126–127.
[5] Morton Dauwen Zabel, *Craft and Character* (New York, 1957), p. 260.
[6] John A. Meixner, *Ford Madox Ford's Novels: A Critical Study* (Minneapolis, 1962), p. 7.
[7] Ford Madox Ford, "There Were Strong Men," *Portraits from Life* (Boston, New York, 1937), pp. 205–206.
[8] Douglas Goldring, *Trained for Genius* (New York, 1949), p. 31.
[9] *Ibid.*, pp. 22–24, 40.
[10] Richard M. Ludwig, "The Reputation of Ford Madox Ford," *PMLA*, LXXVI (1961), 548.
[11] Zabel, p. 253.
[12] Herbert Gorman, "Ford Madox Ford: The Personal Side," *Princeton University Library Chronicle*, IX (April, 1948), 121.
[13] Richard Aldington, *Life for Life's Sake* (New York, 1941), pp. 149–151.
[14] Goldring, p. 252.
[15] Cassell, pp. 5–8.
[16] Goldring, pp. 204–205.

[17] *Ibid.*, pp. 95–97.
[18] Ford Madox Hueffer, *Memories and Impressions*, published in England as *Ancient Lights* (New York, London, 1911), p. xiii.
[19] Ford Madox Hueffer, *The Critical Attitude* (London, 1911), pp. 175–176.
[20] Hueffer, *Memories and Impressions*, pp. 72–73.
[21] *Ibid.*, pp. 25–26.
[22] *Ibid.*, p. 10.
[23] Ford Madox Hueffer, *The Pre-Raphaelite Brotherhood, A Critical Monograph* (London, 1907), pp. 81–82, 94–95, 121.
[24] Ford Madox Hueffer, *Rossetti, A Critical Essay on His Art* (London, New York, 1902), p. 86.
[25] Hueffer, *Memories and Impressions*, pp. 69–71.
[26] *Ibid.*
[27] *Ibid.*, pp. 68–69.
[28] Hueffer, *Rossetti*, pp. 32–33.
[29] Hueffer, *Memories and Impressions*, p. 12.
[30] *Ibid.*, pp. 133–135.
[31] Ford Madox Ford, *The March of Literature from Confucius' Day to Our Own* (New York, 1938), pp. 772–773.
[32] Hueffer, *Memories and Impressions*, p. 224.
[33] *Ibid.*, pp. 265–267.
[34] Ford Madox Ford, *Return to Yesterday, Reminiscences 1894–1914* (London, 1931), p. 41.
[35] Ford Madox Ford, *It Was the Nightingale* (Philadelphia, London, 1933), p. 156.
[36] Ford Madox Ford, *The English Novel from the Earliest Days to the Death of Joseph Conrad* (Philadelphia, London, 1929), p. 25.
[37] Hueffer, *The Critical Attitude*, pp. 118–120.
[38] *Ibid.*, p. 118.
[39] Ford, "There Were Strong Men," *Portraits from Life*, p. 205.
[40] Ford, *The English Novel*, pp. 27, 53.
[41] Hueffer, *The Critical Attitude*, pp. 27–28.
[42] Ford Madox Hueffer, *Thus to Revisit, Some Reminiscences* (London, 1921), p. 120.
[43] Ford, "There Were Strong Men," *Portraits from Life*, pp. 207–209.
[44] Ford, "H. G. Wells," *Portraits from Life*, p. 118.
[45] Ford Madox Hueffer, *The Heart of the Country, A Survey of a Modern Land* (London, 1906), pp. 49, 77, 105, 111.
[46] Ford, *Return to Yesterday*, pp. 146–147.
[47] Hueffer, *The Heart of the Country*, pp. 162–163, 168, 185, 190–193.
[48] Ford Madox Hueffer, *The Soul of London, A Survey of a Modern City* (London, 1905), pp. 148–149.
[49] Ford Madox Hueffer, "London Revisited," *English Review*, pp. 180–181.
[50] Hueffer, *The Critical Attitude*, pp. 104–105.
[51] Hueffer, *Memories and Impressions*, pp. 171–172.
[52] Ford, "Stephen Crane," *Portraits from Life*, pp. 21–22.
[53] Hueffer, *Memories and Impressions*, pp. 324–325.
[54] Ford Madox Hueffer, *The Spirit of the People, An Analysis of the English Mind* (London, 1907), p. 166.
[55] *Ibid.*, pp. 151–153.
[56] Ford, *Return to Yesterday*, pp. 106–107.
[57] Hueffer, *The Critical Attitude*, p. 9.

[58] Ford, "H. G. Wells," *Portraits from Life*, p. 123.
[59] Kenneth Young, *Ford Madox Ford*, number 74 in series entitled "Writers and their Work" (London, New York, 1956), p. 13.
[60] Robie Macauley, "Observations on Technique: Some Notes on a Lecture Given by Ford Madox Ford at Olivet College in June, 1938," *Shenandoah*, IV (1953), 49.
[61] Hueffer, *Thus to Revisit*, p. 36 as quoted by Paul Wiley, *Novelist of Three Worlds: Ford Madox Ford* (Syracuse, 1962), p. 54.
[62] Wiley, pp. 62, 69–71.

2.

The Early Novels and the Ineffectual Hero

THE WORLD of the pre-War novels was marked by many of the traits depicted in the author's non-fiction. There was a pervasive sense of commercialism, self-interest and social decay. Scheming and hypocrisy, financial scandal and political corruption had become the norms of behavior, and swindles such as the Greenland Affair depicted in *The Inheritors, An Extravagant Story* or the political manipulation shown in *Mr. Fleight* seemed to Ford to have become more and more commonplace. There was also a sharp decline of religious faith, a decline to which Ford himself called attention in the fantasy, *Mr. Apollo, A Just Possible Story*, in which the Victorian world was symbolically levelled to the ground by a visiting god. In such a world the heroic figure, whether ineffectually idealist or cynically corrupted, was of little consequence. The idealist had become so detached from reality and so caught up in his own rhetoric that he was virtually paralyzed, even in his personal relationships. And the later corrupted hero, rather than leading society had simply allowed himself to be swallowed by it. As both these heroes came to seem increasingly hollow, Ford made them responsible for what seemed to him a foregone social collapse. Their recurrent failure to confront either themselves or their world become the predominant theme in his novels of the pre-War period.

Yet along with his sharp indictment of the hero, Ford began to develop even in his early novels the double perspective which had been evident in his non-fiction and which was to become a distinctive style in his major works. Because he had not yet refined it to the level of stylistic and psychological subtlety which he was later to achieve, and because in the early novels his major aim was to establish with some finality the failure of the conventional hero, this dual perspective was far less central here than in the major novels. Yet in spite of a strong rejection of both the post-Victorian hero and his world, the author was able to suggest in varying degrees the psychological factors behind the hero's ineffectiveness and thereby to mitigate slightly the sense of blame. The idealistic hero, in particular, was regarded by Ford with a mixture of pity and resentment. The novelist saw, for example, that behind the indiscriminate altruism of George Moffat, the title figure of *The Benefactor*, there lay a

growing dread of personal inadequacy and a painful sense of guilt. Even so corrupt a figure as Mr. Blood, the caricatured political boss of *Mr. Fleight*, was shown to be motivated by a mixture of boredom and cynicism that stemmed from the lack of coherent direction in his world. By making us aware of such underlying factors, Ford was able to temper condemnation with complexity, and at least in the case of the idealistic heroes, to grant a certain virtue by comparison with the encroaching commercial world.

In the major novels, this response to the public hero and the development of the private alternative became increasingly complex, and Ford was able to utilize a subtle psychological focus to convey this complexity and to evoke a multiple response. In the novels written before the War, however, his interest remained comparatively external. While the beginnings of a psychological focus were evident, the concern of the early novels was primarily with the ineffectiveness of the hero and the degeneration of his world. Ford's early idealistic heroes were not shown as bedeviled by the same kind of intense inner struggle that was to characterize Edward Ashburnham, for the author was still primarily concerned with the social implications of their personal failures. The early novels were marked by a limited double focus, and by a small degree of pity and understanding, but their prevalent tone was one of bitterness, softened sometimes by compassion and sometimes by profound regret.

Seen chronologically, the hero in Ford's pre-War novel exhibits a progressive deterioration, so that if these novels are regarded as a group, a general pattern becomes evident. The first heroes, George Moffat and Don Collar Kelleg, are sincere if misguided idealists, and their main failure lies in their detached inertia. By contrast, the later pre-War heroes have themselves become corrupt, and their virtue has shrivelled almost wholly to rhetoric. These corrupt heroes are portrayed by Ford in novels that are largely satirical in tone, and in which the emphasis is on the corruption of the society as a whole. The pattern is, of course, not wholly linear. For example, Etchingham Granger of *The Inheritors* is in his corruption closer to the later heroes than he is to George Moffat. And yet Granger's corruption is impulsive rather than premeditated, for it is motivated by his desire to follow the seeming wishes of a woman whom he is incapable of approaching directly. In like manner, the hero of *The Nature of A Crime* succumbs to his own degradation as a result of suppressing his feeling for a woman whom he fears will not accept his love. On the other hand, the corruption of the later heroes, such as Count Macdonald or Mr. Blood, stems not from impulse or desire, but out of a conscious moral cynicism. And it is a corruption that is far more willful than that of the inept lovers. There is, in other words, a shift in tone and emphasis in the later works of Ford's pre-War period. The coloring is often that of satire, and the problems are rendered in a more social con-

THE EARLY NOVELS AND THE INEFFECTUAL HERO

text. The later heroes also move from the realm of a rather secluded aristocracy to that of politics; and whereas their influence seldom extends over an entire society, they become transition figures between the aristocratic hero and his counterpart, the politician, who was to figure so strongly in Ford's work after the War, and who was to add to the ineptness and the rhetoric of the hero, the greater power that made him so much more ominous. But the full threat posed by the hero-turned-politician was not perceived by Ford until the years of the War; and in his work prior to that seeming climax the condemned hero, no matter how corrupt, was made to typify an aristocratic rather than a professional political class.

Ford's early novels are qualified by an uneven technique. Although they include unquestionable achievements, they are less remarkable for these than for the introduction of subtleties which Ford was to develop later. Many of the novels are constructed with the very omniscience that Ford wanted to avoid, and the characters are not clearly motivated. Often they remain types, seen only through their surface behavior; and sometimes, most noticeably in *An English Girl*, their motivations are ambiguous and confused. Ford has unfortunately left little evidence as to the reason for this technical unevenness. The most obvious cause would seem to be his prolificness, his tendency to write too much and perhaps too hurriedly. On the biographical level, we know that the early years of the century were for him ones at first of severe depression and later of the divorce scandal involving Elsie Martindale, his first wife, and Violet Hunt. But any connection would be conjectural, and we also know that during this period Ford produced novels such as *Mr. Apollo*, *A Call*, and *The Benefactor*, which are much more complex in theme and far more successful in execution than the majority of his pre-War novels. One might attribute the unevenness of Ford's work before *The Good Soldier* to artistic growth, if his novels after the Tietjens series did not often show the same faults of weak plot and characterization. The qualitative pattern of Ford's work seems to build up to a gradual peak, to reach this peak with *The Good Soldier* and the Tietjens novels, and then to go into a period of uneven decline. It may be significant that during the period of his best fiction, the years from 1915 to 1928, the quality of Ford's non-fiction degenerates. It would seem that he chose to give more time to the writing of his major novels, and that he found that genre the most appropriate medium for the attitudes he then wanted to express.

During the years before the War, Ford was only beginning to develop the novel as a means for directly rendering reality. Some of his novels during this period, including by his own admission the historical ones, were mainly exercises in which he could work out the problems of atmosphere, character, and detail. Others, such as *A Call*, were fully realized works, which could stand very much on their own. But for the most part

Ford's view during these early years was still too explicitly tendentious to fit securely in the confines of the impressionist novel. Unlike the major works, these early novels were for the most part reflections of ideas already developed in the non-fiction. Each of these two genres was at this stage of Ford's writing essential to a full understanding of the other. The early novels can thus be seen either as stages in Ford's intellectual development or as germinal groupings toward the techniques which were to reach maturation in *The Good Soldier*. Paul Wiley views them in the latter sense, and suggests "that with the exception of possibly two or three, most of them show a concentrated attempt to arrive at a form of the Affair suited to" Ford's "conception of society in his times."[1] But techniques such as the use of the "affair" were embodiments of Ford's ideas, and the early novels as a group can be examined with some profit chronologically for the evidence they provide both of continuity and change in Ford's view of the pre-War world.

While most of Ford's novels written before the War reflect his view of a decadent present, the works of historical fiction, although conceived as experiments in technique, are revealing in their contrast of this present with a far from idealized past. These novels of the past embody Ford's sense of the roots of his present world, and in one case, his repudiation of the Pre-Raphaelites' romanticized medievalism. They are marked by the central Fordian attitudes toward the hero, and frequently develop their situations through the structure of the "affair." As Wiley notes, they are basically affairs with a difference of locale.[2] Their main emphasis is, however, on the rendering of scene and on the creation of a historical atmosphere through the elaborate use of essentially visual textures. Ford himself remarked in his book on Conrad that historical novels were "a fake more or less genuine in inspiration and workmanship, but none the less a fake," and the genre, he added, was "just for practice in writing."[3]

The focus on atmosphere is especially evident in *Romance*, the novel which Ford wrote with Conrad in 1903, and which Meixner sees as "plainly much more Conradian than Fordian."[4] Meixner draws this conclusion from the book's emphasis on pirates, smugglers, physical adventure, and violent death, elements which often formed the atmosphere in Conrad's more important works. The book has even less of a social context than the other historical novels, where Ford was attempting in part to trace this historical development of the modern world, which he had sketched briefly in *The Spirit of the People*. In this development, there were two kinds of heroes: the sincere disciple of a dying faith, such as Katherine Howard in the court of Henry VIII; and the rising Machiavellian opportunist, such as her adversary, Thomas Cromwell. The reign of Henry VIII, depicted in the Katherine Howard trilogy, was one of the focal points where both the medieval and the modern worlds converged and hovered in their balance. The medieval world, typified by Katherine,

THE EARLY NOVELS AND THE INEFFECTUAL HERO

had its ideals, however imperfect, of chivalry and faith. The modern world, typified by the devious Cromwell, replaced these with deceit, Machiavellian behavior, moral relativism, and a placing of gain over good works. These two worlds form the essential conflict of the Katherine Howard novels.[5] The conflict helps define Ford's view of the modern world, and this view is strengthened by the other historical novels. Their setting, however, prohibits any direct observations of the hero in Ford's own society; and they remain, by Ford's own acknowledgement, exercises in the rendering of texture and atmosphere.

Yet in one historical novel, the fantasy *Ladies Whose Bright Eyes, A Romance*, Ford attempts a direct confrontation between modern society and the medieval world. The latter clearly has the advantage on the grounds of faith, but one of the real triumphs of this novel is that Ford's typically double view is always maintained. Ford's medieval world, unlike the Pre-Raphaelite version, is also shown in its filth, its lustiness, its intrigue and, in some instances, even its lack or misuse of faith. And the ending of the 1935 edition states even more clearly than that of the earlier 1911 version that we cannot return. Sentimental medievalism definitely is not the answer. The final point made by the novel when the publisher, Sorrell, and his nurse, Dionissia Morant, attempt to redirect their present lives, is that it is not so much the time or the place that matter, but the kind of people and their own specific and circumscribed involvements.

The device which the book uses to structure the contrast of societies is to place back in medieval times a commercial publisher, Sorrell, a modern man with few ideals and little faith. While on a train, he is given an old medieval relic, the Tamworth Cross, by Mrs. Lee-Egerton as security against a loan. After the train crashes, Sorrell, actually hospitalized and in a coma, believes himself to have awakened in the Middle Ages, where he is taken for the Greek slave who was to bring home the cross, gained in the Crusades and entrusted to him by his dead master. As Sorrell, the supposed slave, travels toward his master's castle he comes upon three men hanging from a tree, thus immediately directing our view to some of the brutal realities of the period. Sorrell is naturally upset, but the nun with whom he is travelling takes the sight very much in course.[6] A realistic image of the Middle Ages is also rendered by the scene of the two knights of Coucy and Stapleton in a room with their mistresses, one of whom has been purchased from her mother.[7] The local castle is not a very clean place, but Ford uses this detail to underscore the inclusive faith of the medieval people. After a rather elaborate bath, Sorrell asks two ladies how they put up with the stench of the courtyard. One of them replies that "it would be beyond human strength to imitate the spotless whiteness of the courts of heaven. There there is neither eating or drinking. Consider that you are amongst the mortal inhabitants of this earth."[8] Thus even the less pleasant details of their lives these people justify in

terms of faith, and significantly it is a faith that is characterized less by heroism than by a ready acceptance of human limitations.

These two aspects of the Middle Ages—faith and acceptance of human limitations—are brought together in the struggle of the various factions for the Tamworth Cross. As a religious relic, it has a real value in terms of their faith. But it becomes the cause of power struggles, even among the religious orders, and on its behalf Sorrell is sexually enticed by the Lady Blanche de Coucy. Sorrell, however, soon finds a way of personally transcending the jealousies of the local inhabitants, and he adopts, under the tutelage of old Sir Ygorac, the ethic of chivalry. This ideal is marked by generosity and self-effacement, and motivated by a strong trust in God. Ygorac asks Sorrell as a holy man to cure some of his maladies, and Sorrell answers: "Ah gentle knight, we are in the hands of God and His little angels. Of how much I may care or of how little, that I cannot tell you, but I think that surely the cure under God lies more in you than in me. For your faith will make you whole . . . according as it is great or little. This I believe to be the truth of the very truth."[9] Ygorac compliments him on his knightly courtesy, and this sort of knightly faith becomes the most strongly affirmed quality of the Middle Ages. Sorrell begins to find his modern world, where no "single man that I know would have been able to black his own boots," extremely passive.[10] And his own skepticism before he has been taught by Sir Ygorac is in marked contrast to the faith of the Lady Dionissia, the dreamy, self-contained woman who lives by arranged marriage with the Knight of Egerton, and with whom Sorrell falls in love. She dislikes his explaining the cures which he affects as "natural suggestion," and insists that he is actually an "agent" of God.[11] Just before Sorrell awakes from the Middle Ages, he has committed himself to both the knightly ethic and the Lady Dionissia; and a blow from her husband, who finds them together, is Sorrell's last sensation in the medieval world.

The novel appeared in two versions, one in 1911 and one in 1935. The major alteration which Ford made in the later version was in the ending, and the two different conclusions suggest Ford's changing orientation toward the present at different periods of his life. In 1911 he was primarily reacting against the modern world which he saw around him, and the mood of the earlier ending is comparatively passive. The book ends on the love which Sorrell, now back in the twentieth century, and his nurse, Dionissia, suddenly feel for each other. She tells Sorrell that all they can do is take their chances on "what we find in each other" and seize the particular moment. Happiness is something they will have "to find . . . from day to day as if we were homeless wanderers. . . . We have our glorious moments and even if our lives go to pieces, if disasters come, and ruin, and death, we shall have had our glorious moment, and that's all there is in life, and that's all there ever was."[12] Sorrell, however, wants to

simulate a medieval castle on the land he has inherited. Missing from both their plans is the sense of a future which so strongly dominates the 1935 edition.

In this later version, Sorrell finds his publishing work meaningless, and decides to go to the Soviet Union to become a mining engineer, because there they are "beginning."[13] Russia is important not for its political system, about which nothing is said, but because it is a society with a sense of purpose, of things to do, and in this sense stands in contrast to a tired and too-commercial England. After Sorrell has told Dionissia of his plans, she adds that it is necessary for man to go "back to a beginning of everything," that is, to go back to faith. Now, man has "nothing but doubts into which to go forward." Once he has faith, however, he can "go forward with courage." Dionissia and Sorrell decide to go into Russia, into the future, together, "to go forward—don't they say: over the graves."[14] Their attempt to reconstruct a future built on a renewal of personal involvement is very much in accord with the theme of limited heroism which Ford developed in his other writing of the post-War period.

In the 1911 ending of *Ladies Whose Bright Eyes* the solution for Sorrell is still rather tenuous, and the strongest impression is his sense of an unsatisfactory present. It is this sense that dominates all of Ford's early non-historical fiction. The novels as a whole focus on both the ineffectual hero and the corrupt society, but the corruption is often rendered through the degeneration of a small group of potentially great men. As an impressionist, Ford wanted to show that which he could readily observe, and as a believer in the inconclusiveness of modern life, he wanted to show a situation that was clearly circumscribed in time or place, and yet had little sense of a beginning or end. The structure of the "affair" which he developed was perfectly suited to the demands of his art, and all of Ford's early novels employed this structural device in varying degrees. When, in a satire as *The Simple Life Limited*, he departed most noticeably from the "affair" and used a more conventional narrative structure, Ford relied much more on situational contrivance and much less on the complex development of character. It can be seen that the "affair" was strikingly appropriate to his view of his world, and that its use was particularly conducive to eliciting other desirable qualities in his art. The very inconclusiveness of its situation meant that the supporting characteristics had to be more fully developed, if the novel was to have any shape at all. Thus, the complexity of characters and ideas became the distinctive element of Ford's artistically mature novels during the years before the War.

The Inheritors, An Extravagant Story, written with Conrad in 1901, shows the weakness of Ford's early work. The novel is too complex and ambiguous in its symbolic implications and insufficiently complex in its

character development. On one level, it tells the story of the further corruption of an already-ineffectual young aristocrat. But he is corrupted by a girl who claims to be from the Fourth Dimension, and the intended symbolism of the whole Fourth-Dimensionist group is unclear. On another level, the novel is an allegorical treatment of British politics around the time of the Boer War. The different levels of meaning are further confused by the ambiguity of the Dimensionists as symbols; and this ambiguity also leads to an ambivalence in the characterization of Etchingham Granger, the susceptible aristocratic writer. For if the Fourth-Dimensionists are simply a symbolic culmination of the opportunism that is undermining modern society, an opportunism of which Granger is very much a part, then Granger, the artist-hero, can be held responsible for his own degeneration. But if the Dimensionists are to be taken at their word as a deterministic and supernatural force, then Granger is less to blame, for certainly before he meets the girl, he is less corrupt than most of his society. The nature of the Dimensionists is never clarified, and the novel wavers constantly between fantasy and social criticism.

The Dimensionists are a group of people or beings who intend to take over English society, and ultimately the world. Their major characteristic is their openly professed ruthlessness and utter lack of sympathy or altruism. They intend to inherit, without violence, the whole social structure, which is weak and "worm-eaten with altrusim and ethics."[15] Their view of English society is obviously an irony, and yet their lack of altruism is simply an extension of traits that Ford perceived in that very society. The Dimensionists also resemble the society they wish to supplant in their characteristic of internal competition. Although they see no opposition outside their own group, the girl admits to Granger that "We fight for our own hands."[16]

As for Etchingham Granger, he is a younger writer who considers himself to be above the backbiting of his world. He regards with contempt the commercial writer, Callan, who "had an appropriate attitude for every vicissitude of his life."[17] And yet he becomes involved in the Dimensionist scheme by accepting through Callan a job on the newspaper run by Fox, who is later revealed to be one of the supplanted group. This is the first step in Granger's deterioration; for if he accepts with Callan's aid a job the nature of which he despises, he differs little from the commerical writer for whom he professes so much verbal scorn.

The corruption of the society of which Granger is only a small part—although a potential leader because of his position as artist and aristocrat—is shown by the devious imperialism of the Duc de Mersch and even more by the business alliance between de Mersch and the highly respected foreign minister, Churchill. De Mersch is a simple villain, but Churchill and Granger are moralizers, who in spite of their professed appearances allow themselves to become implicated in that very collapse

which the Dimensionists anticipate. The girl herself tells Granger that the discrediting of Churchill in the scandal over de Mersch's Greenland Affair is really a plot to bring down all that Churchill stands for, "all the old order of things."[18] As for de Mersch, he seldom appears as a character, but his history of previous "international philanthropic concerns," such as an " 'All Round the World Cable Company' that united hearts and hands," as well as his involvement in the Greenland Affair marks him as a man skilled in the combination of rhetoric and graft: "Somewhere at the bottom of these seemingly bottomless concerns, the Duc de Mersch was said to be moving, and the *Hour* certainly contained periodically complimentary allusions to their higher philanthropy and dividend-earning prospects."[19]

De Mersch's schemes bear a strong resemblance to the verbose and greedy imperialism that had come to a head in the policies of Prime Minister Joseph Chamberlain just before Ford and Conrad wrote this book. Ford saw imperialism as a political extension of the false heroics which he had discerned in the rhetoric of the Victorians. And the tendency of this imperialism to encompass more and more areas of society is depicted there through the alliance of Churchill and de Mersch. Churchill, as the Dimensionist-girl explains to Granger, has "been thinking a good deal lately that his day is over . . . and so—oh he's going to make a desperate effort to get in touch with the spirit of the times that he doesn't like and doesn't understand."[20] In his susceptibility, Churchill would scarcely seem to be the man whom Wiley sees as standing "for the old order of honor and integrity in government."[21]

Ford's strong indictment of Churchill makes Granger's final act, when he allows the Dimensionist plot to continue by permitting the publication of an article which will expose the whole Greenland swindle and thereby cause Churchill's fall, less a betrayal of Churchill than of himself. Granger allows the article to go through because of his attraction to the Dimensionist-girl, since he thinks that his action is in accord with what she desires, and will therefore draw her to him. He wants to "show her" that he has "co-operated loyally with the powers of the future, though I wanted no share in the inheritance of the earth." But this very attraction only confuses the novel further, for the roles of the two characters and the moral overtones of their relationships become distressingly inconsistent. At one point Granger argues with the girl that she does care for him; and she admits that she does, but adds, "Don't you see, you would influence me; you would be—you are—a disease—for me." But Granger still professes an insatiable love, whereupon she accuses him of inaction: "If you have wanted me I have been there. It is too late."[22] If the girl is only a force, or a symbol of the direction of society, then Granger's love for her is almost ludicrous. If she is human, then many of her own statements become grotesque. The unresolved attraction can be read as the first of a

series of failures by Fordian heroes to commit themselves in emotional situations. This failure will become crucial in other novels; but here the ambiguous and even contradictory nature of the situation dulls the effect.

Granger by the end of the novel is involved in the Dimensionist scheme to wreck the old order, but he is motivated by his feelings for an ambiguously-symbolic character who says that as her object of possible love, he is a "disease." And Granger, for all his efforts, is left only an outsider, cut off from both the past and the future. "I seemed," he says, "for a moment to see myself a tenuous, bodiless thing, like a ghost in a bottomless cleft between the past and the to come. And I was to be that forever."[23] Granger's own fate is not wholly consistent with the scheme of the novel. If by letting through the crucial article and knowingly exposing Churchill, he goes along with the Dimensionists and forsakes any loyalty to the man who, although corrupt, has befriended him, then why is it impossible for him to become a part of the future? He would seem to have relinquished those virtues which would set him apart from the Dimensionists. Perhaps he is still distinguished by his hopeless love, but as it stands the question is simply another area of ambivalence in the novel.

Some of the lack of internal coherence can perhaps be attributed to the differing intentions of Ford and Conrad. In his book on Conrad, Ford tells how he had thought of the work as "an allegorico-realist romance," which "showed the superseding of previous generations and codes by the merciless young who are always alien and without remorse." However, says Ford, "the moment Conrad spoke, he spoke with the voice of the Conrad who was avid of political subjects," and the novel moved in the direction of "a political work, rather allegorically backing Mr. Balfour in the then Government."[24] Jocelyn Baines, in his biography of Conrad, ties the characters of the novel to their historical counterparts, and identified de Mersch as King Leopold II of Belgium; Churchill as Balfour and the Dimensionist, Gunard, who supersedes Churchill as Joseph Chamberlain.[25] But the intent of the authors still remains in doubt, for Conrad himself, writing to Ford in 1903, says of *The Inheritors* that "the authors," by introducing the Dimensionists, "tried to remove the work from the sphere of mere personalities. They attack not individuals, but the spirit of the age—the immoral tendencies arising from a purely materialistic view of life."[26]

The Inheritors remains, then, a novel in which many of the prevalent Fordian themes, the corrupted aristocratic hero and his failure to make an emotional response, the materialism of society, and the irresponsibility of politicians, are hinted at, but never fully, coherently developed. Wiley, accepting the book as a primarily political novel, says that its main fault lies in its attempt to convey, by an extreme condensation, meaning enough for a political novel the size of *All the King's Men*.[27] In the broadest sense of the term, *The Inheritors* is a political novel. It attempts

to see the political structure as part of a larger social and moral decay. However, in actuality the various issues and levels of meaning are far more diverse, and the novel is marred by a confusion which considerably lessens its impact.

This diversity of focus was largely overcome in Ford's next novel of contemporary society, *The Benefactor, A Tale of A Small Circle*, written in 1905. Here the author achieved his first psychologically-complex portrait of the ineffectual hero; for the picture of George Moffat is a study of the idealist trapped within himself. Moffat is driven by a constant altruism, and his feelings are probably as honestly altrusitic as those of any can be. His failure stems from the fact that his ideals cloud his perception of reality, and he becomes relatively insensitive, both to the deceptions and the needs of others. He seems always to misdirect his generosity, placing it upon hack writers who ultimately turn against him, pushing it too frequently on people such as Reverend Brede, whom he is incapable of helping and who only leave him with the burden of guilt for the ill effects of his efforts, and finally withholding it from Clara Brede who would demand from him a really specific and self-sacrificing commitment. Outside of George's abstractions, the world is highly imperfect, and this imperfection impinges on his private sphere through the opportunism of the literary hacks, and finally through the madness of Reverend Brede.

George's assumed role of benefactor is from the beginning presented in ironic terms. We learn that "George Moffat excused his incorrigibility by his tradition," but that "His sister Mary said that meddlesomeness was at the bottom of his character. George had attempted to advise her in her first love affair.... The first lover, worn out by George's subtle handling, had accepted an official position on the Gold Coast, and had died there. Unfortunately, he had never had a successor, and Mary had not spoken to her brother for twenty years."[28] George's almost obsessive altruism has also ruined his first marriage. His wife, before the novel begins, has left him, because she simply could not comprehend his indiscriminate generosity, and could not see that it did any good. Dissension has also been caused by her suddenly becoming religious while George had remained an agnostic.[29] Although this point is not developed, George's lack of faith would seem to indicate in Ford's view, judging by the emphasis on faith in other novels, a certain instability and insecurity beneath his altruism. This theme of insecurity is in fact borne out by the novel, and we see that behind George's idealism, unknown to him, there lies a great deal of guilt and self-doubt. In part, he desires to be worshipped, and is looking for "the perfect disciple."[30]

George's basic problem is that he does not really know how to communicate with people. He is himself torn by difficulties and an apprehensive questioning of his own worth. But while he expects and pushes

others to share their problems with him, he is unwilling to share his with them. Instead, his mistaken idea of responsibility causes him to assume the role of the hero: "George was determined to play the great man, if by that pose he could give pleasure. . . . He was the old great man, exerting himself to be delightful to the young."[31] George has been brought up in a tradition of altruism, and this tradition links him to a time that is past. But paradoxically, his very altruism does not allow him to do good in the tangible areas where he might be most successful. The association of George with the type of the great man, with tradition, and with a blind idealism suggests a strong link between George and the Great Victorians so strongly criticized by Ford.

George's real ties are with the past, and he dedicates himself to reviving this dying order through the person of the mad Reverend Brede. This representative of a faith that is supposed to comfort others is himself tormented by guilt, and walks around complaining that no one understands him, blindly crashing into hedges, and threatening to cut his own throat. The source of his guilt is the death of his wife. "The doctors had told me," Brede tells George, "that in her state of health the least excitement would kill her." One day Brede had grown angry at a servant boy for not properly cleaning his boots: "I could have throttled the oaf. I caught hold of him." Then he had heard a scream, and Mrs. Brede was dead.[32] As with George himself, idealism turned to guilt becomes for the clergyman an obsession and prevents his dealing effectively with any more immediate reality. But his madness, like that of the Reverend Duchemin in the first of the Tietjens novels, also indicates the breakdown of the old values, religious faith included, and suggests the increasing unlikelihood of a solution on their terms.

The futile involvement with Brede, his total madness, and George's ensuing guilt, make George's relationship to Clara extremely difficult and precarious—even more so than if he were playing the great man to her alone. In their early discovering of each other both Clara and George lack confidence in themselves. Clara apologizes for her family, views it as "neurotic," and tries to keep her father out of George's way, so that George can write. George replies to her that his work "doesn't count. I used to blow little tunes on an oat straw; but it all went years ago." But while Clara grows in their relationship, George does not. The girl begins to develop an intelligent self-interest; "No one," she thinks, to herself, "seemed to think that she could suffer. . . . Why did no one—even George, who could see into so many hearts—ever see that she needed sympathy, help, counsel?"[33] George, in his own ineffective way, tries to give her this sympathy, but he can only regard her like his other projects, as one to be pitied and helped. Once she confesses to him her fear that she will never succeed, and he replies that he had always thought her "so tremendously effectual." She fears that he is only trying to comfort her,

and George feels toward her "a sudden and immense tenderness of pity."[34] Pity, however, is a detached reaction, with an implication of superiority; and George can never really accept Clara's opening up to him because he is unable to open up to her. He comments to her at one stage, "Isn't it a pleasure to know that you're human if—as I'm sure I hope will be the case—I'm to go on seeing a good deal of you." Yet later, after he had admitted to himself his love for her, and when he is burdened with financial difficulties and the possibility of selling his home, George does not take Clara into his confidence, does not show her that he, too, is human. His only concern is "not to make a fool of himself—not to 'yelp.'" Consequently, when she learns of his difficulties through a newspaper account, Clara is naturally resentful of George for not taking her into his confidence.[35]

The climax of the novel comes with Reverend Brede's final madness, and George's ensuing guilt and emotional paralysis. George has persuaded Brede to preach again, despite the minister's overpowering sense of his own guilt. But in the middle of his first sermon, Brede goes totally berserk, and George has to take him to an asylum, even though this seems to him "a continuing misery, a long blackness—and a treachery."[36] Now there is nothing between George and Clara—only George's guilt and his idealized sense of self. After taking Brede away, George feels joyously anticipative at the thought of returning to Clara. But once he is with her, and Clara is obviously ready to commit herself to him, "The image of poor Brede came to him: strong, vigorous in his tirades, crying out for sympathy, and indefatigable. That was how he would live in their hearts for as long as they lived." George tries to speak to Clara of "that forgetfulness . . . that getting outside ourselves into communion with a spirit that absorbs us," but goes on to say that "It's only action that is a difficulty." Just before he goes to her, "the black and tremendous figure of her father" appears once more, and George draws back, saying, "No, I must go. It would be a calamity for us all." Clara is for the moment stunned and incredulous. "She could not believe that her attraction would not hold him." She feels "A violent passion against the universe," and as the novel closes she can only ask with bitterness, "Self-sacrifice . . . Doesn't that ever end?"[37]

The inability to transcend the conceptualized self, whether idealized or not, and to respond to a particular person in a specific situation, is one of Ford's strongest and most consistent indictments against the hero. The scene, such as the one above, in which the hero fails to respond to the affections or needs of a woman—or even his own needs—occurs again and again in the author's novels, until it becomes a major thematic device. The situation of potential love between two people embodies many of Ford's central values: it is specific, immediate, and emotionally expressive, and although clearly circumscribed, it is far-reaching in its potential for

the regeneration of an ethical society. The paralysis of the hero in such a situation clearly indicates the failure of his abstractions. *The Benefactor* is important, then, in that it is the first of Ford's novels in which this crucial scene is developed; and in this novel it is so central to Ford's intent that it is placed at the very end, along with Brede's final madness, as one of two events that comprise the climax of the book.

In *An English Girl, A Romance,* published in 1907, the themes of the ineffectual and the paralyzed idealist are taken up again, but the characters and issues are less fully developed, and the novel ends in an apparent contradiction of itself. The hero, Don Collar Kelleg, is made to seem rather comic in his grandiose schemes for righting all wrongs committed by his late tycoon father, as well as many of the wrongs of American society in general. He remains comic because his internal motivations are never developed, and we see only a slightly adolescent exterior. The major difficulty in this novel, however, is that Ford's attitude toward Don becomes confused at the end, and this confusion is due to an apparent indecision as to which of two frequent themes to develop. The novel, for most of its course, pokes gentle fun at Don's social idealism. But suddenly at the end, Ford's scorn turns upon Eleanor Greville, who has been betrothed to Don up to this point, for her refusal to follow her fiancé when he decides for a second time to return to America to attempt his reforms. At this point, Ford condemns Eleanor for her English want of emotion, and in developing this point turns to praising Don's schemes as change and repudiating Eleanor for intellectual stagnation. The two themes simply do not work together, and all that can be said is that the novel achieves for the most part a general if ambivalent disapproval of Don's socialism.

Don's native faith in people is shown early in the novel. He remarks that "The huge—the infinite—mass of the people are good, decent, hardworking, and awfully idealist. Think of their record! They want Liberty, they want it as they want the air they breathe. And that's fine. It *is*." But Don's optimism is only theoretical, and on the trip to America, which occupies a good part of the novel, it undergoes a disillusioning test. On his first visit to Coney Island, Don wanders in a "dizzy gloom. This, he said, was the best they could do then! And there wasn't a trace of refinement, of intellect—even of thought."[38] Don had made the trip in order to redress the wrongs of his late and wealthy father. To Don, his father typifies "American business methods," and he wants "to drive that sort of thing out of the world." But even these plans are temporarily thwarted when the son in America finds that although his father has left him a huge amount of money, he is completely powerless to touch the trusts.[39]

The major part of the novel is concerned, then, with frustrating in various ways Don Kelleg's idealism. During the American trip, Don is disillusioned in three ways. First, he discovers that Kratzenstein, the

barber from whom Don's father had once stolen a mine, does not want his or any help. The man wants nothing that he cannot get by his own initiative or by stealing, and all that he asks of Don is that he rig the market for him on some worthless stocks.[40] Second, Don finds that in spite of his professed democratic faith, he cannot accept—and is repelled by—the popular culture of Coney Island. He wants only to return to England. Mr. Greville, Eleanor's father and the book's voice of common-sense Toryism, explains to his daughter that Don is "a poet. But he's like me in being hopelessly out of date with his time." After voicing one of Ford's major criticisms of the idealist, Greville continues by saying that Don really wants "the American people to go in for certain European virtues—for Poetry and The Higher Thought and Rational Dress." But, he adds, "How can they? America is made up of men who've fled from him just as much as they've fled from me. It's made up of people who left Europe because they could not stand Tory restraints or Poetic restraints."[41] Coney Island leaves Don highly discouraged, and his third frustration, the thwarting of his intentions by his father's will, only strengthens his resolve to return to England.

Up to this point the novel, if it lacks depth, is at least clear in its intent. But once in England, Don's idealism gets the best of him, and he decides to return to America, even though Eleanor will not follow him. The scene would seem to be set for another instance of the hero's inability for specific emotional response. But this time, it is not Don that Ford criticizes, but Eleanor. And strangely enough, the condemnation is made by Don's half-brother, Canzono, who in the previous parts of the book had represented the idea of living for the moment, of having "the taste of the present" on one's lips.[42] At the end of the novel Canzono reverses his position, and becomes an advocate of the future. He calls Eleanor "cowardly" for her refusal to go with Don, and asks of Don's striving: "Wasn't his craving to get at the best in life an action—wasn't it heroic?" And now his main criticism of Eleanor centers on her English reserve: "you are afraid of your own emotions: you are afraid that if you become passionate you will lose dignity. That's why you insist on maintaining your frigid exteriors."[43] *An English Girl*, for all its weaknesses, is perhaps important in that it is the first of Ford's novels in which the indictment of the English for their lack of passion is given explicit statement. It is a theme that Ford handles much more effectively in many of the important later novels.

While *The Benefactor* and *An English Girl* are basically studies of the hero as a type, and deal with English society indirectly, in *Mr. Apollo* Ford attempts a broader picture and writes a fantasy on the visit of a god to early twentieth-century London. As in *Ladies Whose Bright Eyes*, the use of fantasy allows the author to depart from a strict rendering of reality, and to make a more direct statement on the need for faith in the

post-Victorian world. The lack of a working faith was one of the problems which this world had inherited from the Great Victorians, and *Mr. Apollo*, despite certain obvious contrivances, is an effective presentation of this problem. There is in the novel no fully developed mortal hero, only a series of characters representing different responses to the god and to life in general. Mr. Apollo himself is inevitably heroic, by his very nature as a god; but he cannot be taken as a comment on the human hero, since this nature is itself so special. By using a Greek rather than a Judeo-Christian deity, Ford is able to avoid any sectarian connotations, and to emphasize his belief that it is quite possible to conceive of more than one god, and that the important response is not the selection of the proper god, but the basic act of faith itself. The god must, however, embody the quality of transcendence, of being greater than the human, and of thereby imparting a sense of human limitations. In this way, Ford's gods are distinguished from an elevated humanist ideal. A large part of the novel's appeal stems from its point that faith is dependent on man's recognition of his own smallness, and his willingness to receive comfort from the very recognition of his limitations. Thus faith begins for modern man with the awareness of his own unheroic limitations. He must recognize, even if he can never know a reality outside the self.

The novel itself falls into five parts. In the first, Mr. Apollo appears, is arrested and put on trial for disturbing the peace, and finally strikes the arresting constable dead for his inhospitality. In the second, the god encounters the equally inhospitable and self-inflated clergyman, the Reverend Todd. Todd is set against the simplicity and generosity of his wife and the honest curiosity of his daughter and her fiancé. At the end of the section Todd, an advocate of the heroic "muscular Christianity" of the Victorian period, is transformed into a bay tree and made to disappear. In the third section, Mr. Apollo encounters a generally likeable and searching group of young intellectuals at the home of Alfred Milne and his wife. In the fourth part, the god goes with Milne to a successful newspaper, and agrees to do a story which the paper never publishes. This agreement leads Milne to quarrel strongly with Apollo, since he cannot believe that the proposed public declaration of godhead is really true. Finally, in the fifth part, Milne is home without Apollo and very sick. But in answer to Mrs. Milne's prayers the god comes to aid him, and the Milnes are appointed Apollo's priests on earth.

The two persons first met by Apollo in the beginning of the novel are the two least sympathetically seen. The legalistic policeman and the opportunistic clergyman are both figures representing authority in their society, and neither can fully accept Mr. Apollo as a god. "Police Constable 742 L" when Apollo arrives is congratulating himself on the orderliness of his area, for "this pleased his will-ordered mind."[44] The descending god is an unforeseen interruption of his complacency, and the

THE EARLY NOVELS AND THE INEFFECTUAL HERO

officer arrests him for disturbing the peace. Since hospitality and generosity are the virtues Apollo is most seeking in man, he punishes the officer by striking him dead. This act, early in the novel, also serves to establish Apollo's divinity and awesomeness. In court, the god meets the Victorian clergyman. Todd has "no thoughts of his own material advantages," nor yet that "this personage ... might ... exalt him where preferment is to be obtained. That came, of course, later. For the moment he had merely the feeling that he would like—without loss of self-respect, of course—to fawn again this presence as a rat rubs itself against a man's legs."[45] The officer had simply responded out of blindness and a disturbed complacency, and save for its function in establishing Apollo's identity, his death is rather unjustified. The Reverend Todd, by contrast, is a self-centered parasite, and easily the pettiest character in the book. The irony of giving this distinction to a clergyman in a religious novel is obvious.

In strong contrast to the devious minister, there is the spontaneous newsboy, whose agile and rhythmic involvement in his work as he runs and calls through the streets gives Mr. Apollo great pleasure.[46] The boy's behavior is immediate and unself-conscious, and it is these qualities that the god admires. Also in contrast to her husband, there is the lonely and sympathetic Mrs. Todd. Apollo goes home with the clergyman, and when his wife sees the god, "to her lonely soul the sight of this stranger was so good to look upon, was like a warmth in that chilly room, a companion in her loneliness." In her generosity, she worries over Mr. Apollo's comfort: "Poor dear; it is evident a person used to *his* surroundings will find these highly dismal."[47] Apollo, wanting to punish Reverend Todd for his inhospitality, and reasoning that Mrs. Todd will be happier without him, changes him to a bay tree. Mrs. Todd, however, needs someone to serve, and she prays for her husband's return. She wants "to hear him speak but ten words," and toward the end of the novel the god grants her request, but declares that if the minister's first ten words are egocentric, then he must remain for the rest of his life dumb like a tiny child. In a marvelously bitter and comic scene, the Reverend Todd falls into the room and utters his ten words: "I have done nothing to be ashamed of, mark that!" He lies on the floor, unable to do anything but move his fingers "convulsively, like an unweaned child's, out and in to the palms of his hands."[48]

The Todd family encompasses two extremes, but neither the Reverend nor Mrs. Todd gives any serious thought to the significance of Apollo as a god. Mrs. Todd is simply generous, and her husband simply does not care. The serious and sometimes questioning thoughts, and thus the representation of a prevalent modern attitude, are left to the circle gathered around Alfred Milne and his wife. This group is made up primarily of young educated people, teachers and other professionals, and their response is sufficiently serious and openminded so that they are seen with considerable sympathy. Alfred Milne himself has moved from the posi-

tion of "a militant, a harshly full-blooded atheist to that of a weary and gentle agnostic. He was not startled; he was not regretful; he accepted the change as he accepted the diminution of his youthful ideas." As for Mrs. Milne, she has revealed to her husband "that she could not—she dare not—any longer believe that when we died we went into nothingness."[49] The Milnes' flat is the meeting place for their circle of friends. "They came and they talked of Hygiene, of Aesthetics, a little of Music, a great deal of Socialism, hardly at all of Religion, but then with a frenzied animation, for several were Roman Catholics, and charged the deniers of Romish miracles with lack of perception, of logic, of the historic sense."[50] Typical of the group is Carver, a young science student, whose father had been a jobbing gardener for aristocratic neighborhoods. Carver's background and his need to assert himself have given him a hostile disputatious manner, and as a further sign of defiance he has a tendency to force a cockney dialect. At first, he opposes Mr. Apollo, and is particularly adamant in denying the miraculousness of certain demonstrations which the god performs. But Apollo is able to convince Carver that "by your hasty words and unlovely manner you have injured the cause you have at heart." And the god's most significant miracle is that he is able to effect a total change in Carver's attitude and behavior, so that Carver himself becomes a more sympathetic character.[51]

The only member of the Milnes' circle who remains hostile to Mr. Apollo, and even then on a primarily philosophical level, is Mr. Clarges, one of the few older men. Clarges represents the aggressive Victorian denouncer of religious faith, and embodies a major mode of Victorian heroism. Mrs. Milne challenges him by saying, "if, as you say, you destroyed revealed religion in the last century, you left the field open to doubts and speculations." But Clarges, for whom the very idea of uncertainty would be an admission of failure, replies: "We said there was no immortal principle; we said that evolution accounted for all things upon a natural basis . . . We were definite; we knew. . . . We denied all metamorphoses from those of the Scriptures to those of Ovid or the *Arabian Nights*. We *knew*." Because he knows, Clarges has spent his time "exposing Charlatans for forty years." His almost too-anxious defiance is illustrated in a dream which he relates to Mr. Apollo, and it is a dream that typifies what Ford saw as the presumption of the Victorian period. "I dreamt," Clarges relates, "I was in a desert with Huxley and Tyndall. And we saw a great globe of fire coming towards us. And it was the Godhead. And Tyndall fell down on his face and cried out, 'Holy, Holy: Lord God Almighty.' And Huxley said, 'Mind! I never said there wasn't a god, I only said I did not know.'" "And you?" Apollo asks him. Clarges answers that he is "not one to boast," even of his dreams. But Apollo, to Clarges' astonishment, correctly finishes the narration of the dream: "You

uttered these words: 'Shall I have been denying God for forty years to eat my words now?' And you took up a stone and cast it at the great light."[52]

The doubts of Margery Snyde, another member of the group, are of a totally different sort. Margery is a serious Roman Catholic, and when Apollo performs his miracles, she thinks him an emissary of Satan, and flees. But Apollo tells her:

> Child . . . God in his mercy is other than you take Him to be. The universe is very wide, and in it there is space for many gods . . . And you do well . . . for I tell you this; that though your doings be indifferent to God, who, being God, is awfully needless of your prayers and help, yet, in so far as you are true to your God, you help yourself.[53]

And the god expresses a similar view to Clarges, remarking to him that "the universe is so very great—being infinite—and in it there is room for a multitude of gods—even for an infinite number."[54] The point made by this argument is that it is not necessary to profess the "truth" about God, but simply to have faith, a faith which has its basis in man's longing and recognition of his own limitations. Mrs. Milne feels this longing at a time when Alfred is in great despair, and in "need of the proof that he was lovable." His wife wants more than anything to comfort him, but does not know how to begin. "She felt herself suddenly as it were his mother, and again for the first time, there came into her head the idea of an appeal—for his sake—to some one, to something, that was greater and more potent than they two."[55]

But if the need for faith and the sense of a limited self are the key attitudes advanced by the novel, Alfred Milne is the one character who would like, but finds it most difficult, to acquire these attitudes. When Mr. Apollo agrees to write an article for Lord Aldington's paper, Alfred finds this tangible profession of divinity beyond the scope of his belief and approval. He returns home, without either his guest or his faith, and becomes seriously ill. Strangely enough, the presence of the god had increased Alfred's own confidence in himself, perhaps because he no longer needed to make god-like demands of himself. In order to recover, Alfred needs sunlight and air, and he can get neither because of the smoke and grime from Victoria Mansions, a large slum complex across the street. This significantly-named structure is, in relation to the Milnes' own apartment building, "not so high, but infinitely more grimy, and tenebrous, of a brown-coloured brick covered with soot." Its inhabitants are "a squalid and ferocious population," who Mr. Apollo finds extremely "inhospitable." Consequently, during Alfred's illness, the god answers his wife's prayers and helps cure the sick man by levelling Victoria Mansions

to the ground.[56] Symbolically, the corrupt squalor of urbanized Victorian England has been destroyed, and the way is clear for the sunlight of a new faith, for which Alfred Milne and his wife will be the first priests.

In a consideration of the Fordian hero, *Mr. Apollo* is an important novel in that it so openly condemns Victorian England and proposes an alternative faith, an integral part of which is the recognition of human limitations. This recognition is the first state of a self-awareness that will be the prerequisite to the development of the limited hero.

In his final collaboration with Conrad, *The Nature of a Crime*, Ford returned to a reconsideration of the paralyzed hero. The hero of this later work differs from previous characters such as George Moffat in that he is less conventionally moral and far more self-analytical. He is still heroic in his sense of his own importance, but his egoism is of a precarious and psychologically-complex sort. The collaboration first appeared in the *English Review* for April and May, 1909, under the pseudonym of Baron Ignatz von Aschendorf. It was not published in book form—and then against Conrad's wish—until 1924. In the Preface to the hard-bound edition, Conrad links the intent of the book with that of *The Inheritors* by saying that it "contains the crudely materialistic atmosphere of the time of its origin." He also notes that it is " a piece of work in the nature of an analytical confession."[57] The device of using for the novel letters written by the narrator to a woman with whom he is in love allows the authors to penetrate the narrator's mind and to show his sense of self-importance. His confession achieves an admirable complexity, a curious picture of psychological dualism, that is particularly disturbing. The book is short, but in sustained tone it is an adroit piece of literary craftsmanship.

The hero is ineffectual. Until the end, he can make no commitment to the woman he professes to love. But he has also been much more corrupted than previous Fordian heroes, and he adopts the ethical mode of the very society that he writes of with such spite. His crime is part of his conscious defiance of this society, and along with his constant self-denigration, it forms one of the two motifs of his confession.

The narrator, as he reveals in his first letter, is in love with a woman who is currently in Rome with her husband. Instead of doing anything about his feelings, however, he has attempted to forget her by embezzling funds from a wealthy young man to whom he is legal advisor, and then using these funds for gambling. As the novel opens, he believes himself about to be discovered, and so plans suicide, the final act of defiance. He writes to the woman:

> It is, of course, no disclosure to tell you that I love you. A very great reverence is due to youth—and a very great latitude is due to the dead. For I am dead; I have lived only through you for how many

years now! And I shall never speak with you again. Some sort of burial will have been given to me before the end of April. I am a spirit. I have ended my relations with the world.

It is only now that he tells the woman for the first time that he loves her. Since it will not be realized and never had been, his love remains on the level of an abstraction—unreal—and he writes her that with the thought of suicide, the world and other people seem "unreal" to him as well.[58]

The criminal feels himself entirely of his time, "altogether of my time —lacking courage for a swoop, as a bird respects a ragged and nerveless scarecrow. Altogether a man of my time." But because he is continuously engulfed in his self-awareness, and because he has been incapable of commiting—or even declaring—himself to the woman he loves, he has found his only refuge in "abasement," in defying the society which he hates by immersing himself in its corrupt and materialistic values. "Perhaps I was mad. I gambled. I gambled first with my own money and then with money that was not mine." Thus, he has embezzled funds from his wealthy charge to sustain his "abasement." He recognizes his own lack of moral values, and admits that even if "there had been kingdoms to conquer, a crusade to preach . . . I should not have had the courage to go beyond the sound of your voice." And as for faith, although he senses that "Reason forces one to believe in an Omnipotent Ruler," he is himself "unable to believe."[59] All that is left for him is a perverse and defiant pleasure in his own cleverness and degradation. And he convinces himself that his failure to commit himself to the woman is really restraint, and then elevates this supposed restraint into an ideal. He writes to the woman that "I am ready to give my life for this Ideal: nay more, I am ready to sacrifice you to it, since I know that life for you will remain a very bitter thing. I know, a little, what renunciation means." And he asks her to bear all this, "for the sake of my ideal of you."[60] Ford and Conrad have created here a magnificent irony: this self-deceiving, valueless hero is willing to "sacrifice" the woman with whom he is in love to a false ideal which is actually a substitute for his professed lack of ideals. The spiral of abstraction and deluded self-awareness here becomes almost grotesque.

In the midst of his renunciation, gambling, and embezzlement, the narrator tries to justify himself by a sense of moral superiority over his victim. This is a significant psychological detail, for we can observe the narrator attempting to transform his own sense of chaos and inferiority into feelings of superiority that even he will believe. His response is simply another case of heroic self-inflation. The narrator writes that he regards Edward Burden, his charge, as gross and insensitive to the "tiny vanity" of his fiancée. He remarks that if he were Burden, "I should bend all my energies to giving her opportunities for displaying her charm, her

discreteness or her coquetry." Burden, the narrator feels, is in fact "dragging her down" to his own "social or material necessities." Earlier he had noted that he resented Burden for the certainty of his life, and that he felt "toward him: a little like a deity, a little like an avenging Providence."[61] The narrator carries over his sense of acting as a god into his justification of the embezzlement. He says that he hates "all the Edward Burdens of the world—because, being the eternal Haves of the world, they have made their idiotic rules of the game. And you and I suffer: you and I, the eternal Have Nots. And we suffer, not because their rules bind us, but because, being the finer spirits, we are forced to set ourselves rules that are still more strict in order that, in all things, we may be truly gallant."[62] It is obvious that the narrator is easily able to delude himself, and to live in terms of verbal abstractions, without any sense of his own limitations or the realities of his situation. And this self-declared "deity," for all his sense of mission, is about to take his own life until he is stopped by a sudden change of feeling.

This change is significant because it takes the form of a sudden awareness of specific and everyday sensations, and the discovery of these sensations brings the narrator back to a desire for life. He had been walking on the street, and since he was about to die, the world "had lost all interest." Suddenly, however, everything became "Vivid: that is the word. I watched a newsboy throw his papers down an area, and it appeared wonderfully interesting to discover that *that* was how one's papers got into the house. I watched a milkman go up some doorsteps to put a can of milk beside a bootscraper, and I was wonderfully interested to see a black cat follow him. They were the clearest moments I have ever spent upon the earth—those when I was dead." And this new involvement in the particulars of life inspires the narrator to make a commitment—although a partial one—to the woman. He writes at the end that he will "put Burden's estate absolutely clear within the year and work out, in order to make safe money," a "new and comparatively sober scheme," provided that she will consent to be his, "to the extent of sharing our thoughts alone." Finally, he tells her that "I stand reprieved—and the final verdict is in your hands."[63] This is a much stronger commitment to the woman than he has ever previously made. And yet the narrator still cannot completely engage himself, and he qualifies his final action by the response of the girl. The sense of himself as providential is gone, but full engagement in a specific situation has not yet been attained.

The Nature of a Crime, although one of Ford's shorter works and a collaboration with Conrad, can be seen finally as an effective study of a self-inflated, almost paranoiac hero, with all the complexities of personality which paranoia entails. Thus the narrator until the end is not only like George Moffat, ineffectual; but unlike Moffat, he is much more susceptible to corruption by his society. He is in this sense closer to

THE EARLY NOVELS AND THE INEFFECTUAL HERO

Etchingham Granger, but his debasement, unlike Granger's is sustained over a long period of time, and is part of a continuous double personality. Troubled by both a strong sense of inferiority and a compensating sense of grandeur, the narrator reacts throughout the novel with both hypocrisy and introspection. And although both leave him unable to respond to the woman, the introspection complicates our own response to the hypocrisy, for we acquire some insight into the double nature of the narrator's statements. He is given a complexity that takes him far beyond caricature and forces us to take him seriously, even as one of ourselves.

A new dimension is added by Ford to the ineffectual hero in *A Call: The Tale of Two Passions*, written in 1910; and this novel, too, is marked by considerable psychological subtlety, at least in the portrait of the main character, Robert Grimshaw. In Grimshaw we have for the first time in Ford's work a figure whose false idealism is based on a presumed role of social correctness, and the only fault of the novel as a whole is that some of the other central characters are not as clearly motivated. Grimshaw's insistence on propriety sets his behavior apart from the less social altruism of George Moffat and anticipates the theme of convention which is central to *The Good Soldier*. The responses on the major characters, such as Katya Lascarides and Pauline Leicester, are to an extent reactions to Grimshaw's own inaction. But except for their dependence on Grimshaw's responses, these other characters are not as clearly motivated. They can in themselves establish no counterforce to Grimshaw's ineffectuality, and in fact grow to assume much of this ineffectuality themselves.

Robert Grimshaw, with his marked predilection for self-denial and social propriety, typifies even more than the others the English society of which Ford wrote in *The Spirit of the People*, and which was marked by its inability to deal with situations involving passion by its much too strong concern for propriety. This code of behavior can inspire a false heroism when it becomes for people such as Grimshaw a mode of life rather than a controlling restraint in specific situations. In *A Call* the code so distorts reality for Grimshaw and destroys his freedom that he is finally forced to submit to the dominant Katya on her terms, and is left with only a useless insight into his own dilemma.

As the novel opens, we see that Grimshaw has yielded Pauline Lucas to his friend, Dudley Leicester, because he thought it the proper thing to do. He admits to Ellida Langham, the sister of Katya Lascarides, that he has "now given" Dudley "What was dearest and best to me." Grimshaw has only recently broken an engagement with Katya, because he cannot accept her terms of marriage. He confesses to Ellida that while "Katya could give me companionship," Pauline could "have given me worship." But Grimshaw has, in spite of his preference, given Pauline away to Dudley, after already having put Dudley's estates in order. Now, as he tells Ellida, he had given Dudley Pauline because "that's how Society has

to go on. It's the sort of thing that's got to happen to make us the civilized people that we are." Pauline becomes another instrument for the raising of Dudley Leicester: "She'll make a man of him. She'll give him a career. He'll be her life's work." Grimshaw goes on to link his behavior to that of his class: "We're all—all of us, in our class and our day, doing the same thing. Every one of us really wants the moon, and we've got somehow to get on with just the earth, and behave ourselves."[64]

If Grimshaw's lack of overt passion is based on a mistaken sense of responsibility, Dudley Leicester, the object of his responsibility, is almost an emotional vacuum, a void into which Grimshaw pumps effort like wasted air. Dudley has "never done anything," and he has no comprehension of "personal attitudes in those around him. The minute jealousies, the very deep hatreds, and the strong passions that swelled in his particular world of deep idleness, of high feeling and want of occupation—in this world where . . . there were so many things to feel—Dudley Leicester perceived absolutely nothing, no complexities, no mixed relationships."[65] One of the ironies of the novel lies in the priority which Grimshaw, who is at least potentially a leader, gives to the needs of the idle and insensitive Dudley, who can do little but follow. Grimshaw misdirects his energies and represses his feelings because he is misled by a distorting sense of convention.

Katya Lascarides, the woman with whom Grimshaw has recently broken an engagement, is herself dominated by her own abstractions. At the start of the novel, which begins after the engagement has already been broken, we learn that Katya has gone to Philadelphia, where as a psychologist she is fulfilling her sense of responsibility. But the idea of good works is not the only inflexible ideal by which Katya is motivated. She wants also to follow her mother's example of a common-law marriage. Nonetheless, as she returns on the ship to England, her thoughts about Grimshaw indicate that she is far more susceptible to his influence than she will admit. She wants to escape from her own inflexibility by having Grimshaw overpower her, and to herself asks him, "Oh, Robert Grimshaw, why don't you bring me to my knees."[66] Once in England, she tells Grimshaw that her mother had insisted on a common-law marriage because she wanted to trust her husband "absolutely." For this same reason, Katya professes to want a similar arrangement. But Grimshaw, despite his claim to "want you with all my heart" will not accept her terms. Ironically, the very fact that she has expressed affection for him had, he claims, given him the strength to refuse her. He feels more certain of an affection which both have only skirted, and Katya can do nothing but ask sardonically, "If I'd refused you, you'd have given in?"[67] Both Grimshaw and Katya are too imbued with the particular inflexibilities, Katya with her goal of common-law marriage and Grimshaw with his

concept of correctness, to be able to respond to their need for each other. And if Grimshaw is caught between his attraction to both Pauline and Katya, he commits himself to neither, but only makes an act of wasted sacrifice which leaves him nothing but frustration and jealousy.

Grimshaw's jealousy leads to the central incident from which the book receives its title. One night, after he is married to Pauline, Dudley goes home with Etta Stackpole Hudson, his one-time fiancée. She taunts him and he follows her inside. While there, Dudley hears the phone and answers it without thinking, only to learn that his voice is recognized by the "invisible man" on the other end of the line. Dudley goes into "a sudden panic" and hangs up the receiver. But the mystery of this call slowly drives him mad. The caller remains unknown until the end of the book, when Grimshaw admits to Pauline that it had been himself. When he had seen Dudley with Etta Stackpole, he had been overcome by bitter and passionate jealousy: "This sort of marriage of convenience, was," he had thought to himself with regard to the one he had arranged for Dudley, "the sort of thing that in their sort of life was frequent and successful enough, and having been trained in the English code of manners never to express any emotions at all, he had forgotten that he possessed emotions. Now he was up against it." The call itself had been compulsive: "The whites of his eyes gleamed below the dark irises, his white teeth showed, and as he clasped the instrument to him he appeared, as it were, a Shylock who clutched to his breast his knife and demanded of the universe his right to the peace of mind that knowledge at least was to give him."[68]

This incident shows that Grimshaw's sense of propriety is essentially a veneer, covering a passion which when suppressed too long can only erupt in such an expression of pent-up feelings. And while Grimshaw's sense of propriety and responsibility is the most clearly delineated, other characters are in part similarly motivated. Pauline, already the victim of Grimshaw's sacrifice, tells him at one point that she has known of Dudley's meeting with Etta Stackpole. But she has decided that life will not give her what she wants, and therefore she will play for Dudley the role of "Nursery Governess."[69] Grimshaw himself tells Etta at one point that he had intentially diverted Dudley from her, even before Dudley had married Pauline. He adds that his Greek ancestry on his mother's side has given him "a sense of responsibility. I can't bear to see chaps of my class—of my class and my country—going wrong." All the main characters in the novel use their sense of propriety to avoid a direct confrontation of their own emotions. Grimshaw tries to speak to Etta about her suspected relationship with Dudley, whom he thinks to have been "carrying on an intrigue with you all that time." Grimshaw is of course mistaken, and Etta, who sees through him, observes that he *"wanted* to believe that" Dudley "was mean and deceitful" so that he could again

claim Pauline for himself. But Grimshaw cannot yet bring himself to admit his responsibility for the phone call and Dudley's subsequent madness, because this would be an admission of his own emotional core.[70] Thus, his sense of responsibility is confined to the sphere of social expectation, and it becomes a means by which he can evade the burden of himself.

The strongest spokesman against this illusory and abstract responsibility is a Greek Orthodox priest whom Grimshaw meets one day. The priest advises Grimshaw to think less of propriety and more in terms of his immediate actions: "And to do what you want, unless obviously it is evil, is to follow the dictates of the instincts that God has placed in you." Grimshaw asks if the priest means to say that "we should not think too much of the effects of our deeds?" and the priest answers, "Not too much. . . . For then we shall lose much Christian charity." The implication here is that too great an awareness of consequences drives one further into the self and lessens the ability to respond empathetically to others. The priest counsels Grimshaw to seek meaningful human relationships:

> Bring one unto the other, that mutual comprehension may result. That is the way of Christian fellowship; that is the way to bring about the peace of God on earth.[71]

Unfortunately, it is this very sensitivity to and expressiveness in significant human relationship that Grimshaw most lacks. At one point, he is walking with Katya, trying to convince her to help cure Dudley's madness. For Grimshaw, this conversation is both an evasion of Katya and an alleviation of guilt; but when he says to her, "It's that other thing you must end," she thinks he is speaking of their own impasse with each other. When she learns the truth, however, Katya exclaims, "No wonder you can't give in to me if you've got to be thinking of him all the time." And later when Ellida advises Grimshaw to bring Katya "to her knees," he only replies that he is "tired out."[72]

Grimshaw's fatigue stems from the despair and frustration of never having brought himself to fully express his true feelings. Most of his encounters have ended with an evasion of the emotion behind them. Only to Pauline does he finally begin to express some of his doubts, but she has by this time closed herself to any compassion toward him. She feels that he has "ruined all our lives," and tells him that "If you were the only man in the world, my dear, I would never look at you again." She feels that their situation can never end for the good, and points ironically to the useless propriety which their class has assumed:

> That again . . . is our day and our class. And that's the best that's to be said for us. We haven't learned wisdom; we've only learned how to behave. We cannot avoid tragedies.[73]

THE EARLY NOVELS AND THE INEFFECTUAL HERO

The English, as Ford sees them, do not and cannot avoid tragic situations. But they do, by virtue of their weak emotional response, avoid that direct confrontation of situations, of themselves, or of each other, that would give them the stature of tragic heroes. If they assume any heroic stance at all, it is a heroism of rhetoric or of adherence to their social codes, and this sort of heroism is meaningless in its very evasion of the tragic confrontation. The encounter with crisis should force upon the tragic hero a strong sense of his own human limitations. The rhetorical hero, facing no criteria for measurement except the values which the group attaches to his words, persists in his own self-inflation; and when he does encounter a situation which might measure his capabilities, he emerges with little knowledge of himself.

The conclusion of *A Call* is a good example of the anti-tragic nature of the Fordian world. Grimshaw ends the novel in much the same way that he began. He is, if anything, forced into a role of greater passivity. Pauline will have nothing to do with him, despite the fact that she freely admits that she remains attracted to him. She, too, resigns herself to a life of expected duty. Grimshaw admits his role in the mysterious phone call, and he is left humbled by Katya, to whom he must submit on her own terms. There is no real sense of resolution, and except for Katya who has her conquest, the lives of the characters will go on much as before. In his epilogue to the novel, Ford remarks on its inclusiveness, and speaks of the technique of the "affair:"

> For me, as you know, a book must have a beginning and an end. But whereas for you the end is something arbitrarily final, such as the ring of wedding bells, a funeral service, or the taking of a public house, for me—since to me a novel is the history of an 'affair'—finality is only found at what seems to be the end of that 'affair.' There is in life nothing final. So that even 'affairs' never really have an end as far as the lives of the actors are concerned.[74]

In a truly heroic world, there would be a resolute ending because the hero would have met the situation directly, even if only to be killed by it. But as Wiley remarks, "an important feature of *A Call* and a presage of *The Good Soldier* is its evidence of Ford's grasp of a form distinct from that of heroic tragedy and adopted to the restraints of an unheroic world."[75] *A Call* is Ford's most skillful handling of the structure of the "affair" before *The Good Soldier*, although it does not achieve the complicated texture of the later work. The "affair" was, however, a device that Ford was temporarily to abandon until that later novel, which he considered the culmination of his craft. After *A Call*, Ford turned his attention to four novels of satire, three of which were built on a dislike of the emerging political hero, a figure who was to appear far more frequently in his writings after the War.

THE LIMITED HERO

In Ford's pre-War political satires, the heroes are not yet full-time politicians. They are motivated by the same self-interest as their more professional successors, but their sphere is quite special and still detached from national policy. In contrast to later Fordian characters, they have not yet become mass leaders, and consequently their role is not so much one of manipulating and controlling the public as of satirizing their private foibles and personal gain. These early political figures can even seem to Ford slightly ridiculous, for at this state they have not yet inflicted the great War upon the world.

The first of the political novels, *The Simple Life Limited*, appeared in 1911. With this work Ford temporarily abandoned the depiction of complex characters, creating instead a set of broadly sardonic caricatures. This and his next novel he published under the pseudonym of Daniel Chaucer. Naumberg has verified the pseudonym as Ford's by citing a letter from Ford to Violet Hunt in his first edition copy of *The Simple Life Limited*. It is dated Giesse, April 9th, 1911, and is signed "Daniel Chaucer."[76] Wiley suggests that in these two novels, "when Ford mocks living individuals thinly disguised ... the ridicule cuts deep enough at times to suggest a reason for his publishing the book under the pseudonym of 'Daniel Chaucer.' "[77] Both the use of the pen-name and the grossly-portrayed characters suggest a rather embittered and predominantly satiric attitude toward the new and burgeoning variant of the hero.

The Simple Life Limited is very much one of Ford's weaker novels. It is an attempt to satirize the socialism of men such as William Morris, who advocated a return to an economically and productively simple existence, and whom Ford regarded as rather like children. In its satire, however, the novel relies too heavily on caricature and coincidence, and both the characters and action are badly motivated. Ford's attitudes are rendered by taking a group of Simple Lifers and juxtaposing them against other characters or situations with which they can be contrasted. These contrasts generally serve to highlight the unreality of the so-called Simple Life. On the one hand, for example, there are Simon Brandson and Horatio Gubb, two of the leaders of the colony and both rather comic individuals, and on the other Gerald Luscombe, the landowner on whose estate the Simple Life Colony settles, and who without any doctrine treats the peasants far better than do the colonists, who turn them off their land. One contrast is brought together in the person of Gubb's son, Hamnet, who changes from a Simple Lifer to an early limited hero when he decides to live alone in the woods. The Simple Life scheme finally appears as an amusing aggregation of characters, none of whom are capable of making any utopia achieve the promise of its name.

The plot of the novel is largely a succession of devices which continue to show the childishness and hypocrisy of the colony. The first scene

opens with the strange marriage of Hamnet Gubb and Ophelia Brandson, who will later be forced to separate by their parents because marriage is against the rules of the community. But now the young couple (their names suggesting the two Shakespearean characters whose love was thwarted by the moral chaos of their parents' world) approach the house of Gerald Luscombe. They denounce him as a property owner, but Luscombe only asks them in out of the rain. Hamnet continues his harangue, but suddenly Ophelia asks Luscombe to rent them a cottage. Luscombe informs them that he would have to evict the present occupants, and Hamnet replies, "You could find them another cottage. . . . We have decided that that one would exactly suit us," and Ophelia adds that they "desire . . . to lead the Simple Life." The attitudes of the couple are further revealed as Hament tells Luscombe that the "principle" of his existence is "protest," and Ophelia adds that theirs is "a union of reason. We enter upon it without any passion; it is purely utilitarian."[78] The same defiant attitude is adopted by the four Lee children, daughters of Mrs. Lee, an ardent Simple Lifer who is having an affair with the romantic fugitive, Brandetski. The girls' father, Mr. Lee, is a financier who in the city assumes the name of Henry Augustus Pierpoint. Two of the children side violently with their mother; the other two with their father, and none of them wants to grow up and become a woman.[79] Ironically, the childish self-indulgence of the utopian adults has inspired anything but childlike innocence in their children.

The two most interesting members of the colony are Brandson and Gubb, its leaders. Each is essentially a rhetorician, but the motives behind their rhetoric are different. Brandson is the theoretician of the group. Born a Slav, he had worked as superintendent of a British railway in Africa, where his policy had been that "the only thing for the subordinate races was the whip." Later he had become a writer, and but for his laziness might have been great. One day in a fit of rage he had beaten out the brains of a dog over whom he had tripped; and the recollection of the incident had stayed with him and hampered his writing.[80] In his period of greatest inactivity, Brandson had met Horatio Gubb, a solicitor, "a close disciple and friend of the late Mr. William Morris," and "a parasitic gentleman, who fattened entirely upon the associations and upon the ideas of such distinguished people as would permit him to enter their homes." Gubb, after Morris' death, had begun to waver in his socialism, but his support of the Boers in the Boer War, begun for business reasons, had lost him most of his clients.

Gubb soon discovered Brandson's ability to play the role of prophet, and established a subscription fund for him, which also proved somewhat profitable to himself. From this fund the colony had grown.[81] Gubb had then conceived the idea of forming a company which would let out land to the inhabitants of the colony. Yet the motive behind Gubb's scheme at

the time was not profit. Rather, he wished "to be the actual organiser, the dictator of a prosperous 'going' concern along lines of a sufficient idealism to gain for himself a certain sphere of influence." He wanted to be able to stop almost always having "to adopt the attitude of a sort of today." Nevertheless, by the time that Gubb is attempting to convince Luscombe to make further investments in the colony, Ford comments that "The Simple Life paid. It paid well. It paid very well." And Luscombe points out that it "paid a dividend of eight and a half per cent upon the first year's workings."[82] Both Brandson and Gubb, true to their tradition of simplicity, make their own clothes, but "Gubb had always the air of being a plump and prosperous stockbroker disguised, to please himself, as a convict."[83]

Gubb's dedication to the colony is a strange mixture of opportunism and fanaticism. He is able to make the community into a paying venture, or to oppose Hamnet's marriage to Ophelia because it will make the community appear disunited while they are negotiating for new land, and at the same time he can voice his opposition through the argument that marriage is "contrary to the principles of the Simple Life." He can utilize the needs of the colony as a reason for almost anything because, as he tells the young couple, "it is your duty to sacrifice your individual wishes to the good of the whole community."[84] Thus Gubb and Brandson head a community built out of inferiority feelings, based on rhetoric, and elevated to a comic heroism. As for its roots, the colony is not even in touch with the farming class to which it claims to be returning. The local villagers, whom the colonists had forced from their homes when they took over their portion of Luscombe's land, view the Simple Lifers as "foreigners because they were not local men," and they think nothing of yelling at or stoning the colonists. They even attack Brandson.[85] And hostile villagers are not the only problem which the community faces. Luscombe, after an experimental investment of five thousand pounds, refuses any further support for the colony, not because it is a financial failure, but because he is disappointed by evidences of the colonists' dissipation. Gubb himself appears at his most blatantly opportunistic when he is trying unsuccessfully to argue with the landowner. At this point, Ford might have gained a trenchant satirical effect by allowing the colony to dissipate away or to prosper through a scheme of outright profiteering. But instead he introduces a highly melodramatic climax which, while it links the colony to a foolish romanticism, weakens the earlier satire both by overpowering it and by straining credibility.

The climax appears in the form of Cyril Brandetski, a self-dramatizing romantic who has served in Russia as a spy both for and against the Czar. He is currently fleeing the Russian police. Symbolically, Brandetski links the colony to the world of political intrigue and romantic revolt, a world to which it is indirectly related by its professed Utopianism. But as a

character in the story, Brandetski seems contrived and artificial. He often seems a ludicrous beast-like man, flaunting about in a fury of self-indulgent emotionalism. For example, although he is having an affair with Mrs. Lee, Brandetski soon becomes obsessed by the image of Ophelia, and he says to Hamnet, "All these days I am fevered, I am torn with agony." After this declaration, "The Russian shrieked, clenched his fist to the sky, turned, sprang over the low gate, crashed through the low gate, crashed through the brambles and then disappeared amongst the black shadows of the firwood."[86] His passion for Ophelia grows more and more intense, and leads to the climactic episode of the book. This episode begins with a testimonial ceremony which has been arranged by Mrs. Lee for Mr. Gubb. Ophelia disrupts the proceedings, however, by delivering a surprise speech in which she criticizes the Simple Lifers as people who are "afraid to face life."[87] After this speech, Brandetski, who has by now convinced himself that Ophelia is an agent of the Russian police, attacks and threatens to kill her. Ophelia is saved by Hamnet, but the distraught Russian melodramatically sets fire to the colony and then kills himself. The tone of satire is lost in the action, and the novel is reduced to a level of unnecessary triteness.

After the excitement, Hamnet retires alone to the woods, where he becomes a precursor of the limited hero. He is by now separated from Ophelia, who has married a theatrical producer, and he proposes that the Simple Life is "to know the life you like and to have the courage to lead it. You don't have to organize: you don't want to make it the Simple Life Limited: you just want to go ahead. If you think about Life it isn't Life." Hamnet's goal is now to become completely spontaneous, to do away with self-consciousness. The secret, he tells Brandson, is to act in accord with one's impulses, which come in phases, so that one day a person may live in the woods while the next he may be "up in London dashing about in motor cars."[88] Hamnet's reduction of the Simple Life to the private sphere is very much in line with Ford's position, as is his admiration of the artist's response and his view of himself as "an artist in Life." But Hamnet is still in revolt against the over-organized life of his father's venture, and his position lacks the coherent self-definition which was later to mark the limited hero. The novel remains primarily a critique of the organized Simple Life, and Hamnet's final statement of a spontaneous alternative is less a program than a mark of his revolt.

The political overtones of Ford's next two novels, *The New Humpty-Dumpty* and *Mr. Fleight*, are far more ominous. Each of these two novels takes the theme which most preoccupied Ford before the War—the breakdown of the Great Man—and links it to the theme of political corruption by having a potentially virtuous figure become the one most fully corrupted. The same subject had previously been treated by Ford and Conrad in *The Inheritors*, but in that novel too many characters had

been introduced in too short a space and the impact of Granger's deterioration had been blunted by a confused development as well as by the use of fantasy. In Ford's other pre-War political novel, *The Simple Life Limited*, the characters as we have seen were little more than caricatures. In *The New Humpty-Dumpty* and *Mr. Fleight* the surface quality is retained, in that the novels never probe the psychological motivations of their characters. But the note of ridiculous comedy which had marked the treatment of the Simple Lifers is gone, replaced now by a greater sense of foreboding, and of consequences that are far less removed from the realm of the possible.

In *The New Humpty-Dumpty*, which appeared in 1912 also under the name of Daniel Chaucer, Ford shows the inability of political action to come to grips with human imperfection, or "the dark forest" of the human heart. The book was in fact originally to be called "The Dark Forest," and this proposed title suggests that the novel's implications are more than political.[89] The plot centers around a proposed counter-revolution in the small republic of Galizia. The attempt to restore the monarch is backed by various monied interests, including the English Lady Aldington and a wealthy American, Dexter, for purely mercenary reasons. They employ as organizer of their scheme Count Sergius Macdonald, the Humpty-Dumpty who will by the end of the novel tumble from his high wall. Macdonald himself is a great man without any reasons for greatness. He is admired for his seeming aristocratic virtues, but it soon becomes evident that these virtues are merely a veneer covering "the dark forest," the soon-exposed area of his vulnerability. Like the other ineffectual heroes in Ford's work, however, he does not recognize these limitations, but lives instead under an aura of heroism. He professes, for example, to take part in the counter-revolution only out of an aristocratic curiosity, but in actuality he is motivated by what turns out to be a superficial interest in Lady Aldington. Thus, the counter-revolution is quickly seen as a commercial plot, led by an aristocrat without values who quickly becomes inflated with his own position, and who is in the end assassinated. It is scarcely the sort of beginning that, even if successful, would lead to a very stable government.

The idealized image of Macdonald is used by the others to justify the counter-revolution, for if the plot is to succeed, it must be masked by a veil of heroic words. The theoretician for the group is the converted Fabian, Herbert Pett, whose motives are about as noble as his name implies. Mrs. Pett explains Pett's theories, which are a reversal of common socialist doctrine, to a group of counter-revolutionaries:

> It struck Herbert . . . that if you've already got a stratum of society that does its duty automatically and efficiently, we Socialists were on the wrong track. We were trying to pull down when we ought to have

been trying to lift up. What struck Herbert was that *he* ought to have been trained to act as Macdonald acted, not that Macdonald ought to have been levelled down to act like Herbert, or rather not to act at all.[90]

There is a double irony in Pett's theory. First, it is an adulation of the heroic figure, and especially of a particular hero who is hardly as elevated as Pett professes to think. And second, Pett had originally cultivated Macdonald in order to take advantage of the Count's wealth and to advance his own position. Pett, that is to say, wants to raise Macdonald so that he can raise himself.

And the man whom Pett chooses to idolize is scarcely deserving of the image. He is basically a man without values or goals, generally bored, and liable to quickly jump from one impulsive role to another. He joins the counter-revolutionary plot partly out of interest in Lady Aldington, but quickly forgets her in the momentum of his own game of heroism. His ideas are a mixture of naive faith in mankind and a cynical acceptance of human baseness. He is "perfectly willing to allow" the wolf-like, predatory nature of "his fellow beings," and yet "always at the bottom of his heart there was the feeling . . . that all humanity, if you could understand them . . . were at least as chivalrous as himself." His acceptance of political executions is revealing:

> That a Russian Czar or a royal bureaucracy should execute a hundred and fifty thousand political prisoners a year did not disturb this serene philosophy. For that was part of their game—of their particular political game, and as you would expect nothing else, it was neither dishonest nor disappointing.[91]

But though he seems aware of both sides of human reality, it is as if two sides remain for him forever separated. He has no faith to support his idealism and to counter his cynicism—to reconcile them in a comprehensive and realistic view of man. Without this reconciliation, his cynicism can easily allow his involvement in political schemes, all the while leaving his spineless idealism undisturbed. Some sense of the split in Macdonald's thought is revealed unintentionally by Lady Aldington, who sees him as the embodiment of chivalry, but also regards him as "quixotic."[92] Don Quixote was of course not the culmination of the chivalric ideal, but a comic late-comer in whom the sense of the ideal and the real was also off balance. And Lady Aldington would tend to see the Count in his most favorable light, because of her love for him and her desire "to feel in herself nothing but humility."[93] The dichotomy in Macdonald's belief, his tendency on the one hand to idealize man and on the other to excuse the worst, leaves him incapable of exercising any moral influence on the counter-revolution, even if he should desire to do so. He is, that is to say,

ineffectual in specific situations, and himself highly vulnerable to corruption.

The Galizian scheme is politically successful, but its ultimate value is dubious. It leads immediately to three situations of violence or attempted violence: Macdonald wants to murder the ex-president, who has already agreed to step down; Macdonald's embittered wife, whom he has divorced, plots to pour vitriol over his face; and Macdonald himself is shot in the back. The climate of violence and corruption engendered by the counter-revolution thus manifests itself in a revealing extension of chaos and instability.

The underlying darkness of the political plot is played against a background of "the dark forest" as seen in the private lives of the major characters. And this linking of social and individual deterioration was a theme that Ford was to carry into his major novels. In both *The Good Soldier* and *Parade's End* sexual and marital estrangement are seen as underlying factors of the sick society; and in *The New Humpty-Dumpty*, beneath the political action there is the nominal marriage of Count and Lady Macdonald, as well as Macdonald's purported but basically egotistic love for Lady Aldington. Ford constructs in this novel an interesting variation on the scene in which the hero fails to respond to a woman in a particular situation. On the day of the counter-revolution, Macdonald leaves Lady Aldington alone in the bullring, with a crowd that is hostile and impatient because the bulls do not appear. When he finally returns, she tells him that she "was going mad." Macdonald replies that he "had to" leave, in order to discredit the Galizian president by seeing that the bulls did not appear. But the president has already agreed to the whole counter-revolution, and Lady Aldington says that she would not have had the heart "to disgrace that wretched broken man so utterly." At this point, Macdonald invents a beautiful romantic fabrication and says that he really kept the bulls from appearing because he knew that Lady Aldington would "hate to see the bulls killed."[94] Later in the same day, after they have married, Macdonald again deserts Lady Aldington in order to threaten to shoot the already-deposed ex-president. Other Fordian heroes, such as George Moffat or Don Collar Kelleg, at least deserted their women out of actual feelings of guilt or idealism; and if they were mistaken, they were at least honest. But Macdonald, inflated by his own heroic role, deserts Lady Aldington for a scheme that is basically opportunistic, leaves her in order to perform acts that are not really necessary, and lies to her in the bargain. There is little left but the rhetoric of the counter-revolution, a rhetoric that dominates Macdonald's death scene which becomes almost a parody of verbal heroism. He insists that his death be attributed to "a necessary disease," and that "there musn't be any bloodshed on the King's threshold"; and he can voice this final wish despite his just having left Lady Aldington in order to threaten

the already-deposed president with assassination. Macdonald's last words, which he utters to Lady Aldington, are in themselves an ironic travesty of their real meaning. He reminds her of "the dark forest! The dear dark forest," but while he speaks of this human characteristic frequently, the "new Humpty-Dumpty" forgets to apply his words to his own actions.[95] Thus what might have been a meaningful awareness becomes for Macdonald simply another set of words.

The ending of the novel is thus developed with trenchant irony, and its final effect is disturbing. Still, if the book achieves complexity by playing the surface of political corruption against the background of "the dark forest," the characters are in spite of this too often developed only on the external level. Count Macdonald's aristocratic qualities are simply spoken of, and never seen; the reasons for his corruption, his susceptibility to power, are seldom shown in depth; and the attraction which Lady Aldington feels toward Macdonald, even after his lies and desertions, is never justified. *The New Humpty-Dumpty* is handled well enough to be taken seriously, but lacks sufficient depth of detail to rank as a major statement on the corruption of the hero.

The same virtues and weaknesses are present in *Mr. Fleight*—and the themes of this novel are also similar to those of *The New Humpty-Dumpty*. Once again Ford draws, in the character of Mr. Blood, an aristocratic figure who had become bored and morally detached; and again, the context is one of corrupt politics. The one significant change in *Mr. Fleight* is that Mr. Blood, despite his own detachment, is much more openly cynical and vicious than Count Macdonald. What little virtue remains is centered in the figure of Aaron Rothwell, the wealthy soap manufacturer who wants Mr. Blood to bring him political fame. Rothwell is a basically honest and sincere businessman, who lacks the courage of his inclinations and wants to fly politically upwards. He becomes the willing victim of the detached Mr. Blood, the leader who draws rather than gives blood, and who delights in manipulating people. This bored aristocrat is beyond even self-interest, but likes to toy with egotism in others. Both characters immerse themselves in corrupt politics, and through them Ford seems to imply that the political sphere is compounded of two elements— blood and climbing.

As the novel begins, Aaron Rothwell, or Mr. Fleight, asks Mr. Blood to transform him into a public hero. He already has considerable wealth from his family fortune, "So it does not seem right that I should be nobody."[96] The climb to political fame thus dominates the book's structure, and from the start Mr. Fleight errs in being false to his better self. He is forced by so doing to relinquish his private values, such as the desire, which he never has the courage to follow through, "to keep a small shop."[97] Even his use of the name, Mr. Fleight, to hide his Jewish origins is a denial of self, and only describes his most undesirable trait.

Mr. Fleight's problem is that he wants to fly too high and, furthermore, in the wrong direction.

Mr. Blood by contrast has relinquished no personal values, for he has none. In fact, he is more than blatant in his perverse ethics, and seems to find little in his actions save a diversion for his boredom and curiosity. He is an aristocrat, but this only leaves him less to do. He makes no pretense of responsibility, but simply does the corruption of his society one better by playing with the positions of others, and thereby almost playing God. He is, that is to say, a controlling figure without direct involvement or any principle of control—a kind of idealist in reverse. Mr. Blood represents an older type of English gentleman who once stayed home and hunted foxes, "and would not have cared a halfpenny whether the nation was going to ruin, just as to-day he cared even less." He is, Ford goes on to say, "an anachronism, and an inactive one at that." He cultivates people out of a sense of curiosity and amusement, and he decides to help Mr. Fleight in his aspirations as an "experiment." He tells his subject that he wants to test his scheme for "the way a man like you might climb," and he adds that the plan will be rather costly. Among other things, Mr. Fleight will have to spend "£150,000 a year for sheer bribery" and "at least £12,000" so that he can "have an expensive wife for the social side of things."[98] He goes on to arrange Mr. Fleight's climb in two ways. First a candidacy is bought from another contender, and then the new candidate is introduced to some of the literary crowd, so that he can start the necessary influential magazine. Mr. Blood does not even blink at the corruption of the arts.

Mr. Fleight's mentor is the more disturbing of the two figures, simply because he represents the remnants of the traditional ruling class. Some of the self-inflation of his position remains, but none of the substance, and Mr. Blood's heroic potential reverts to an almost total cynicism. He confesses that he feels himself an amused god:

> You seem such an extraordinary ignorant lot of people. You're all climbers, more or less, and I am so exactly where I want to be that I seem to sit on a pinnacle. If it amuses me to stick a finger down into the middle of you and give some of you a lift, why shouldn't I?[99]

But if he is a god, Mr. Blood is also a parasite. He views society as "an extraordinarily cruel and disordered machine"; and in this society it is the business of each man "to extract the last drop of blood" from the people below him. The concept of struggle, he regards as the "more scientifically honest" way of looking at things.[100] In line with this view, Mr. Blood regards the poor as a "race," to be treated as "dogs . . . incurably outside" the higher strata of society.[101] Even Mr. Fleight is ultimately used by the Bloods. Reginald Blood, Mr. Blood's brother, confesses that their candidate is an "instrument" in "the usual attempt of the richer classes to get

THE EARLY NOVELS AND THE INEFFECTUAL HERO

the poorer into their power by hook or by crook." Reginald regards Mr. Fleight as a Jew and an outsider, and thereby a supposedly unaffiliated candidate who can draw votes without himself becoming committed.[102]

Mr. Fleight is noticeably uncommitted, but this has much less to do with his religion than with his own failure to adhere to his deeper values. His lack of commitment, itself symbolic of his society, is brought out through his relationship with the small shop-girl, Gilda Leroy. Under the name of Aaron Rothwell, Mr. Fleight develops a friendship with the Leroys. This friendship not only becomes an outlet for his real name, but also for his real and usually suppressed self. He claims to visit the Leroys only to get "the comforts of home," and he professes to them his dislike of social climbing:

> It's a weary sort of nonsense. There's the palm plants and the marble staircases; and the Christian wife you've purchased, standing at the top in white satin to receive 6,000 guests, whilst the invisible orchestra plays the Prieslied out of the Meistersingers. . . . And you yourself are just the dirty little Jew in the shadow of your wife, grinning and holding out your hand, which more than half the people won't take. And the remainder will be licking your boots because they'll all suppose you've got half the jobs in the kingdom to give away.[103]

At the end of the novel, when he has won the election, Mr. Fleight ironically realizes that his detested dream has come true. His Jewishness has not left him unaffiliated. It has only added additional emphasis to the irony of his seeking fame in a culture he professes to despise. It is also a measure of that culture's degeneration that it can lure with its most cynical values those outside its sphere.

As a would-be hero, Mr. Fleight fails much as do the other Fordian heroes to commit himself to a woman. This time the woman, Gilda Leroy, kills herself when she overhears Mr. Fleight deny to her mother that he has any serious intentions. Gilda's response is a bit melodramatic, but her death also suggests that Mr. Fleight has killed a better part of himself. And this suggestion is enhanced when Mr. Blood insists that the candidate suppress his emotions until after the election, and that he assuage his guilt by giving Gilda a fancy funeral.[104] But despite his ability to adopt the emotional coldness and opportunism of English society, Mr. Fleight will never really be accepted as anything more than an "instrument." His alienation is emphasized when he is attacked one night, outside the Leroys', by an anti-Semitic mob, who "had for a long time resented the visits of an insignificant-looking Hebrew to their neighbourhood."[105] The mob is simply the violent base of the society to which Mr. Fleight aspires; and by succeeding, he becomes a part of the very mob that attacks him.

The novel reaches its ironic climax with Mr. Fleight's political victory.

THE LIMITED HERO

At a massive party to celebrate the launching of the influential magazine, the candidate learns that he has won by default, and must therefore affect his new social role. The expensive Christian wife has been purchased, and has just gone off to the garden with the Chancellor of the Exchequer. And Cluny Macpherson, one of the writers for the influential journal, expresses the moral laxity of the age, and then proceeds to give it his stamp of approval. He says that "We are all friendly agnostics" and nothing more. "We haven't . . . got any religion," and science no longer attempts "to prove anything." Still, the English are "a nice pleasant lot," even if they no longer "write letters abusing each other in the *Times* . . . And," concludes the poet, "I'm sure it's much better like that."[106] This age, as Ford saw it, had simply the vestiges of the Victorian moral fervor, which had been steadily weakened by its unreality. But that fervor, although it had become rhetoric, had at least been an involvement of sorts. What it had been superseded by was the mere spineless tolerance praised by Cluny Macpherson, and this lack of involvement in turn left only a society in which corrupt Mr. Fleights were used and encouraged by cynical Mr. Bloods. The old aristocratic values clearly had little relevance or influence, if they were heard at all.

The decline of these aristocratic values was lightly satirized by Ford in one of his few pure farces, *The Panel*, which appeared in 1913, and was simultaneously published in America as *A Ring for Nancy*. The book is a minor effort, and relies on such stock comic devices as mistaken identities and bedrooms with sliding panels in between. It is interesting for us only to the extent that some of Ford's characteristic attitudes toward the hero find their way into the highly-contrived plot. Major Edward Foster is pursued by four ladies, and in the course of what was meant to be a brief vacation, before he marries one of them, he encounters them all in the same house. The Major has given up the woman with whom he is really in love, Lady Mary Savylle, who had appealed to him "because she was simply the only girl he had ever met who didn't care what she did." Still, despite the attraction of her unconventionality, he had been bound by his own conventional sense of honor, and had "given up courting her since both his parents had died and he had found himself penniless."[107] While avoiding Lady Savylle, the Major, looking for someone to talk to, has met and become engaged to the morally-overbearing Olympia Peabody, an "enormously wealthy" American who had taken up residence "in a Bloomsbury boarding house . . . in order to study the serious problems of British vice at close quarters." But even Olympia Peabody's morality is largely rhetoric, for she confesses to "a natural hatred for most people," and her professed altruism disappears as she begins to set her sights on Edward.[108]

In this context of rhetorical fronts, Lady Savylle, disguised as Nancy, her personal maid, watches over and keeps her grip on Edward. As

THE EARLY NOVELS AND THE INEFFECTUAL HERO

Nancy, she discusses Edward's desertion of her ladyship, and condemns him for his rules, as well as his desertion of Lady Savylle for Olympia Peabody. The Major screams at her, "Was it me that should go running to a woman I couldn't support?" and her reply is a bitter denunciation of Edward's proud heroism:

> Yes, damn your Irish honor! . . . and damn your black, novel-reading Papist pride! It was your duty to come crawling to the woman you adored; it was your duty to give her the pride and joy of tending you, and you, you give it to another woman! You give it to the wicked stranger and she gets all the pride and joy of tending you who have tried like a hero, and ruined your poor eyes like a scholar and ruined your life like the black evil fool that you are.[109]

In her condemnation of Edward's heroism, of his "rules" which hold him back from responding to her, Lady Savylle could easily be Clara Brede speaking to George Moffat or Pauline Leicester reproaching Robert Grimshaw. And the themes of heroism and alienation in all of these novels anticipate the more complex treatment of the same themes in *The Good Soldier*. In *The Panel* Lady Savylle finally gets Edward, but only because the usual inconclusiveness of the Fordian world is lightened by the conventions of farce.

Two major themes are finally predominant in Ford's novels up to *The Good Soldier*. First, there is the increasing corruption of society, and the simultaneous confusion of values. And secondly, there is the ineffectiveness of the hero. This figure undergoes a progressive deterioration in Ford's work throughout this period. The earlier heroes, such as George Moffat and Don Kelleg, are moral in themselves, and are ineffectual because of the very abstractness and detachment of their morality. But in the later heroes, who are themselves products of the earlier detachment, morality has become either hypocritical, as with Count Macdonald, or suppressed, as with Mr. Fleight. At the furthest extreme, it has been supplanted by the overt cynicism of Mr. Blood. Exceptions can of course be found to this pattern. The corrupted hero, Etchingham Granger, who appears in 1901, is closer to figures such as Count Macdonald or Mr. Fleight than he is to George Moffat. Still, the overall direction is evident; and it is also clear that the hero is centrally implicated in Ford's condemnation of the pre-War British society.

Critical opinion has thus far assumed a false dichotomy between the early Fordian heroes and their society. The heroes have not been sufficiently blamed, but have instead been placed in opposition to their decaying world; and the extent to which Ford himself blamed them for this decay has not been perceived. John A. Meixner, for example, writes that "Ford's perception of social decay, indeed, is his largest and most pervasive theme," and finds Ford's world marked by the decline of the "classic

Christian gentleman," "the ideal individual for Ford . . . the man of goodness and true gentility whose primary aim is helping those in need." Meixner finds "significant representations of the ideal" in Churchill of *The Inheritors,* in Don Kelleg, Mr. Fleight, and "most fully" in Count Macdonald. The leader of the Galizian counter-revolution is seen by Meixner as a new type of Fordian hero, the decisive figure who is capable of action and who will "evolve eventually into Christopher Tietjens."[110] Richard Cassell, although recognizing George Moffat's paralyzing guilt, views both George and Clara as "equally victims of a graceless society," and also regards *Mr. Fleight* as a picture of the not altogether admirable encroachment of the monied Jew into British politics." which the "tired feudalists" like Mr. Blood have abandoned. Mr. Blood himself is for Cassell "the true chivalric gentleman of the traditional ruling gentry."[111] And Richard W. Lid finds the crucial difference between the wavering Don Kelleg and Christopher Tietjens to be only that "Tietjens is sure of his ground" and "Don is not."[112] It is puzzling to find so many good critics, all failing to see the extent to which Ford condemns his early heroes for the breakdown of their world. One can only conclude that the sense of social decay in the pre-War novels is so strong that it overshadows for these critics the nature of the heroes, many of whom are not developed with the complexity that Ford was to achieve in his later works. Yet, given the lack of detailed characterization, it is still difficult to see how Count Macdonald can be considered an early Christopher Tietjens. Ford himself must, however, have sensed the need for a stronger psychological focus in his novels; for this focus, only hinted at in the minor novels, was to become the most striking feature of *The Good Soldier,* the first of his major works.

NOTES

[1] Paul Wiley, *Novelist of Three Worlds: Ford Madox Ford* (Syracuse, 1962), p. 131.
[2] *Ibid.,* pp. 91–93.
[3] Ford Madox Ford, *Joseph Conrad, A Personal Remembrance* (London, 1924), p. 186, as cited by John A. Meixner, *Ford Madox Ford's Novels: A Critical Study* (Minneapolis, 1962), p. 81.
[4] Meixner, pp. 27–28.
[5] Wiley, pp. 101–102.
[6] Ford Madox Ford, *Ladies Whose Bright Eyes, A Romance* (London, 1935), p. 47.
[7] *Ibid.,* p. 177.
[8] *Ibid.,* p. 105.
[9] *Ibid.,* p. 295.
[10] *Ibid.,* p. 253.
[11] *Ibid.,* p. 255.
[12] *Ibid.* (1911 edition), p. 361.

[13] *Ibid.* (1935 edition), p. 349.
[14] *Ibid.*, p. 350.
[15] Ford Madox Hueffer and Joseph Conrad, *The Inheritors, An Extravagant Story* (London, 1901), p. 13.
[16] *Ibid.*, p. 29.
[17] *Ibid.*, pp. 22–23.
[18] *Ibid.*, p. 125.
[19] *Ibid.*, p. 78.
[20] *Ibid.*, pp. 63–64.
[21] Wiley, pp. 140–141.
[22] Hueffer, *Inheritors*, pp. 154, 188–189.
[23] *Ibid.*, p. 209.
[24] Ford, *Conrad*, p. 141.
[25] Jocelyn Baines, *Joseph Conrad: A Critical Biography* (London, 1960), pp. 239–240.
[26] G. Jean-Aubry, *Joseph Conrad, Life and Letters*, I (New York, 1927), 312–313.
[27] Wiley, p. 141.
[28] Ford Madox Hueffer, *The Benefactor, A Tale of a Small Circle* (London, 1905), pp. 8–9.
[29] *Ibid.*, p. 12.
[30] *Ibid.*, pp. 45–46.
[31] *Ibid.*, p. 69.
[32] *Ibid.*, pp. 37–39, 72–73.
[33] *Ibid.*, pp. 61, 89.
[34] *Ibid.*, p. 188.
[35] *Ibid.*, pp. 217, 249, 301.
[36] *Ibid.*, pp. 331, 335, 339.
[37] *Ibid.*, pp. 341–349.
[38] Ford Madox Hueffer, *An English Girl, A Romance* (London, 1907), pp. 17, 260.
[39] *Ibid.*, pp. 33, 281.
[40] *Ibid.*, pp. 248–254.
[41] *Ibid.*, pp. 268–269.
[42] *Ibid.*, pp. 171–172.
[43] *Ibid.*, pp. 301–308.
[44] Ford Madox Hueffer, *Mr. Apollo, A Just Possible Story* (London, 1908), p. 3.
[45] *Ibid.*, p. 28.
[46] *Ibid.*, p. 44.
[47] *Ibid.*, p. 58.
[48] *Ibid.*, pp. 269–270.
[49] *Ibid.*, pp. 80–81.
[50] *Ibid.*, p. 93.
[51] *Ibid.*, pp. 110, 115–127.
[52] *Ibid.*, pp. 108–109, 111–112.
[53] *Ibid.*, p. 142.
[54] *Ibid.*, pp. 194–195.
[55] *Ibid.*, pp. 148, 306–307.
[56] *Ibid.*
[57] Ford Madox Ford and Joseph Conrad, *The Nature of a Crime* (London, 1924), pp. vi–vii.

[58] *Ibid.*, pp. 3-4.
[59] *Ibid.*, pp. 9-11, 17, 23.
[60] *Ibid.*, pp. 30-31.
[61] *Ibid.*, pp. 25, 51-52.
[62] *Ibid.*, pp. 82-83.
[63] *Ibid.*, pp. 84-87, 93-94.
[64] Ford Madox Hueffer, *A Call: The Tale of Two Passions* (London, 1910), pp. 14-15, 33-34.
[65] *Ibid.*, p. 46.
[66] *Ibid.*, p. 102.
[67] *Ibid.*, pp. 121-123.
[68] *Ibid.*, pp. 77, 278-284.
[69] *Ibid.*, p. 128.
[70] *Ibid.*, pp. 163, 180-184.
[71] *Ibid.*, pp. 215, 217, 222.
[72] *Ibid.*, pp. 251-253, 257.
[73] *Ibid.*, pp. 275-276.
[74] *Ibid.*, pp. 298-299.
[75] Wiley, p. 158.
[76] Edward Naumburg, Jr., "A Collector Looks at Ford Madox Ford," *Princeton University Library Chronicle*, IX (April, 1948), 145-146.
[77] Wiley, p. 159.
[78] Daniel Chaucer, pseud., *The Simple Life Limited* (London, 1911), pp. 7-8, 27, 28, 43.
[79] *Ibid.*, pp. 177-195.
[80] *Ibid.*, pp. 69-77.
[81] *Ibid.*, pp. 77-79, 80-90.
[82] *Ibid.*, pp. 92-93, 119-120.
[83] *Ibid.*, p. 54.
[84] *Ibid.*, p. 101.
[85] *Ibid.*, p. 226.
[86] *Ibid.*, p. 329.
[87] *Ibid.*, p. 342.
[88] *Ibid.*, pp. 384, 387-388.
[89] Daniel Chaucer, pseud., *The New Humpty-Dumpty* (London, New York, 1912), p. v.
[90] *Ibid.*, pp. 75, 421.
[91] *Ibid.*, pp. 303-304.
[92] *Ibid.*, p. 319.
[93] *Ibid.*, pp. 333-334, 400, 414.
[94] *Ibid.*, pp. 400-401.
[95] *Ibid.*, p. 432.
[96] Ford Madox Hueffer, *Mr. Fleight* (London, 1913), p. 3.
[97] *Ibid.*, p. 92.
[98] *Ibid.*, pp. 9, 20, 21, 87.
[99] *Ibid.*, p. 189.
[100] *Ibid.*, p. 249, as cited by Richard Cassell, *Ford Madox Ford: A Study of His Novels* (Baltimore, 1961), p. 102.
[101] Hueffer, *Fleight*, p. 253.
[102] *Ibid.*, pp. 212-213.
[103] *Ibid.*, pp. 109, 298-299.
[104] *Ibid.*, p. 245.

[105] *Ibid.*, p. 149.
[106] *Ibid.*, p. 304.
[107] Ford Madox Hueffer, *A Ring for Nancy* (Indianapolis, 1913), pp. 75–76.
[108] *Ibid.*, pp. 40, 42, 191.
[109] *Ibid.*, pp. 165–166.
[110] Meixner, *Ford's Novels*, pp. 84–85, 96–97, 108–109.
[111] Cassell, pp. 119, 137–138.
[112] Richard W. Lid, "Tietjens in Disguise," *Kenyon Review*, XXII (Spring, 1960), 268–271.

3.

Heroism and Responsibility in
The Good Soldier: *The End of a Phase*

THE GOOD SOLDIER, which appeared in 1915, brought to a culmination Ford's rendering of the ineffectual hero in the society before the War. The themes of the earlier novels were here restated, though with greater complexity, both in treatment and implication. The good soldier, Edward Ashburnham, embodied the rhetorical heroism of George Moffat as well as the verbal hypocrisy of Count Macdonald; but Ford's picture of Ashburnham was complex enough to place him between and yet above his two predecessors. Furthermore, the lives of all the characters in this novel were sharply undercut by their society, by the disintegration of a context in which Ashburnham's aristocratic role might once have been meaningful and sufficient. Ironically, however, the very way of life of Ashburnham and those around him augmented this disintegration of their world. Behind their increasingly chaotic lives lay the one English characteristic most strongly criticized by Ford—the inability to cope with passion, and the evasion of all emotion under a mask of convention and responsibility. Ford intended *The Good Soldier* to be both the technical and thematic climax of his literary career. And when he turned again to the novel, after the War, it was to begin the development of the limited hero as an alternative to a world which in his view had gone beyond the breaking point.

But *The Good Soldier* is more than a heightened recapitulation of Ford's earlier accomplishments. In technique alone, it is one of his most finished performances; and the very self-consciousness of the technique is used by Ford to reflect one of the dominant traits of John Dowell, the narrator. Dowell is a man turned inward upon himself, and his self-consciousness is both his major strength and weakness. The style of the novel, with its mixture of verbal cleverness and hesitancy, and with its constant turning back and forth upon action and significance, is an accurate rendering of Dowell's mode of response. The narrator vacillates between the public heroism of an Ashburnham and his own unsure self-awareness, which because of its uncertainty cannot act as a counterforce to public heroism, but can only assert itself verbally and after the fact.

The dual nature of Dowell's response complicates our attitude toward him, for it evokes our simultaneous sympathy and condemnation. Dual

THE END OF A PHASE

characteristics are also evident in the other characters, and the prevalence of this double point of view is, in fact, the main quality which sets *The Good Soldier* apart from Ford's previous novels. For along with the presence of themes from the earlier works—the ineffectiveness of the hero and the breakdown of his world—and in spite of an intensification of these themes and a much stronger sense of social collapse, the entire Ashburnham affair is rendered by Ford with a greater sense of pity and compassion, and a much greater sense of the dilemmas in which the characters are caught than is found in any of his previous work. While the early novels contain brief intimations of their heroes' difficulties, and while some of these earlier heroes are made to seem superior to their corrupt and encroaching world, the double perspective is overshadowed in Ford's pre-War work by a sense of bitter disappointment and a predominantly critical point of view. In *The Good Soldier*, by way of contrast, the double attitude takes precedence over any bitterness, and the result is a novel that approaches the dimensions of tragedy. The emphasis is as much on suffering as on failure, and by this suffering—by the difficulty of the struggle which most of them wage with varying degrees of ineffectiveness—the characters are ennobled even as they move closer and closer to their futile and inconclusive end. The choices which confront them are far more difficult than those faced by the heroes of the earlier novels, and often there are no desirable choices at all.

The narrator, huddled within the seeming security of the Ashburnhams' small and once-coherent world, finds that this world has been an illusion, undermined by marital infidelity, moral and emotional inertia, and a false and evasive responsibility. And yet, while each of the participants helps in some way to perpetuate this illusion, each of them, even the insensitive Leonora, attempts within the scope of a severely restricted vision and response to rectify the situation. As their very responses drive them deeper and deeper into an unending spiral, the choices which they face become progressively narrow in their possible consequences. And as we sense the futility of all this suffering, even as we condemn the Dowells and the Ashburnhams for the ineffectiveness of their perpetuated illusions, our pity and admiration are also evoked. All the while that they move toward a foregone failure, their inept struggle imparts to these characters, and particularly to Ashburnham and the narrator himself, a complexity and a dualism that gives their inconclusive end a note of stifled tragedy, of dignity that has lost the moral point which might have made it valid.

In *The Good Soldier* Ford is able to sustain this intricate point of view by shifting the focus of the novel from the breakdown itself to the consciousness of the characters involved. Thus, he is able to render the simultaneous struggle and self-delusion which these characters experience as they sense the crumbling of their once-ordered world. The use of

THE LIMITED HERO

Dowell as a narrator helps him in this task. For in addition to voicing the psychological texture of the period through his own doubts, Dowell is sufficiently sensitive to the details if not always to the implications of the situation, so that he can tell us something of the other characters' minds as well. He catches the complexity of Ashburnham's response, particularly as he wrestles with his passion for Nancy Rufford; and thus, despite his disenchantment with the "good soldier," Dowell is able to distinguish his responses from those of the more commonplace Leonora. Dowell's view of Ashburnham has, of course, its ironies; but it perceives a vestige of nobility in this hero, which sets him apart from a world which has even less. Ashburnham's inner turmoil suggests a potential for moral response, which might have been realized had either he or his world been able to discern a workable moral base.

In the final analysis, however, Ashburnham, like many other Fordian heroes, is crippled by his own heroism. His responses are marked by the same illusion and moral hesitancy evident in those of the emulative Dowell. The narrator, as he gradually surpasses Ashburnham in our esteem, does so not by his ability to find a solution to his difficulties, but simply by a greater awareness of the problem. Dowell's introspective awareness, moreover, sets the tone for the novel as a whole. In *The Good Soldier* Ford achieves through the combination of tone and structure a verbal texture totally different from anything he has yet accomplished, and it is through this texture that he is able both to complicate and control the responses of his readers, and to involve them directly, through the sense of recognition, in the problems which are posed. This texture, given shape in Dowell's narrative, might well be called the rhetoric of bewilderment. It is rhetorical in the sense that the statements of so many of Ford's heroes are rhetorical—that is, it is a verbalization of feeling and intent supported by very little active response. But in the case of Dowell, there is at least a partial reason for the lack of action; for Dowell is honestly unable to locate a solution, and he rises above Ford's other heroes in that he is, within the limits of his awareness, honest in his expression of this bewilderment. He does not pretend to any greater certainty than he actually feels, and in the light of this uncertainty, Dowell's verbalization embodies a form of action, in that he is at least trying to make coherent a situation in which he feels essentially powerless. He can piece together the dilemma, and to an extent abstract its causes; but he can see these causes or a possible solution only in part. Most of the implied solutions can only be inferred from his commentary, or from the situation itself; for Dowell by the novel's end has pieced together as many of the questions and fragments of the past nine years as he is able, and he falls back into the role which he has inherited from the still-admired Ashburnham. Dowell remains, ultimately, part of the world

of the novel. His awareness can carry us only so far, and beyond that point we must interpret for ourselves.

The tone in which *The Good Soldier* is phrased is more than anything a reflection of its narrator's new level of awareness at the end of nine years of nearly constant illusion. The Dowell who tells the story has only recently learned the truth, and he is anxious to discover its significance. To do so, he must of course comment on himself as a participant, as well as on the other characters in the novel. He must attempt to make judgements, to delve beneath the surface and discern the manifold pattern of cause and effect. But Dowell, as we shall see, is able to make these judgments only in part. He is unable to fully commit himself because he is just as bewildered as anyone else in the book. He is, however, more acutely aware and consciously articulate in his confusion than the others; and this awareness, itself the source of his major strength, allows him to perceive the relevance of the pervasive uncertainty and sense of loneliness to the crisis that now dominates his mind.

The frequent contradictions in the narrator's thought are a sign of his own confusion and inability to take a decisive stance. Yet he can at times use his awareness of this very confusion to achieve some of the book's most significant insights. Such is the case in his view of love, which he sees as an alleviation, however precarious, of basic anxiety, and as a renewal of the feeling that one's very existence may have justification. In his attainment of such insights, Dowell extends the function of his narrative tone beyond the mere delineation of his own responses. This tone assumes, in fact, three functions in the novel: it renders Dowell's personality at the time of his narration; it helps us to perceive, largely through Dowell's eyes, a similar although less articulate bewilderment in the other characters; and it embodies a central commentary, made by both Dowell and Ford, on the nature of the world in which the events of *The Good Soldier* occur.

Dowell longs for the certainty of the old proprieties and illusions. He is incapable of the conscious restructuring of his life that would ready him for the role of the limited hero, and thus he is able to rise only in part above his fallen world. He can be honest with himself only to a certain extent, and then on a predominantly verbal level. His is a mind incapable of full commitment, turned back upon itself after nine years of unknown hell. He is aware of the irony of these past nine years, but he is unaware of his ironic final position. The structure of the novel allows Dowell to voice his sense of bewilderment, and to express the only internal insights about the situation just ended. But by making Dowell a participant as well as a narrator, Ford condemns him almost as strongly as he does the others. We are able to observe the narrator's own lack of passion, and to see that he has been more than a simple victim. And Ford's obvious criticism of

Dowell cautions us against fully accepting his narration of events, and to look for omissions in his observations and responses.

Even though his confusion sets the tone of the novel and becomes one of its central truths, Dowell is still very much subject to the double perspective that Ford maintains throughout the work. Even at the end, he simply takes on the life of Edward Ashburnham, and thus falls into the ironic role of a greatly-reduced good soldier. Ashburnham's responsibility, or what remained of it, had been false, almost a mockery of his degeneration and growing isolation, and Dowell as the novel draws to a close is tired and even more alone. He is left to watch the now mad Nancy—as clearly a victim after her involvement as before she had been an innocent bystander. Dowell, finally with Nancy but unable to bring their relationship to the expression of a love he once had felt, is living under an actual responsibility, and is therefore, less false than Ashburnham had finally become. But with Nancy's derangement, Dowell's responsibility is like a death watch in an empty room, for Nancy is incapable of communication, and although not yet dying is already dead.

Possibly because of its complexity and its repeated motif of bewilderment, *The Good Soldier* has evoked considerable controversy among its critics. These differences, centering especially around the question of genre, reflect the many dimensions to be found in the novel. For while essentially a work of personal and social disintegration, *The Good Soldier* moves inside the consciousness of its characters and gives an indication of the tensions to which they are subject. This struggle imparts to them a very real, though partial dignity, and evokes the sense of compassion characteristic of tragedy. Moreover, this inner focus heightens our sense of recognition and takes us beyond the point of comic detachment, particularly since the characters' uncertainties often seem very much our own.

A recurrent critical question has centered on the significance of the situation presented by Ford. This significance hinges on whether the characters and events become symbolic, and, if so, on the nature and scope of their references. E. V. Walter sees the novel as a picture of English society in a transitional stage, between impending breakdown and total collapse.[1] But Wiley, who sees the novel as pervaded by an irony which "expresses Victorianism in the final stage of self-consciousness with respect to the hypocrisies of its conventions," contends that "although the main characters are Anglo-Saxons, the scheme of the novel is international, the chief locale being the central European wasteland."[2] Robie Macauley, on the other hand, de-emphasizes the social significance of the novel, sees Dowell as "an ordinary American from Philadelphia," and suggests that Ford "meant to say . . . that the saddest story is the perpetual story of love between man and woman, love that can never quite arrive at understanding and decays."[3] It is one of the triumphs of

THE END OF A PHASE

The Good Soldier that all these themes are present. Ford's main focus is clearly on the breakdown of British upper-class society, but it is a society whose life is cosmopolitan, and therefore has international ramifications. The action of the novel centers, moreover, on personal disintegration; but we have seen that while Ford's use of the "affair" entailed this smaller focus, Ford regarded the "affair" and the personal disintegration which it rendered as symbolic and symptomatic of a larger breakdown. In this novel, and in the Tietjens series as well, Ford establishes even more clearly than in his earlier works the close link between the personal and the social tragedies.

The Good Soldier is then a rendering of social disintegration, seen through the focus of the "affair." Dowell, himself, with his tendency to introspection, is constantly pondering the significance of events, and in this way tends to universalize them. His own awareness of bewilderment marks him as a more localized type, and he comes to represent a rather prevalent human response in a world falling apart at its roots. It is in fact Dowell who most evokes our own sense of recognition and involvement, for he is able to articulate much of our own bewilderment. There has nevertheless been considerable critical controversy over how Dowell should be regarded, over how seriously his articulation should be taken, and over the nature of Ford's own attitude toward Dowell's world. This controversy has centered around the question of genre, since genre is often a means by which the writer can structure his attitudes within a recognizable framework. Mark Schorer, for example, in his introduction to the novel, sees *The Good Soldier* as "a comedy of humor," in which the controlling humor is "phlegm," manifested in "a world without moral point," and in "a narrator who suffers from the madness of moral inertia."[4] Cassell finds himself in general agreement with Schorer, and contends that "Even though the Ashburnham affair evokes tragic implications, we are never allowed to react to the story with the emotions usually accompanying a tragedy of the classical type." Dowell "moves the story into the realm of the comic and ironic."[5] Wiley also finds in the novel a tragic potential, but feels that the structure of the "affair," in accord with Ford's view of his world, embodies an anti-tragic point of view. Tragedy is an attitude and a genre that lies in the past, implying a sense of finality that no longer exists. Wiley cites Dowell's remark that he is calling his tale " 'The Saddest Story' rather than 'The Ashburnham Tragedy' just because it is so sad, just because there was no current to draw things along to a swift and inevitable end." Wiley then adds that these "words are, to be sure, typical of Dowell in his want of tragic insight and recourse to banalities like 'sadness'; yet the story is in the end his story, and his halting definition ironically fits with an account of human bungling monstrous to the point of imbecility." Wiley also regards the events on which the novel comes to a close, "Leonora's second

marriage, Ashburnham's suicide," and "Nancy's madness," as "banalities proper to an 'Affair' " and incapable of inducing "tragic catharsis."[6]

Theodore Dreiser, however, reviewing the novel for *The New Republic* in 1915, thought its theme "tragic in the best sense that the Greek knew tragedy, that tragedy for which there is no solution," but added that the book did not reach tragic proportions because the characters, particularly Dowell, were not defined with sufficient clarity.[7] Departing strongly from Schorer's view, John A. Meixner makes the strongest case for viewing the novel as tragedy. Meixner contends that "*The Good Soldier* is, at its core, a tragedy. It tells a lacerating tale of groping human beings, caught implacably by training, character, and circumstances, who cruelly and blindly inflict on each other terrible misery and pain: 'poor wretches,' as the narrator says, 'creeping over the earth in the shadow of an eternal wrath.' " Yet Meixner qualifies his classification of the novel as a tragedy by adding that "around this awful core, and without diminishing its power," Ford has subtly "placed a context of comic irony. This context—which Mr. Schorer has made the center of the book—Ford uses . . . to provide the novel's ultimate commentary on the nature of human life in the twentieth-century world. *The Good Soldier* epitomizes in a classic way the altered tragic vision of our modern sensibility."[8]

While most of the critics thus see the novel as falling somewhere between the poles of comedy and tragedy, with Schorer making the strongest statement for the former and Meixner for the latter, Hugh Kenner, taking a different approach, argues that Ford never resolves the problem of genre or attitude in this novel, and finds the only resolution to lie in the very task of writing which Dowell undertakes. And Kenner adds that "Ford, one uneasily supposes, doesn't himself know what this attitude is to the situation he presents. The gap between presentation and 'values' is never bridged. Ford's presented values are those of the craftsman; the man Ford, most compassionate of novelists, is himself in an impasse, an impasse of sympathy for all sides."[9] It is clear that most critics of *The Good Soldier*, although they may isolate a particular genre for emphasis, see the novel finally as a modification of traditional generic attitudes. Kenner simply goes one step further, and claims that none of the conventional genres is utilized, and that consequently no attitude is resolved. This lack of resolution may apply to Dowell's own estimate of the situation, but lack of resolution is an aspect of Dowell's character. Furthermore, it is necessary to remember that while Dowell is the narrator, and thus embodies the novel's visual points of view, he is also a character in its plot. One of Ford's strongest technical achievements in the novel is this presentation of two simultaneous points of view—that of his narrator as well as his own. Thus, Dowell's bewilderment has a very real validity as a condition of mind within the novel. It is a quality of the world and a part of the problem portrayed. But it is not necessarily

THE END OF A PHASE

Ford's point of view. It is in fact unlikely that the author, had he been without a coherent attitude, could have exercised upon this work the degree of control so immediately evident. The question of attitude must therefore be broken down to a group of questions; and by so doing it is possible to see *The Good Soldier* as approaching very nearly the characteristic attitudes of tragedy, but as also embodying significant and ironic qualifications in the rendering of its predominantly tragic heroes.

The question of tragedy hinges on the dignity of the characters and the degree of struggle which they wage against their circumstances. And most of the central figures of *The Good Soldier* do engage in struggle. The irony arises from the fact that they never carry the struggle through to the point of resolution. Certainly Dowell, with his growing awareness of the total predicament, is more than a comic character. His very attempt to discover the meaning of the situation and to commit it to paper is an effort to overcome the moral impotence which he feels in himself. He finds only fragments of meaning; but his search is genuine. Despite his insights, however, Dowell will not and probably cannot commit himself to a means of solution. At one point, he wants to convince himself that the illusory Ashburnham had actually been as real as he once seemed, before the illusion was shattered. And the Ashburnham in whom Dowell would like to believe is actually a more typical, ineffectual hero than Dowell himself, a hero whose public and private selves are quite disparate.

Yet even Ashburnham is presented with sufficient complexity to make credible a sense of internal struggle. For one thing, he is pushed out of his feudal role by the unsympathetic opposition of his wife, Leonora; and his various affairs with other women are in part an attempt to regain through a woman some sense of self-respect. And he struggles to maintain his older, public self, which asserts itself in his final refusal of Nancy Rufford. This scene, in which Nancy offers herself to Ashburnham out of a sense of duty, has, however, many levels of meaning, and it also registers Edward's inability to cope with an emotional situation. Still, whatever the complexities inherent in Ford's overall view, the refusal is viewed by Ashburnham himself as an act of honor and heroism, and is thus an indication of his own internal struggle. Ashburnham's final vestiges of dignity are ineffectual in his specific circumstances, but they are nonetheless real and sufficient reason to view him with sympathy.

Thus in *The Good Soldier* Ford sustains a constant moral and psychological dualism. He endows his characters with a mixture of tragic heroism and moral inertia, examines the relationship between these qualities, and finally questions the value of the heroism itself. The heroic qualities do give the characters a social position, which makes their fate more crucial than it would be, were they entirely degenerate and of inconsequential status. And although their heroism is offset by the evidence of moral deterioration and inertia, the most telling irony is gained by Ford's

disapproval of both, so that the answer to the bewilderment of Dowell is seen not to lie in the public heroism of which Edward Ashburnham is the final and corrupt embodiment.

It is Ashburnham who is most clearly related to Ford's other ineffectual heroes, and his heroism shares with that of the earlier figures the quality of false responsibility. Ashburnham is the sort of man who always fulfills and perhaps even surpasses his expected social duties. He is—until his wife assumes the management of his estates—rather like a benevolent father to his tenants. Thus he plays the part of the dutiful aristocrat, or the good soldier, but this role is so external that it is gradually undermined by Ashburnham's own private life. The sense of responsibility becomes for him a means of publicly veiling and evading the private sphere of passion and emotion. The role of the good soldier is thus at least in part a social ceremony—one that becomes increasingly irrelevant, and leaves only an abyss which drives Ashburnham from one woman to another, and finally to end his life. The ceremony is one in which many other characters in the novel participate. Dowell, for example, plays in his marriage the part of dedicated nursemaid to his supposedly sick wife; and Leonora, instead of directly meeting the problem of her bad marital relationship, takes over her husband's estate, and without quite realizing it kills his last small vestige of self-respect. Ashburnham's frenzied series of affairs can be attributed in large part to Leonora's cold and businesslike act. And if we look at the responses of the main characters as a group, a pattern becomes evident. All are ineffectual in their private lives, and for each of them marriage has become a state of alienation. And each of them assumes a role of false responsibility as a means of evading—perhaps even out of blindness to—the personal breakdown. The pretense of responsibility comes to dominate their social lives, until at varying points for each of them the facade collapses and there is no more illusion. Edward kills himself, Leonora marries Rodney Bayham and entrenches herself in the new order, and Dowell is left alone, to watch over Nancy Rufford.

There are two characters in the novel whose main function is to evoke a bi-polar historical dimension. Nancy Rufford's faith and innocence recall a mode of life that can barely survive in a faithless world whereas Florence Dowell embodies the blatant self-interest that eats away at everything for which Edward once stood. Nancy thus embodies an older world that has already vanished, whereas Florence foreshadows a new one that is about to take its place. Ashburnham, Dowell, and to a lesser extent Leonora are caught in between, and do not really belong to either. But Florence and Nancy, in addition to suggesting a historical context, are persons as well, and as such act upon and react to the major characters. In these relationships, they are pulled along by the momentum of Edward's corruption, until Florence kills herself and Nancy is left to an inarticulate madness. As symbols, then, Nancy and Florence measure the inability of

either Dowell or the Ashburnhams to come to terms with two conflicting worlds. But as persons they measure the ineffectiveness of these characters, particularly Edward, in immediate relationships. And Nancy at the end helps to add a final ironic note. She is left under the care of Dowell, who thus preserves a symbol of the past and at the same time lives in a passionless relationship with the woman for whom he once had felt a never-articulated love.

While related to Ford's earlier novels in its thematic condemnation of false responsibility, *The Good Soldier* differs from books such as *The Benefactor* or *A Call* in the degree of its complexity and in its steady crescendo of chaos and bewilderment. The choices for Robert Grimshaw or George Moffat had been relatively simple, with external obstacles at a minimum. But although the characters of *The Good Soldier* experience greater struggle, they are often confronted by a more difficult series of choices, none of which may seem inherently desirable. For example, Dowell does not respond emotionally to his wife. But Florence's capacity to react to Dowell with any honesty or sympathy, even if he did so, is at least dubious. Then again, Dowell admits his interest in Nancy to Leonora, after his wife has killed herself. But Dowell's ability to express emotion is small, and even had he attempted expression to Nancy, he would have clashed with Edward, whose interest in his ward was by this time becoming almost obsessive. And Edward himself becomes less and less responsible in his personal involvements, and yet all the while maintains at least in Dowell's eyes the surface of the good soldier. But again if Edward had attempted depth in any of his affairs, his success would have been tenuous at best; for the women with whom he becomes involved— Leonora, his wife, the mercenary La Dolciquita, the extremely ill Masie Maidan, and Florence Dowell—are for the most part themselves incapable of full and sustained emotion. Edward's struggle is ineffectual, and often meagre; but the choices open to him, particularly in the context of his own awareness, seldom offer very clear moral alternatives.

This difficulty and often impossibility of clear choice is a major factor in Ford's double perspective. Each action and circumstance seems to drive the characters deeper and deeper into the spiral of their own ineffectiveness, and this is true even of those actions which express honest struggle. The lack of straight narrative, and the piling of situation on situation and character on character, all seen through Dowell's mixture of compassion, shock, and bewilderment, builds up to a sense of increasing chaos, of spiral upon spiral, that is almost grotesque in its intensity. The tone of tragedy has been heightened almost to the point of madness. But this madness comes, ironically, not from the fury of cosmic rage, but from the confused whimper of the characters' moral impotence.

The novel is divided by Ford into four parts, even though the overall structure is that of Dowell's effort to recollect and piece together events.

The progression is one of thought rather than conventional narrative, and Dowell's attempt to understand becomes part of the action of the novel. In the first section, Dowell recalls Ashburnham's two most significant affairs, prior to his intense attraction to Nancy Rufford. After beginning to trace the relationship between Florence and Edward, and detailing the latter's affair with Masie Maidan which had preceded it, Dowell draws his impressions of the major characters, and inadvertantly tells us something about himself. The second part builds toward one of the climactic events of the novel, Florence's suicide after she senses Edward's growing interest in Nancy, and after Dowell meets in the lobby of the spa at Nauheim the man in whose house Florence had conducted part of a previous affair. Before recounting her suicide, Dowell summarizes his dead relationship with his wife, and also gives a picture of Ashburnham as the good soldier up to August 4, 1914, the day of Florence's death. Part Three focuses on Edward's growing attraction to Nancy. It begins after Florence's death, when Dowell recounts his own brief interest in Nancy, which is quickly overshadowed by that of Ashburnham. In this section Dowell also sketches the arranged and unfortunate marriage of Edward and Leonora, up to the intrusion of Florence. Finally, the fourth part contains Edward's climactic refusal of Nancy, his later suicide, Nancy's madness, and the final irony of Dowell's own assumption of Edward's role in a greatly reduced sphere. By the end of the novel, Dowell's world is of necessity limited and rather private. But Dowell does not consciously reduce and internalize his response; the reduction is forced upon him. He does not, as does Christopher Tietjens, offset his disillusion by assuming the role of the limited hero.

Ford looked upon *The Good Soldier* as the culmination of his technique, and certainly as a triumph of craftsmanship it surpasses any of his work before or after. In a dedicatory letter to Stella Bowen, Ford wrote:

> So, on the day I was forty I set down to show what I could do—and *The Good Soldier* resulted. I fully intended it to be my last book.... So I regarded myself as the Eel which, having reached the deep sea, brings forth its young and dies—or as the Great Auk I considered that, having reached my allotted, I had laid my one egg and might as well die. So I took a formal farewell of Literature in the columns of a magazine called the *Thrush*—which alas, poor little auk that it was, died of the effort.[10]

And in a letter to Percival Hinton, an English admirer, in 1931, Ford wrote that he still regarded *The Good Soldier* as his "best book technically, unless you read the Tietjens books as one novel, in which case the whole design appears. But," he added, "I think the Tietjens books will probably 'date' a good deal, whereas the other may—and indeed need—not."[11] Ford was probably thinking that the Tietjens novels were too

closely tied to a specific historical event—the First World War—while *The Good Soldier* reflected a broader contemporary atmosphere. But the Tietjens novels, perhaps because their technique is less ostensibly self-conscious, remain more vivid as experiences, while *The Good Soldier*, although remaining one of Ford's major achievements, calls attention to itself mainly through its technique—a technique which admittedly renders an inconclusive and fragmentary society, but which is still at times too meticulously contrived to allow the reader a full empathetic response.

The broken, inconclusive and chaotic nature of the novel's world is suggested by its use of *progression d'effet* and by its radical departure from a straight narrative pattern. Events are given as they are recalled in Dowell's mind, and the narrator is constantly picking up strands of thought and referring them backward and forward and then back again. The structure is that of his own groping attempt to understand. Dowell himself admits that he does not "know how it is best to put this thing down," and concludes that he will just imagine himself "for a fortnight or so at one side of the fireplace of a country cottage, with a sympathetic soul opposite me. And I shall go on talking, in a low voice while the sea sounds in the distance and the great black flood of wind polishes the bright stars."[12] This structure of recollected thoughts, particularly in the broken sequence which Dowell's thought assumes, enhances the sense of a situation that has not yet reached its end. And Meixner notes the way in which Ford uses other devices to the same effect. For example, he begins *in medias res*, and thus attempts "to grip the reader's attention by presenting as forcefully as he can an emotional conflict at the peak of its intensity, and then having aroused the desire to know more about it, to develop the background which led to the situation. His special skill is in so presenting the expository material that the tension is not quickly resolved, but keeps pulling the reader on and on."[13] Meixner is here discussing the Tietjens novels, but his comments apply equally well to the strategy of *The Good Soldier*. Actually, the peak of conflict occurs before the novel begins, and is the impetus for Dowell's very efforts to put everything down. This peak occurs when Dowell discovers the reality in which he has lived for the past nine years, and the cumulative effect arises out of his efforts to derive some semblance of coherence from what he has discovered.

One of the effects which builds upon itself throughout the novel is that of Dowell's increasingly double view of Ashburnham. For nine years, even during the time of his affair with Florence, Ashburnham had been for Dowell a figure to be admired and imitated. And even after Dowell comes to know the reality, he fights his disenchantment with a desire to retain the appearance, or at least to assure himself that it had once been real. Behind Dowell's double view, moreover, lies Ford's own complicated attitude, and his implicit condemnation of some of the very heroic traits

of the good soldier that Dowell most admires. And both implicitly and explicitly, Ashburnham stands in the novel for the old order, so that his deterioration symbolizes the breakdown of a cohesive society built upon an ineffectual base.

Early in the novel Dowell sketches Ashburnham as the good soldier, but then, ironically, counters his own sketch with a final sentence:

> ... Edward Ashburnham was the cleanest looking sort of chap;—an excellent magistrate, a first rate soldier, one of the best landlords, so they said, in Hampshire, England. To the poor and to hopeless drunkards, as I myself have witnessed, he was like a painstaking guardian. And he never told a story that couldn't have gone into the columns of the *Field* more than once or twice in all the nine years of my knowing him. He didn't even like hearing them. ... You would have said that he was just exactly the sort of chap that you could have trusted your wife with. And I trusted mine and it was madness.[14]

The passage illustrates the complex point of view through which Ford controls the novel. Dowell worships Ashburnham for his deceptive public image, an attitude which, as the many ironies of the novel make clear, Ford does not share. And while Dowell, in his disenchantement, partially condemns Ashburnham, he does not perceive the connection between the public appearance and the private reality. Even Leonora admires the public Edward, despite her constant knowledge of his indiscretions. Once she admits to Dowell: "To do my husband justice there could not be a better man on the earth. There would not be room for it along these lines." Dowell is still totally ignorant of Edward's degeneration and says to Leonora that "there are not any other lines that count"; and asks her jokingly, "you're not going to accuse him of not being a good husband, or not being a good guardian to your ward?" And a few lines later he swears that Edward is never attentive to another woman, "not by the quivering of an eyelash."[15]

As for Ashburnham himself, until Leonora by taking over his estate had deprived him of his role, he was able to exist in a world nicely circumscribed by the proper words and actions. As Dowell remarks, "all good soldiers are sentimentalists—all good soldiers of that type. Their profession, for one thing, is full of big words, courage, loyalty, honour, constancy." And he goes on to say that Ashburnham did at times during their nine-year acquaintance "discuss what he would have called 'the graver things.' Even before his final outburst to me, at times, very late at night, say, he has blurted out something that gave me an insight into the Sentimental view of the cosmos that was his. He would say how much the society of a good woman could do towards redeeming you, and he would say that constancy was the finest of the virtues. He said it very

stiffly, of course, but still as if the statement admitted of no doubt."[16] Ashburnham is thus endowed with many of the typical qualities of the Fordian hero, false responsibility and a predilection for rhetoric; and despite the fact that his deterioration is of a deeper and more private sort and his world more complex than had been the case with his predecessors, Edward Ashburnham is a direct descendent of the earlier ineffectual hero, only intensified in all his traits.

One of Ashburnham's distinguishing characteristics is the great disparity between his public and private roles, at least in the earlier stages of his deterioration. George Moffat is ineffectual largely because of his moral position, and his failure, however mistaken, occurs in a context of public morality. And Count Macdonald, although on the one hand a sentimentalist, is also a professed cynic, and his efforts at maintaining a role of public morality are never so strong as those made by Ashburnham. Ashburnham is finally destroyed by his inability to come to terms with his private deterioration, and his public role gradually becomes an evasion of the issue. He does not fail only out of adherence to his principles, but is rather an example of the *homo duplex* of whom Ford spoke in his volume of war propaganda, *Between Saint Dennis and Saint George, A Sketch of Three Civilizations*. In this book, which appeared in the same year as *The Good Soldier*, Ford said that "any public man has a dual personality," and that he exists, on the one hand, "with all the incidental private relationships of any other man," but that "in addition," as a public figure, he is "forced to be modified by the traditions of the office which he fills."[17] The "office" which Ashburnham fills is that of the good soldier, and his attempts to maintain at least a semblance of its traditions are the basis for the double view with which he is viewed both by Ford and Dowell throughout the novel.

The problem of Ashburnham's dignity, its degree and kind, still remains, if we are further to distingiush him from previous Fordian heroes. We have already seen that his role of good soldier is regarded by Ford with a mixture of irony and qualified respect. In Ford's view Ashburnham, for all his degeneration, still ranks above his more commonplace and opportunistic wife, and still further above Florence, although his affair with Dowell's wife is a measure of his degradation. Ashburnham's vestiges of aristocratic dignity become admirable simply because his society has dropped so far below them, and is unable to show any clear alternatives to take their place. Meixner finds Ashburnham's dignity so striking, in the context of the novel, that he is able to designate him a "tragic protagonist," as well as "a man much above the ordinary," and a hero who, "if at his introduction seems . . . essentially a creation of comedy," grows steadily in stature throughout "the book until at its close he is an extremely impressive, noble figure." Moreover, "As Dowell makes clear, he was not a precocious libertine, but a sentimentalist. . . . Sentimentality in

fact is Edward's basic human weakness, his fatal flaw—even, as ironically, it is the source of much of his virtues."[18] Meixner comes much closer than most critics to a convincing interpretation of Edward Ashburnham, and Meixner's emphasis on the flaw of sentimentality suggests Edward's need to grasp at a standard of values, however false and misguided they may be. Ashburnham certainly has some of the qualities of the "tragic protagonist." But Ford's double view strongly qualifies any such role. Ashburnham's heroism is fragmentary; it covers a sordid and chaotic reality, and never confronts either this reality or its underlying causes. And Edward's final act of heroism, his refusal of Nancy Rufford, leads ultimately to his suicide and to Nancy's madness.

The history of Edward's marriage to Leonora is an ironic one of false responsibility on both sides and of progressive distrust. The union had been arranged by the two families, so there was little passion to begin with. And both Leonora and Edward had been from the start totally out of touch with each other's needs. Edward's traditions were aristocratic and feudal, while Leonora came from a family of much less established Irish landholders, and consequently had little understanding of Edward's feudal ideals. Dowell recalls the early days of their marriage:

> You see, he was really a very simple soul—very simple. He imagined that no man can satisfactorily accomplish his life's work without loyal and wholehearted cooperation of the woman he lives with. And he was beginning to perceive dimly that whereas his own traditions were entirely collective, his wife was a sheer individualist. His own theory—the feudal theory of an overlord doing his best by his dependents, the dependents meanwhile doing their best for the overlord—this theory was entirely foreign to Leonora's nature. She came of a family of small Irish landlords—that hostile garrison in a plundered country.

Gradually Leonora, finding Edward's feudal responsibility extravagant, had taken upon herself the management of his estates. This was of course a telling blow to Edward's ideals and his self-esteem, and he had turned to a succession of women in an effort to regain some feeling of his own right to exist. The situation grew worse, for while Edward could not withhold from his wife a certain grudging respect, this very feeling "made her seem so much the more cold in other matters that were near his heart—his responsibilities, his career, his tradition. It brought his despair of her up to a point of exasperation, and it riveted in him the idea that he might find some other woman who would give him the moral support that he needed." At this point Ashburnham "went about deliberately looking for some woman who could hold him," and as Dowell remarks with some irony, "there were quite a number of ladies in his set who were capable of

agreeing with this handsome and fine fellow that the duties of a feudal gentleman were feudal."[19]

Leonora's fault lay in her total incomprehension of Edward's needs, whereas Edward's lay in his never confronting his wife with the problem, but in running from it through a frenzy of unfortunate affairs. And, as Robie Macauley points out, "with each attempt to use another woman as a temporary Leonora, Ashburnham has complicated and destroyed the lives of others." His almost desperate grasping at straws of acceptance results finally in the deaths of Masie Maidan and Florence Dowell, and in an "insupportable tension in the mind of Nancy Rufford, who goes mad."[20] Dowell, still half-reluctant to condemn either Ashburnham or his own wife, speculates on the death of Masie Maidan, and decides that with her illness she would probably have died, even if Florence had not come on the scene. Still, says Dowell, "she would have died without having to soak her noonday pillow with tears whilst Florence, below the window talked to Captain Ashburnham about the constitution of the United States (. . .) Yes, it would have left a better taste in the mouth if Florence had let her die in peace."[21] If Edward had been able to reach the depth that he had been denied by Leonora in his other relationships, he might have justified them as attempts to create a more desirable reality. But the other relationships attained only the level of simplest gratification, partly because Edward, with his role of good soldier removed, had little but a superficial self to give.

The affair of Edward and Masie Maidan is a typical instance of the interplay of Ford's characters during the last years of their world. The Ashburnhams and the Dowells had actually become acquainted one day when Florence had accidentally come across Leonora, who just at that moment was boxing Mrs. Maidan across the ears. Leonora had later tried, of course, to veil the incident by saying that she had been straightening a comb in Mrs. Maidan's hair. But the act against Edward's current paramour had really been for her a venting of pent-up frustration and rage. She was "just striking the face of an intolerable universe." For that afternoon she had "discovered that Edward Ashburnham was paying a blackmailer of whom she had never heard something like three hundred pounds a year." The blackmailer was Major Basil, the husband of one of Edward's previous mistresses, and this discovery had been for Leonora a final stab in the back. She had, however, been most disturbed by the possibility that the books of the estate might be thrown off balance. Ironically, Leonora had actually encouraged Edward's affair with Mrs. Maidan. She had, in a striking flourish of false responsibility, paid Mrs. Maidan's expenses from India, where her husband and this woman met, to the health resort at Nauheim. Leonora had justified her actions to herself by saying that "she could trust Masie—she could trust her not to rook

Edward for several thousands a week," and that "she would have welcomed it if she could have come across the love of his life. It would have given her a rest." Leonora had rather perversely resigned herself to feeling responsible for her husband's happiness as well as the state of his books. Her sudden attack against Masie simply indicated that her attitude ran contrary to her actual feelings.

A further irony was piled upon this affair by the fact that Leonora's public boxing of Masie's ears accidentally brought in the woman who was to be her husband's next object of attention. Edward's interests soon began to focus on Florence, who shortly after their acquaintance had begun an obvious flirtation. Masie then had died while trying to strap up her large portmanteau so that she could return to her husband. Her death had occurred on the same day that the Dowells and Ashburnhams had taken together an excursion to an old castle; and she had left a note for Leonora, in which she had expressed surprise at the idea that she was brought to Nauheim as an adulteress, and went on to say that she had heard Edward call her "a poor little rat to the American lady." Leonora, with a final stroke of responsibility and perhaps out of a slight guilt over the fatal results of her project, had not told Edward of the letter. Consequently, for Ashburnham Mrs. Maidan's death had simply ended "the one affair of his about which he never felt much remorse."[22] As for Leonora, she had once hoped that if "through her agency" Masie Maidan could help Edward to "smile again," "he might return, through gratitude and satisfied love—to her." After Florence, however, Leonora had pretty much to give up hope.[23]

Leonora's mixed motivations in the Masie Maidan affair indicate that despite her ostensible aggressiveness and desire to manage situations, she, too, is subject to the same bewilderment that marks almost everyone in the novel. Her responsibility is in part a social response, in part an effort to maintain self-respect, and in part the expression of a vague desire, which she does not know how to fulfill, to have Edward voluntarily return to her. But all of her efforts, instead of bringing him closer, push him back and leave her in a mood of partial resentment and greater resignation. Neither she nor Edward knows how to cope with each other, and together they bring on the progressive worsening of an already bad situation.

Part of Leonora's sense of duty is derived from her English Catholicism, and her religious response becomes for Ford another example of an idealism which distorts the image of actual reality. Dowell explains that "Leonora's English Catholic conscience, her rigid principles, her coldness even her very patience, were, I cannot help thinking, all wrong in this special case." And he goes on to suggest, in a moment of bitterness toward Ashburnham, that Leonora ought to have divorced: "she quite seriously and naively believed that her church could be such a monstrous

and imbecile institution as to expect her to take on the responsible job of making Edward Ashburnham a faithful husband."[24] The idea of divorce as a solution may be an indication of Dowell's own tendency to evasion, but his analysis of Leonora's pervasive sense of duty is very much to the point. The pattern had continued all through her life with Ashburnham. She had, for example, legalized her management of the estate after Edward had run off temporarily with the sensuous La Dolciquita. Leonora and her attorney had made themselves the legal trustees for "all of Edward's property, and there was an end of Edward as the good landlord and father of his people. He went out." After Edward had returned from this diversion, but before his time with Masie Maidan, he and Leonora had "settled down into a model couple and they never spoke in private to each other."[25]

Dowell admits that Leonora could force Edward "to settle all his property upon her" because "in his clumsy, good-natured, inarticulate way he was as frightened of her as of the devil. And he admired her enormously, and he was as fond of her as any man could be of any woman." Leonora, Dowell goes on to say, took advantage of his ambivalence "to treat him as if he had been a person whose estates are being managed by the Court of Bankruptcy." But then the narrator adds, in a thin evasion of judgement, "I suppose it was the best thing for him."[26] And if Leonora did not confide in her husband, but instead continually reduced his opinions and attitudes, Edward did little to help these matters of communication. On the contrary, he took great care to conceal himself and his debauchery from his wife because "he was positively revolted at the thought that she should know that the sort of thing he did existed in the world. . . . He wanted to preserve the virginity of his wife's thoughts."[27] Thus, the Ashburnhams created in their marriage a cumulative habit of evasion and distrust, and all was justified under the name of responsibility, of protecting the thoughts or the fortunes of one or the other partner in their nominal marriage. Beneath the appearance of responsibility, however, there lay a reality of passion and bewilderment, and of bitter hostility that finally, as we shall see, reached a breaking point in the infatuation of Edward for his innocent ward.

As if to underline the major flaw in Edward's relationship to Leonora, the theme of false responsibility is brought out through other characters as well. An amusing instance of the sense of duty magnified to the point of ridiculousness is given in the short picture of Florence's Uncle Hurlburd. On a voyage to the South Seas, he had decided that he wanted to take presents for all the people he might meet on the voyage. "And it struck him that the things to take for that purpose were oranges—because California is the orange country—and comfortable folding chairs. So he bought I don't know how many cases of oranges— . . . There must have been half a cargo of fruit." And Dowell goes on to recall that "to every

person with whom he had as much as a nodding acquaintance, he gave an orange every morning."[28] Mr. Hurlburd is also thought by his doctors to have the same "heart" condition from which Florence and Edward supposedly suffer; but as if to preview the falseness of Florence's disease, Dowell tells us that her uncle actually died of bronchitis. The implications of the pun that Florence has a "heart" problem are obvious, and her supposed condition becomes the basis for Dowell's assumed role of sick nurse, another of the novel's many false positions. Florence had apparently convinced a group of doctors to verify her pretended condition, for with their sanction she could demand Dowell's attentions, and yet send him away when she desired the quiet of another assignment. Dowell recalls that his "whole endeavors were to keep poor dear Florence on to topics like the finds at Cnossos and the mental spirituality of Walter Pater. I had to keep her at it, you understand, or she might die. For I was solemnly informed that if she became excited over anything or if her emotions were really stirred her little heart might cease to beat. For twelve years I had to watch every word that any person uttered in any conversation and I had to head it off what the English call 'things'—off love, poverty, crime, religion, and the rest of it."[29]

Dowell almost states explicitly here that his assumed responsibility was a careful evasion of major issues. Perhaps it might be said that his choice was not an easy one, for he was told by many doctors what he had to do. And to condemn Dowell is hardly to lessen Florence's guilt; for she represents a blatant self-interest which Ford saw as part of the new order, and under her onslaught of deceptions and alibis, Dowell at times seems essentially a victim. And yet, one must wonder how Dowell, with all the best intentions, could have been deceived by Florence over so long a period of time, and it must be concluded that his caring for Florence's "heart" was either an evasion of his passions, or that Dowell started the relationship with only enough passion to become an ineffectual manservant. In any case, this was the first of many illusions under which Dowell was to live for the next nine years.

As a character, Dowell is involved in the deceptions and evasions of his world, but as a narrator his function is more complex. As a character in the plot, believing in and deceived by both Florence and Ashburnham, and seldom able to assert himself in any way, he is as much to blame as anyone for the tortured minuet that marks the end of his world. But as a narrator, recalling and trying to comprehend the past, Dowell reacts to the situation after the fact. Here his honesty in voicing his bewilderment, his efforts to understand, and his frequent compassion add to his dimensions and make him a more believable and admirable character. He becomes, in spite of his very obvious limitations, the most highly regarded person in the novel, and certainly the one with whom we as readers, also trying to comprehend, can most easily empathize.

THE END OF A PHASE

Because of his double role in the novel, and also because his drawbacks as well as his virtues are so evident, Dowell has been subject to strongly varying interpretation. The variance is perhaps the result of *The Good Soldier*'s complex perspective, which ensures that no character receives the author's or the reader's full approval or disapproval. Still, preference for certain characters is evident, and Dowell's role is especially significant in this regard, since as narrator he voices most of the novel's explicit attitudes. If these attitudes are regarded as valid in any way, then Dowell's relative moral priority must be granted. Among the critics, Mark Schorer takes the most unfavorable view and regards Dowell as a grotesque and comic character. He contends that "the book's controlling irony lies in the fact that passionate situations are related by a narrator who is himself incapable of passion, sexual and moral alike." Dowell, he goes on to say, is marked by "a mind not quite in balance." Schorer then questions Dowell's distinctions of blame between Florence and Ashburnham: "For why are Florence's indiscretions crimes, and Edward's, with Florence, follies at worst and, at best, true goodness of heart? Why, after his degradation, is Edward still 'a fine Fellow'? In every case, the 'fact' is somewhere between the mere social convention and that different order of convention which the distorted understanding of the narrator imposes on them."[30] Schorer is correct in noting Dowell's moral indecisiveness, but he does not give sufficient weight to the narrator's efforts to understand. The distinction which Dowell tries to make between Florence and Ashburnham does not specifically refer to their deception of himself so much as it does to what they stand for in the context of the entire novel. Wiley agrees generally with Schorer, and sees Dowell as incapable of piercing beneath the surface of appearances. Hence the double vision of the novel lies in the contrast of Dowell's perceived appearances and the reality beneath them.[31] Like Schorer, Wiley perceives a part of Dowell's response, but loses sight of an important aspect emphasized by Samuel Hynes in a recent article.

Hynes sees the novel as one "which raises uncertainty about the nature of truth and reality to the level of a structural principle." The action of *The Good Soldier* lies, therefore, not in the ostensible plot, but rather "in the action of the narrator's mind as it gropes for the meaning, the reality of what has occurred. . . . This point is clear enough if one considers the way in which Ford treats the violent events which would, in a true melodrama, be climactic—the deaths of Masie Maidan, Florence, and Ashburnham. All these climaxes are, dramatically speaking, 'thrown away,' anticipated in casual remarks so as to deprive them of melodramatic force, and treated, when they do occur, almost as afterthoughts." Hynes, although he gives Dowell disproportionate significance in the novel as a whole, comes closer than either Wiley or Schorer to a fair interpretation of the narrator. Hynes also points out that Dowell's moral

indecision is shared by all the main characters of the novel, so that Dowell is no worse than they, and also that it is Dowell who performs the only two unselfish acts of the book: he crosses the Atlantic to answer Ashburnham's plea, almost at the end, for help; and he travels to Ceylon, when Leonora will not, in order to bring back the deranged Nancy.[32] Though these actions may be ironically trivial in the total collapse, their value must still be recognized. Graham Greene, supporting this point of view, argues that *The Good Soldier* is marked by a quality of "restraint, a restraint which is given to it by the gentle character of the narrator . . . who never loses his love and compassion for the characters concerned."[33] Greene, too, seems to focus on one side of Dowell's dual nature, and yet, as against the other characters of the novel, we do find Dowell marked by the virtues mentioned.

Finally, John A. Meixner, in line with his view of the novel as essentially tragic, looks upon Dowell sympathetically as a type of twentieth-century mind. He sees the narrator as "Prufrock before Prufrock, and not a mere sketch as in Eliot but a full-scale portrait. He is a man who, incapable of acting, is almost entirely feeling—a creature of pure pathos. Lonely and unrooted, Dowell is an alienated being. . . . That was why the Ashburnhams had meant so much to him. They had . . . filled a frightening void." Then, in answer to Schorer, Meixner proposes that "Dowell's absurdity does not induce laughter, but rather a grave sadness. His consciousness will be peculiarly receptive to the ache of the universe." Meixner best catches the mood in which Ford has drawn his narrator. Despite the fact that Dowell is a causal factor in the breakdown of his world, he embodies, nonetheless, the consciousness of this world, and thus summons our compassion. And as Meixner concludes, "The ultimate importance (and final justification) of Dowell in the novel is as a concrete, functioning embodiment of the state of mind formed by the new conditons of the twentieth-century world: alienated and unrooted, helpless and 'less than human,' pathetic and absurd. As symbolic context, Dowell gives the tragedy a remarkably contemporary dimension."[34] Part of our response to Dowell is undoubtedly determined by the fact that we recognize his bewilderment as our own; his world is symbolically very much our own, and his response is at least more articulate than many of us would be likely to make.

Judging by the great diversity of interpretations, it would seem that Ford's narrator can almost represent as many different things as there are critics to interpret him. The weakness of nearly all these readings, however, is that each critic tends to over-emphasize one aspect of Dowell's total personality, and does not take into account the novel's continuous double perspective. Schorer and Wiley, as we have seen, emphasize Dowell's naivete and his desire to preserve the reality of appearances. On the other hand, Hynes, Greene, and Meixner stress his real if

THE END OF A PHASE

partial awareness, his compassion, and his almost frightening alienation. All these qualities can be discerned in the narrator, although in the context of the novel his more positive attributes stand out by comparison. Dowell is, however, like all the persons in this novel seen on many levels. A central distinction must be made between Dowell, the participant, and Dowell, the narrator; but even inside each level a double perspective is evident and mixed responses are evoked. For example, as participant Dowell is bland enough to be totally oblivious to his wife's stratagems, and yet is also responsive enough to travel back from America to England in order to answer Ashburnham's request for help. Similarly, as narrator he almost forces himself to believe in the reality of Ashburnham's appearance, and yet is able to face and express a strong sense of the loneliness and alienation of the other characters as well as himself. Dowell and the other characters of *The Good Soldier* are depicted in accord with the demands of the complex characterization for which Ford in 1922 praised the work of Joyce:

> The mind of every man is made up of several—three or four—currents all working side by side, all making their impress or getting their expression from separate and individual areas of the brain. It is not enough to say that every man is homo duplex; every man is homo x-plex. And this complexity pursues every man into the minutest transactions of his daily life. You go to a bookstall to ask the price of a certain publication. Yes! But part of your mind says to you very quickly: 'This clerk has the nose of my uncle George!' Another part feels that you have plenty of time for your train; another that the fish you had for breakfast is disagreeing with you.[35]

Complexity of character extends of course beyond the disparity of uncles' noses and fish for breakfast, and while it may add psychological and symbolic dimension, it can be the source of much critical disagreement. The many and extremely divergent interpretations of Dowell are strong evidence of this possibility.

One of Dowell's major flaws is a desire to cherish illusion, a desire which results in a major limitation of his awareness. Even his marriage had been a legalized illusion, in which, while Florence was busily arranging her assignations, Dowell had imagined himself a remarkably efficient sick nurse. "You see," Dowell writes, "in those days I was interested in people with 'hearts.' There was Florence, there was Edward Ashburnham —or, perhaps, it was Leonora that I was more interested in. I don't mean in the way of love. But, you see, we were both of the same profession—at any rate as I saw it. And the profession was that of keeping heart patients alive. You have no idea how engrossing such a profession may become . . . and surely, surely, these delusions are necessary to keep us going—so did I, and as I believe, Leonora, imagine that the whole world ought to be

arranged so as to ensure the keeping alive of heart patients."[36] Even here Dowell maintains a double view, for he admits the delusion that was his responsibility, all the while that he lauds its necessity to his psychological self. This necessity arises from his essential aimlessness; for in 1904, when he had met Florence for the first time, Dowell "had no attachments, no accumulations." And even after the marriage he remained merely "a wanderer upon the face of public resorts," who "having nothing in the world to do—but nothing whatever! . . . fell into the habit of counting" his steps, and "would walk with Florence to the baths."[37] His main worries had revolved around an exceeding impatience at missing trains. And since "The Belgian State Railway has a trick of letting the French trains miss their connections at Brussels," Dowell had written "infuriated . . . letters to the *Times* that the *Times* never printed."[38] In this state of impatient boredom, it is easy to see how the care of a "heart" patient could have become for Dowell a fascinating diversion, and a substitute for letters to the *Times* about late Belgian trains.

The same need for something to hold on to, for a "delusion" which was "necessary to keep going," had engendered Dowell's nine-year cultivation of the Ashburnhams, for Edward had been to the wandering American a figure of purpose and stability, worthy of emulation. And this unwillingness to relinquish his idol causes Dowell, even as he writes, to contend that the appearance of Ashburnham during the nine years it had lasted had actually been the reality. Even after his disenchantment Dowell can "swear by the sacred name of my creator that it was true. It was true sunshine; the true music; the true splash of the fountains from the mouth of stone dolphins." And he can ask anxiously, "If for nine years I have possessed a goodly apple that is rotten at the core and discover its rottenness only in nine years and six months less four days, isn't it true to say that for nine years I possessed a goodly apple?"[39] This is not a pat assertion on Dowell's part; it is a question. And as a question it carries the urgency of a stunned and disillusioned man trying to salvage some fragment of his former world. What adulation Dowell has left for Ashburnham is unchecked, even by his memories of Ashburnham's muddled involvement with Nancy, "The most monstrously wicked thing that Edward Ashburnham ever did in his life." For in spite of statements such as this, Dowell admits that "It is impossible of me to think of Edward Ashburnham as anything but straight, upright and honourable. That, I mean, is, in spite of everything, my permanent view of him. I try at times by dwelling on some of the things that he did to push that image of him away, as you might try to push aside a large pendulum. But it always comes back—the memory of his innumerable acts of kindness, of his efficiency, of his unspiteful tongue. He was such a fine fellow."[40] The "large pendulum" keeps swinging back into Dowell's consciousness, until finally he comes to see himself as another Ashburnham. "For I can't

THE END OF A PHASE

conceal from myself," Dowell tells us, "the fact that I loved Edward Ashburnham—and that I loved him because he was just myself. If I had the courage and the virility and possibly also the physique of Edward Ashburnham I should, I fancy, have done much what he did."

Dowell's admiration of Ashburnham is the converse of his evident tendency toward self-denigration, his fear of his virtual impotence; it is an expression of his need to believe in a hero whom he can both worship and emulate. And at the end of the novel, despite a new knowledge of his hero's flaws, Dowell finds himself ironically "in my fainter sort of way ... following the lines of Edward Ashburnham." Dowell's first real tragedy arises from the fact that in spite of his articulate awareness—even in a sense because of it—he can only cling to the pieces of a world that has already fallen apart. His attempt to piece together the past and its significance is an act of meaningful self-assertion, but apart from this effort, Dowell finds "only Hell (. . .) Edward is dead; the girl is gone—oh utterly gone; Leonora is having her good time with Rodney Bayham, and I sit alone in Branshaw Teleragh." Nancy, now mad, is "sitting in the hall, forty paces from where I am now writing. . . . She is very well dressed; she is quite quiet; she is very beautiful. The old nurse looks after her very efficiently."[41]

In effect, at the end of the novel, Dowell remains far less capable of translating feeling into action than even Edward. For the latter's affairs and his suicide, however misguided they may have been, were at least expressions of passion. Dowell, for all his awareness, remains inert. He is present just before Ashburnham kills himself, and senses that Edward, "to the last, a sentimentalist," intends to commit suicide; but he asks himself, "Why should I hinder him?" When Ashburnham sees that Dowell intends no interference, his eyes become "soft and almost affectionate," and he remarks, "So long, old man, I must have a bit of rest you know." Dowell does not know what to say. "I wanted," he recalls in the novel's final sentences, "to say 'God bless you,' for I am also a sentimentalist. But I thought that perhaps that would not be quite English good form, so I trotted off with the telegram to Leonora. She was quite pleased with it."[42]

This final episode, Nancy's telegram from Brindisi informing Edward that she is having a good time, and Ashburnham's subsequent suicide, is handled, in accord with the dominant mode of the narrator, with considerable understatement. And with this inconclusive conclusion to his effort at understanding, we are left at the end of the novel with the double view of Dowell that has been maintained throughout. In the final scene, Dowell's dispassionate and inarticulate resignation emphasize his ineffectiveness, when a stronger response might have saved Ashburnham's life. But Dowell's ineffectiveness is always balanced by his consciousness of his own faults. He expresses frequently his own lack of a clear moral direc-

tion: "I know nothing—nothing in the world—of the hearts of men. I only know that I am alone—horribly alone."[43] And later, as he thinks of himself occupying Ashburnham's position, he asks whether the lives of all men are "like the lives of us good people . . . broken, tumultuous, agonized, and unromantic lives, periods punctuated by screams, by imbecilities, by deaths, by agonies? Who the devil knows?"[44] The triteness of the final question contrasts with the stark imagery of Dowell's perception of life, and indicates the two levels of his response. He is caught between the two, without, as he himself perceives the faith by which he might transcend the crippling paralysis of his own uncertainty. "I don't know," he admits. "And there is nothing to guide us. . . . It is all a darkness."[45] Thus Dowell, for all the irony of his misplaced responsibility and lack of significant action, achieves in his sense of the human condition, a sense built from his own bewilderment and alienation, an especially disturbing degree of insight and articulation.

Dowell's questions and insights into the whole turbulent situation have two functions in the novel. First, they raise the narrator to the rank of a major and admirable character; and second, they extend the significance of the situation itself. Through his speculations, Dowell underlines the symbolic meaning of the story, and suggests its relevance for all our lives. He begins his story with a comment on the difference between appearance and the knowledge of reality. "This," he says, "is the saddest story I have ever heard. . . . My wife and I knew Captain and Mrs. Ashburnham as well as it was possible to know anybody, and yet, in another sense, we knew nothing at all about them. This is, I believe, a state of things only possible with English people of whom, till to-day, when I sit down to puzzle what I know of this sad affair, I knew nothing whatever. Six months ago I had never been to England, and, certainly, I had never sounded the depths of an English heart. I had known the shallows."[46]

In his attempt "to puzzle what" he knows of the affair, Dowell soon relates this particular situation to the general themes of overthrow and instability. He tells us that Edward was descended from an Ashburnham who accompanied Charles I to the scaffold in 1649. And shortly afterwards, Dowell explains that he writes because "it is not unusual for human beings who have witnessed the sack of a city or the falling to pieces of a people to desire to set down what they have witnessed for the benefit of unknown heirs or of a generation infinitely remote; or, if you please, just to get the sight out of their heads." And then he admits, "I can't believe it's gone. I can't believe that that long tranquil life, which was just stepping a minuet, vanished in four crashing days at the end of nine years and six weeks." But suddenly the sense of a more frightening reality intrudes upon his image of the minuet, and Dowell exclaims, "No, by God, it is False! It wasn't a minuet that we stepped; it was a prison—a prison full of screaming hysterics, tied down so that they might not

outsound the rolling of our carriage wheels as we went along the shaded avenues of the Tannus Wald."[47] The sense of the "prison full of screaming hysterics" modifies even Dowell's hatred of his wife. He imagines her, along with Edward and Leonora, on judgement day; and the dominant image is one of Leonora and Edward, together, as for Dowell they should be, while Florence stands aside in the sight of God, painfully alone:

> But what were they? The just? The unjust? God knows! I think that the pair of them were only poor wretches, creeping over this earth in the shadow of an eternal wrath. It is very terrible (. . . .) It is almost too terrible, the picture of that judgment as it appears to me sometimes, at nights. . . . But upon an immense plain, suspended in mid-air, I seem to see three figures, two of them clasped close in an intense embrace, and one intolerably solitary. . . . And the immense plain is the hand of God, stretching out for miles and miles, with great spaces above it and below it. And they are in the sight of God, and it is Florence that is alone.

This compassionate image of a judgement scene, dominated by great empty spaces and loneliness is, however, quickly countered by Dowell's resentment, as the cuckolded husband; for immediately in the following paragraph he admits, "I know that I hold myself back. For I hate Florence. I hate Florence with such a hatred that I would not spare her an eternity of loneliness."[48] Alienation and deception, bewilderment and hatred, such are the elements of the world in which Dowell has lived and which he now tries to comprehend. In his position, as the victim of a deception that has left him with a half-articulated hatred of his late wife, it is very much to Dowell's credit that he can perceive the underlying loneliness at all.

The perception of this loneliness leads Dowell to make what is probably his most acute and disturbing insight. He senses that human love is basically a "craving for identity," a craving made more intense by a world without clear lines of definition, and that love, if it is to succeed, must impart to each of the partners a sense of themselves at the same time that they lose themselves. They need, more than anything else, a reassurance, a sense of being anchored against the emptiness; and it is one of the greatest failures of the Ashburnhams and the Dowells that not one of them is able to convey this sense of worthiness to anyone else. In the light of Dowell's comments, the various affairs of Florence and Edward, and the false responsibility professed by all the characters are nothing but desperate substitutes for a sense of personal worth that they have never found. Dowell suggests a type of specific, personal response which, had it been made by any of the characters, might have altered the outcome of "the saddest story." Dowell's comprehension of the love relationship, at least in theory, thus becomes a controlling idea by which his own circum-

stances can be judged. He voices an insight that can very well be taken as a comment on the action of the entire novel:

> Of the question of the sex-instinct I know very little and I do not think that it counts for much in a really great passion. It can be aroused by such nothings . . . that I think it might be left out of the calculation. I don't mean to say that any great passion can exist without a desire for consummation. That seems to me to be a common-place and to be therefore a matter needing no comment at all. It is a thing, with all its accidents, that must be taken for granted, as, in a novel, or a biography, you take it for granted that the characters have their meals with some regularity. But the real fierceness of desire, the real heat of passion long continued and withering up the soul of a man is the craving for identity with the woman that he loves. He desires to see with the same eyes, to touch with the same sense of touch, to hear with the same ears, to lose his identity, to be enveloped, to be supported. For whatever may be said of the relation of the sexes, there is no man who loves a woman that does not desire to come to her for the renewal of his courage, for the cutting asunder of his difficulties. And that will be the mainspring of his desire for her. We are all so afraid, we are all so alone, we all so need from the outside the assurance of our own worthiness to exist.
>
> So, for a time, if such a passion come to fruition, the man will get what he wants. He will get the moral support, the encouragement, the relief from the sense of loneliness, the assurance of his worth. But these things pass away; inevitably they pass away as the shadows pass across sundials. It is sad, but it is so. The pages of the book will become familiar; the beautiful corner of the road will have been turned too many times. Well, this is the saddest story.[49]

But Dowell is not blind to the frequent imperfections of human love. He is aware that "In all matrimonial associations there is . . . one constant factor—a desire to deceive the person with whom one lives as to some weak spot in one's character or one's career. For it is intolerable to live constantly with one human being who perceives one's small meanesses. It is really death to do so—that is why so many marriages turn out unhappily."[50] This seemingly inevitable deceit works against the type of ideal marital relationship of which Dowell had spoken, for the ideal necessitates a direct confrontation, an openness, in which the partners share with each other their loneliness in order that they may alleviate it. Only such sharing can lead to the intimacy through which the lovers can give each other the desired sense of their own "worthiness to exist." One of the strongest criticisms which Ford makes, and which Dowell implies, against the characters in *The Good Soldier* is that they never attempt this direct confrontation of each other or themselves. Dowell's views on love are, in a sense, a development of Ford's continuous criticism throughout his work of the

hero's inability to respond in an emotional situation. The narrator of *The Good Soldier* simply extends the sense of what such an emotional situation involves.

In the light of the relevance of these insights to *The Good Soldier* and to Ford's work as a whole, it is hard to see how Paul Wiley can refer to Dowell's statements as "an ironical exposure of" his "character through his own words" and a "Victorian parody."[51] The whole tone of Dowell's statements is directly in opposition to that of the Victorian period as seen by Ford, and the narrator's views are also clearly differentiated from those responses which Ford most strongly condemns in the novel itself. Dowell's ability to articulate such insights makes him much more than a comic character, and raises him not only above the other persons in the novel, but even partly above his own inert and usual self.

Ashburnham's breakdown and his heroism, as well as the breakdown of his society, all reach their climax in his tangled involvement with Nancy Rufford; and this climactic episode is also used by Ford to underline the criticism of the English implied both in Dowell's statements about love and in the novel as a whole. Nancy, as a symbol of innocence, is used and ultimately driven mad by both Edward and Leonora, and her madness marks the final incoherence of Ashburnham's world. Although Edward's feelings for Nancy are apparently genuine, he is unable to realize them and his inability is in this case seen by Ford with a noticeably double point of view. Leonora, on the other hand, by this time painfully baffled and embittered, uses Nancy as a means of revenge, and she does so by simultaneously goading Nancy to satisfy Edward's passion and revealing to her all of Edward's previous indiscretions. Ashburnham himself, unable to prevail over his wife's spiteful behavior, is made to typify, especially in his final refusal of Nancy, what Ford saw as the peculiarly English evasion of passion.

The evasion of passion, mitigated by particular circumstances, becomes the dominant theme of the final section of the book. The ironic scene in *The Good Soldier* in which Nancy departs for India is taken almost directly from a similar scene in Ford's earlier definition of English society, *The Spirit of the People*. In that book Ford related how he had stayed one summer at the home of a socially-established couple. The husband, like Edward, had developed an attachment for the young ward. The situation had grown intolerable, and it was decided that the girl should take a trip around the world. It had all been done, "with the nicest tranquillity." The arrangements were carefully made, and the host had asked Ford to accompany the girl and himself to the station, in order to avoid the possibility of a "scene." On the way to the station, they had "talked in ordinary voices," and emotional expression was held to a minimum. Finally, as Ford recalled it, the parting at the station had been "too surprising, too really superhuman not to give one, as the saying is, the

jumps. For P⎯⎯⎯ never even shook her by the hand; touching the flap of his cloth cap sufficed for leave-taking." Commenting on this incident, Ford had seen the two people as doggedly "playing the game to the bitter end." He added that since the girl had "died at Brindisi on the voyage out, and P⎯⎯⎯ spent the next three years at various places on the continent where nerve cures are attempted," "a word or two" at the moment of separation "might have saved the girl's life and the man's misery without infringing eternal verities." And Ford had added in conclusion that "a silence so utter, a so demonstrative lack of tenderness, seems to me to be a manifestation of a national characteristic that is almost appalling."[52] Edward and Nancy's parting scene is almost an exact parallel of the incident in the earlier book, and it implies a similar criticism of the English response:

> There was upon these peoples' faces no expression of any kind whatsoever. The signal for the train's departure was a very bright red; that is about as passionate a statement as I can get into that scene. She was not looking her best; she had on a cap of brown fur that did not very well match her hair. She said:
>
> 'So long,' to Edward.
> Edward answered: 'So long.'
>
> He swung round on his heel and, large, slouching, and walking with a heavy deliberate pace, he went out of the station. I followed and got up beside him in the high dogcart. It was the most horrible performance I have ever seen.[53]

Ashburnham's "horrible performance" with Nancy only culminates an attitude toward passion that runs through the entire novel. Dowell, for example, tells us early in the book that his nine years of friendship with the Ashburnhams "were characterized by an extraordinary want of any communicativeness on the part of the Ashburnhams to which we, on our part, replied by leaving out quite as extraordinarily, and nearly as completely, the personal note."[54] Shortly thereafter, Dowell remarks that "the modern civilized habit—the modern English habit of taking everyone for granted is a good deal to blame" for a condition in which one can live a whole lifetime and yet know almost nothing of "one's fellow beings."[55] Once again, with these observations, Dowell rises above the level of Ashburnham and his world. But as Dowell himself admits, his own marriage to Florence had been marked by the same evasion of passion for which he now criticizes the English. Florence had agreed to marry him because "She wanted to marry a gentleman of leisure; she wanted a European establishment. She wanted her husband to have an English accent, an income of fifty thousand dollars a year from real

estates and no ambitions to increase the income. And—she frequently hinted—she did not want much physical passion in the affair."[56]

Their marriage had begun with an elopement, and Dowell's own indecisiveness, lack of passion, and sexual inexperience had quickly extinguished all of Florence's warmth, which itself had all the duration of a single embrace. Dowell admits that he had been so preoccupied with the details of the elopement "that I must have received her advances with a certain amount of absence of mind. I was out of that room and down the ladder in under half a minute. . . . I fancy that, if I had shown warmth then, she would have acted the proper wife to me, or would have put me back." Dowell gives Florence far too much credit for good intentions, and this is another indication of his tendency toward self-abasement. When Florence had finally come down the ladder, two hours later, she had announced for the first time her prohibitive "heart" condition, and Dowell had been relegated to "the part of a male nurse." Later, on the ship to Europe, a tempest had given Florence reason to declare her condition worse and her husband had received discreet suggestions from the ship's doctor "that I had better refrain from manifestations of affection." And Dowell adds with an intended double meaning, "I was ready enough." In Le Havre, Florence had taken up with the "lugubrious, silent" and "morose" Jimmy, a second-rate artist and her lover for the next two years, during which time "he lived in our flat in Paris, whether we were there or not." Dowell had fallen quickly into a role of moral inertia and false responsibility. He had been told by Jimmy that "what Florence needed most of all were sleep and privacy. I must never enter her room without knocking, or her poor little heart might flutter away to its doom." There is an evident irony in Dowell's tone as he recounts this experience, but just as he begins to suggest that he now sees through himself, he brings in an image that pulls us back to our double perspective, and makes us wonder if he still would not regard entry into Florence's room as a crime. "Why," he exclaims, "I would as soon have thought of entering her room without her permission as of burgling a church."[57] Dowell's false responsibility during his marriage to Florence is of a much more grotesque and almost bitterly comic sort than Ashburnham's; but Dowell, unlike Ashburnham, had no feudal tradition to which he could revert, and when this feudal tradition is lost, Ashburnham's degeneration is much more complete.

As a character, Dowell's expressions of passion are not frequent, but one is significant. On August 4, 1913, Florence had committed suicide. The act had been incited by her sensing Edward's interest in Nancy and by her seeing Dowell with "an odious Englishman called Bagshawe," whom Dowell had met accidentally, and in whose house Florence and Jimmy had met for two years.[58] Dowell recalls that he felt no urge to prevent his wife's death, and little passion or regret after it had occurred:

> I tell you I had no regret. What had I to regret? I suppose that my inner soul—my dual personality—had realized long before that Florence was a personality of paper—that she represented a real human being with a heart, with feelings, with sympathies and with emotions only as a bank-note represents a certain quantity of gold. . . . It is even possible that, if that feeling had not possessed me, I should have run up soon to her room and might have prevented her drinking the prussic acid. But I just couldn't do it; it would have been like chasing a scrap of paper—an occupation ignoble for a grown man.

The final phrase of this passage imparts a double meaning, and tell us something of Dowell's new attitude after he has learned from Bagshawe the facts of Florence's life. Under normal circumstances, his lack of regret and his disinclination to act might be considered failings; but in this case, with the nature of Florence's past now very much in the open, Dowell's response is the beginning of his discovery and recognition of his own feelings. For the first time he allows, although by inaction, some of his hostility toward his wife to come to the surface. He is beginning in a small way to act like a grown man. And it is this beginning that makes even more significant Dowell's remark in passing to Leonora, after Florence's death, that "now" he "can marry" Nancy. Sensing Dowell's attitudes toward both Florence and Nancy, Leonora had begun to tell Dowell of Florence's relations with Edward, of which until this point he had suspected nothing. In order to retain his double view of Dowell, however, Ford has the narrator remind us that until he had spoken to Leonora, he had not even realized that Florence's death had been a suicide, but had blamed it on heart failure.[59] Elliot Gose calls attention to this admission of desire for Nancy, two hours after Florence's suicide, and sees it as a new recognition of passion on Dowell's part, "a realization which liberates his ability to desire, causing in effect a revolution in his . . . personality. It is true that he does not act out his desire, but this fact . . . is important mainly for its irony."[60] Dowell, as is made clear by the novel's inconclusive conclusion, never goes very far beyond the role of "male nurse" in his actions, but the partial recognition of his feelings which he makes after Florence's death is the beginning of the recognition that will allow him to rise above himself through his role as narrator.

The episode of Edward's attraction for Nancy Rufford is used by Ford primarily to make a further condemnation of Edward for his inability to cope with passion, and to show how Nancy herself is buffeted between Edward and Leonora until she finally goes insane. Although from a home in which "her mother was said to have committed suicide owing to the brutalities of her father," Nancy had lived with the Ashburnhams as their ward for thirteen years before the incidents occurred which drove her to the point of madness. "Edward always called her 'the girl,' and it was very pretty, the evident affection he had for her and she for him.

And Leonora's feet she would have kissed—these two were for her the best man and the best woman on earth—and in heaven. I think," Dowell adds, "that she had not a thought of evil in her head—the poor girl."[61] Edward had gradually become obsessed with his love for "the girl," almost as if he were seeking through her a renewal of his own innocence. He had, however, been noticeably torn by an inner conflict over whether to tell Nancy anything of his feelings. One night Leonora had found him, "kneeling beside his bed with his head hidden in the counterpane. His arms outstretched, held out before him a little image of the Blessed Virgin—a tawdry, scarlet and Prussian blue affair that the girl had given him on her first return from the convent. His shoulders heaved convulsively three times, and heavy sobs came from him before she could close the door. He was not a Catholic; but that was the way it took him."[62]

Leonora's reaction to her husband's new interest had been complex and ambivalent. At one time she would pity him, and then she would act from this feeling. But, as Dowell says, "she loathed him another and then she acted as her loathing dictated. She gasped, as a person dying of tuberculosis gasps for air. She craved madly for communication with some other human soul." And it was Nancy on whom she chose to unburden herself. Ultimately, she ordered the girl to go to Edward, not so much out of a desire to ease his struggle, but because she despised his virtue in holding back with Nancy, and she wanted to further despise him by seeing him yield.[63] As for Nancy, she had felt in herself an interest in Edward that was beginning to approach a passion; but Dowell describes her desire in sexual terms, as "an inward flame; desiccating at the soul with thirst; withering up in the vitals," and thus suggests that the interest in Edward may have been on Nancy's part only an adolescent physical awakening. When one night Leonora had "appeared in her doorway, and told her that Edward was dying of love for her," Nancy's "prevailing mood" had not been love, but a "sense of duty."[64] Leonora had played upon Nancy's confusion and her misguided sense of duty. The embittered wife now added the element of guilt, and told Nancy that the satisfaction of Edward's desire "was the price the girl must pay for the sin of having made Edward love her, for the sin of loving her husband. She talked on and on. . . . The girl must become an adulteress; she had wronged Edward by being so beautiful, so gracious, so good. It was sinful to be so good. She must pay the price so as to save the man she had wronged."[65] The horror of this situation can only be appreciated if we realize that Nancy is about to offer herself to the confused Edward out of a sense of guilt and duty, that Leonora is trying to instill in her the same sense of false responsibility that has destroyed both her own life and that of her husband, and that Nancy's faith in both her guardians has been totally demolished.

The scene in which Nancy finally comes to Edward's room and offers herself to him carries echoes of the scenes in Ford's previous novels in

THE LIMITED HERO

which the hero had been faced with the problem of directly confronting and responding to a woman. Nancy is much more forward than either Clara Brede or Pauline Leicester, but her motives are also much more complex. As for Edward, the pressure brought upon him, directly by Leonora and indirectly by Leonora's influence over Nancy, make his choice an extremely difficult one and make his refusal of Nancy partially justifiable—particularly because she herself is coming to him out of a sense of false responsibility. But echoes of similar scenes in *The Benefactor* or *A Call* still sound indirectly in the encounter between Edward and Nancy, and these echoes suggest a partial condemnation, similar to that which Ford had made in the earlier novels of the heroic response.

The climactic situation at Branshaw Teleragh had built up for weeks, with Edward in his state of anguish, Nancy fully confused, and Leonora only adding to the girl's confusion. The talk, Dowell recalls, had been incessant: "You have to imagine horrible pictures of gloom and half lights, and emotions running through silent nights—through whole nights. You have to imagine my beautiful Nancy appearing suddenly to Edward, rising up at the foot of his bed, with her long hair falling . . . in the glimmer of a night-light that burned beside him. You have to imagine her, a silent and no doubt agonized figure, like a spectre, suddenly offering herself to him—to save his reason! And you have to imagine his frantic refusal—and talk. And talk! My God!" In this contest of taut and high-strung feelings, the girl had come to Edward's room. "And that," recalls Dowell, "was the real hell for him. That was the picture that never left his imagination—the girl, in the dim light, rising up at the post of his bed." And Edward Ashburnham, striving for one final time to remain the good soldier, had sent her from the room:

> And he says that he didn't want it; that he would have hated himself; that it was unthinkable. And all the while he had the immense temptation to do the unthinkable thing, not from a physical desire but because of a mental certitude. He was certain that if she had once submitted to him she would remain his forever. He knew that.
> She was thinking that her aunt had said he had desired her to love him from a distance of five thousand miles. She said: 'I can never love you now I know the kind of man you are. I will belong to you to save your life. But I can never love.'
> It was a fantastic display of cruelty. She didn't in the least know what it meant—to belong to a man. But, at that, Edward pulled himself together. He spoke in his normal tones: gruff, husky, overbearing, as he would have done to a servant or to a horse.
> 'Go back to your room,' he said. 'Go back to your room and go to sleep. This is all nonsense.'[66]

THE END OF A PHASE

Edward has three choices in this situation. He can accept Nancy on her terms; he can, as he does, refuse her; or he can attempt to convey to her a sense of his own feelings, and hope thereby to win her over to a fuller and less duty-bound giving of herself. The third solution would have been the most desirable, for it would have brought about an open and perhaps successful emotional encounter. Certainly, circumstances are against such a solution, for Edward is incapable of such direct emotional response and Nancy's mind has already been corrupted by Leonora. Had he been able to meet Nancy openly and fully, Edward might at least have saved what was good in her. His resorting to the role of the responsible hero only puts his own response on the same level as Nancy's offer, and, with awful irony, Edward puts a final seal on the girl's corruption. If, however, he had accepted Nancy on her terms, that would have been the worst solution of all; and, in his own way, he is trying to keep Nancy from further hurt as well as to maintain his own self-respect. Cassell, in fact, sees Edward's "refusal of Nancy as a victory for the generous emotions over the selfish ones," and adds that this victory marks Ashburnham as "the last of a tradition" and the only character in the novel, "able to meet a moral test."[67] But Cassell argues too strongly for the nobility of Edward's refusal, and the ending of the novel—Nancy's madness and Edward's own suicide—seems at least to cast some doubt on this interpretation. In the context of his own moral responses, Edward acts as nobly as he can. His refusal puts him on good terms with convention and propriety. But Edward's "victory" does not prevent Ford from regarding him with a double perspective, and in this light his triumph becomes ironic and the omissions in his response take on significance by their very absence.

After the climactic refusal, Nancy had been sent by Ashburnham back to India. On the way she had sent from Brindisi, the callous telegram which brought about Ashburnham's suicide. And on hearing of Edward's death, Nancy herself had gone mad, and had consequently to be brought back to England by Dowell. Meixner notes that the final image of Nancy suggests the two poles between which she had fluctuated. She can utter only two fragments. The first, the words "Credo in unum Deum Omnipotentum," reflect her once strong faith in an omnipotent God, and are called by Dowell "the only reasonable words she uttered." The second, the expression "shuttlecocks," indicates "how she felt between Leonora and Edward, and that was the way Edward had felt between the women. And that is the word, Ford is saying, for man's buffetted, purposeless existence in the world that has come into being." Thus in the final image of Nancy, Ford juxtaposes the sense of faith and the breakdown of faith that mark the two poles of his own world.[68]

And Dowell, who watches over her, remains to the end a dual figure.

THE LIMITED HERO

We have already seen the significance of his attempt to relate the events of the past nine years, and we have seen as well the acute frankness of some of his insights. And yet, for all these insights, he remains inert and essentially baffled. As he speculates, almost at the end of the novel, on Edward and Nancy, he says at first, "But I am pretty certain that I am right in the case of Nancy Rufford—that she had loved Edward Ashburnham very deeply and tenderly." But in the following paragraph he reflects, "Anyhow, I don't know whether, at this point, Nancy Rufford loved Edward Ashburnham. . . . I don't know." In the next two paragraphs Dowell twice expresses his bewilderment by saying, "I leave it to you." And finally, he condemns Edward by deciding that "It is, at any rate, certain that Edward's actions were perfectly—were monstrously, were cruelly—correct. He sat still and let Leonora take away his character and let Leonora damn him to deepest hell without stirring a finger."[69] Dowell is admittedly confused, but seems unaware that he is contradicting himself. And he scarcely pauses to ask if at any point he might have intervened, or lifted a finger, to try to prevent Edward's damnation or Nancy's insanity. Dowell is left at the close—for the "affair" does not allow a real conclusion—on a dominant note of inertia, strongly mitigated by his attempt to find coherence and significance in the situation—but still marked in large part by the rhetoric of bewilderment.

A society in which the main responses are bewilderment and a paralyzing sense of false responsibility has little chance of survival, and the pre-War British world, the portrayal of which Ford culminated in *The Good Soldier*, was for these reasons unusually vulnerable to collapse. As Ford saw it, the First World War simply marked the passing of a way of life that had already ended, and he felt strongly the need to find something to fill the void. In his next group of novels, and most strikingly in the Tietjens tetralogy, Ford concerned himself with the War and its aftermath, and from this concern there gradually arose the new figure of the limited hero. The germ of this new figure can be seen in the personal awareness and coherence which Dowell, to an extent, achieves. And in his assumption of the writer's role, a role in which, for Ford, the individual's intervention in the world's affairs was circumscribed by the nature of his work, there is a hint of the artistic response that was later to be so central. But if Dowell begins the private response of the limited hero, he himself has no awareness of the significance of this response, and no sense of having even begun to find an answer to his bewilderment. Dowell is not, that is to say, conscious of living a new role, and he in fact does so only in part. Essentially, he remains a searching but baffled man, ennobled by his attempt to find coherence in the world, but like the other figures in "the saddest story" ineffectual. He is marked throughout by a partial tragic dignity, but he is also debased by an adherence to false and conventional

illusions, by an inability to cope with passion, and by a failure to confront specific situations with a concrete and active assertion of a moral, though not necessarily heroic, self.

NOTES

[1] E. V. Walter, "Political Sense of Ford Madox Ford," *New Republic*, CXXXIV (March 26, 1956), 17.
[2] Paul Wiley, *Novelist of Three Worlds: Ford Madox Ford* (Syracuse, 1962), pp. 174–176.
[3] Robie Macauley, "The Good Ford," *Kenyon Review*, XI (1949), 271, 277.
[4] Mark Schorer, "The Good Novelist in *The Good Soldier*," *Princeton University Library Chronicle*, IX (April, 1948), 132.
[5] Richard Cassell, *Ford Madox Ford: A Study of His Novels* (Baltimore, 1961), pp. 162–163.
[6] Wiley, pp. 187–188, 199.
[7] Theodore Dreiser, "The Saddest Story," *New Republic*, III (June 12, 1915), 156.
[8] John A. Meixner, "The Saddest Story," *Kenyon Review*, XXII (Spring, 1960), 237.
[9] Hugh Kenner, "Conrad and Ford," *Gnomon* (New York, 1958), pp. 168–169.
[10] Ford Madox Ford, *The Good Soldier, A Tale of Passion*, Penguin Books edition (Hammondsworth, Middlesex, England, 1946), p. 6; all subsequent page references are to this edition.
[11] Douglas Goldring, *Trained for Genius* (New York, 1949), p. 245.
[12] Ford, *The Good Soldier*, p. 19.
[13] John A. Meixner, *Ford Madox Ford's Novels: A Critical Study* (Minneapolis, 1962), p. 171.
[14] Ford, *The Good Soldier*, p. 18.
[15] *Ibid.*, p. 94.
[16] *Ibid.*, pp. 31–32.
[17] Ford Madox Hueffer, *Between St. Dennis and St. George, A Sketch of Three Civilizations* (London, New York, Toronto, 1915), p. 24.
[18] Meixner, "Saddest Story," pp. 258–259.
[19] Ford, *The Good Soldier*, pp. 138–139, 148–149.
[20] Macauley, "Good Ford," p. 276.
[21] Ford, *The Good Soldier*, pp. 53–54.
[22] *Ibid.*, pp. 53–75.
[23] *Ibid.*, pp. 168–169, 178.
[24] *Ibid.*, p. 61.
[25] *Ibid.*, pp. 156–157, 161.
[26] *Ibid.*, p. 58.
[27] *Ibid.*
[28] *Ibid.*, pp. 24–25.
[29] *Ibid.*, pp. 21–22.
[30] Schorer, pp. 128, 130.
[31] Wiley, p. 189.

[32] Samuel Hynes, "The Epistomology of *The Good Soldier*," *Sewanee Review*, LXIX (1961), 226–227, 229–230.
[33] Graham Greene, Introduction to *The Bodley Head Ford Madox Ford*, p. 12.
[34] Meixner, "Saddest Story," pp. 244–245, 263.
[35] Ford Madox Ford, "A Haughty and Proud Generation," *Yale Review*, XI (1922), 716–717.
[36] Ford, *The Good Soldier*, pp. 49–50.
[37] *Ibid.*, pp. 26–27.
[38] *Ibid.*, p. 49.
[39] *Ibid.*, p. 14.
[40] *Ibid.*, p. 109.
[41] *Ibid.*, pp. 216–217, 232.
[42] *Ibid.*, p. 234.
[43] *Ibid.*, pp. 14–15, 17.
[44] *Ibid.*, p. 218.
[45] *Ibid.*, pp. 18–19.
[46] *Ibid.*, p. 11.
[47] *Ibid.*, pp. 12–14.
[48] *Ibid.*, pp. 69–70.
[49] *Ibid.*, pp. 110–111.
[50] *Ibid.*, p. 113.
[51] Wiley, pp. 185–186.
[52] Ford Madox Hueffer, *The Spirit of the People, An Analysis of the English Mind* (London, 1907), pp. 149–151.
[53] Ford, *The Good Soldier*, pp. 224–230.
[54] *Ibid.*, p. 38.
[55] *Ibid.*, p. 40.
[56] *Ibid.*, p. 79.
[57] *Ibid.*, pp. 82–87.
[58] *Ibid.*, pp. 97–98.
[59] *Ibid.*, pp. 101, 103–104, 116.
[60] Elliot B. Gose, Jr., "The Strange Irregular Rhythm: An Analysis of *The Good Soldier*," *PMLA*, LXXII (1957), 501–509.
[61] Ford, *The Good Soldier*, p. 92.
[62] *Ibid.*, pp. 127–128.
[63] *Ibid.*, pp. 188–189, 199.
[64] *Ibid.*, p. 209.
[65] *Ibid.*, pp. 212–213.
[66] *Ibid.*, pp. 186–187, 222–223.
[67] Cassell, pp. 154–157.
[68] Meixner, *Ford's Novels*, pp. 185–186.
[69] Ford, *The Good Soldier*, pp. 225–226.

4.

Heroism and Responsibility in the Tietjens Novels: A New Beginning

IF JOHN DOWELL, the narrator of *The Good Soldier*, finds himself almost unintentionally in a private world, one in fact forced upon him by the ending of his nine years of illusion, Christopher Tietjens, the hero of the *Parade's End* tetralogy, intentionally redirects himself toward a private mode of response with a full consciousness of what he is doing. And it is in his conscious seeking of this new response that Tietjens departs from all of Ford's previous heroes, and becomes so central as to justify four lengthy novels. The Tietjens series marks a center of change in Ford's thought, a center that is sufficiently crucial to warrant extensive analysis of each of the four books, for it is here that Ford finally proposes an alternative to the earlier ineffectual hero. The Tietjens novels contain the first portrayal of the limited hero; and while the tetralogy grows very clearly out of Ford's reaction to the war experience, it also embodies an answer to the problems of that experience. The primary concern is with Tietjens' growth as a character, with his development from a conventional to a limited hero.

Technically, the most interesting feature of the Tietjens novels is the way in which Ford controls the reader's attitude toward his main character. For although Tietjens is finally seen as a Fordian ideal, he is at the outset little more than a superior country gentleman of the British pre-War variety, who still has an active sense of public expectations and appearances. Throughout the four books, however, Ford maintains a constantly diminishing double perspective. The double view is strongest in the first volume of the tetralogy, and declines steadily as the series progresses. Events are used, by themselves and in contrast to others in order to shift the balance of judgement. Thus, Tietjens at first receives only qualified approval, but by the end of the series grows to embody Ford's most complete affirmation.

Tietjens is never seen, however, with as harsh a critical eye as Ford had fixed upon the characters of *The Good Soldier*. The hero of *Parade's End* may be initially ineffective in his personal encounters, but the complexity of these encounters is soon established, and Tietjens, within the confines of his public role, always acts with dignity. He is superior to both the General Campions of the old order and the Paul Sandbachs of the new;

and even Sylvia, his overly-vindictive and embittered wife, despises him because he is too good. The early Tietjens illustrates the failings of the English gentleman operating at his best. As the novel progresses and Tietjens undergoes and survives the war experience, he learns new ways of effectively asserting himself as an individual, and through Valentine Wannop, the girl for whom he gradually achieves a meaningful love, he learns how to respond specifically to another person. The War, as the final crumbling of the post-Victorian world, forces Tietjens, as it did Ford, to cope with reality on new terms. Tietjens is never entirely Ford, but his response continually moves toward the author's position. For with the War, the breakdown became an incontrovertible matter of fact; and as a result, a new way of life became not only desirable, but an immediate necessity.

Underlying Ford's portrayal of Christopher Tietjens are his attitudes toward the First World War and its causes, attitudes which sharply reflect his views on conventional heroism in its military and political manifestations. Many of the works in which Ford develops these views have been neglected by scholars, perhaps because—due to the circumstances under which they were written—they have been dismissed as mere propaganda. As a result, the significance of these works in the evolution of his views has been vastly underrated.

The War itself is the focal point of Tietjens' change. It was a war that seemed to Ford simply the climax of the heroism that had preceded it. Germany, as he argued in his two volumes of war propaganda, had in the nineteenth century developed hero worship and national glorification into a massive cultural trait, which it then tried to push on the rest of Europe. The German spirit was the culmination of a sickness that had already infected the western powers during the previous century. And although as a propagandist for the British Government, Ford had to place the major blame on Germany, his view of the War embodied a clear indictment of the English as well. In the propaganda books there was an explicit statement of ideological kinship between the Germans and the Great Victorians. And English society, as Ford showed it in the Tietjens novels, had become so weakened by its own decline from rhetoric to self-interest, that it could find little but chaos with which to meet the war situation.

In Ford's view, English public heroism was preferable to its German counterpart only in that it never took the form of aggressive worship of the state. And although in his propaganda books he lauded the English spirit of correctness, it is evident in the Tietjens novels that Ford's view of the War included a strong disapproval of both societies. The two volumes of propaganda, particularly the second, *Between St. Dennis and St. George, A Sketch of Three Civilizations*, were notable not only for their rejection of German nationalism, but also because they marked the beginning of Ford's turn toward French culture as a manifestation of

limited heroism. In the "travel" books of the 1930's this culture came to symbolize for Ford an entire way of life. And in the Tietjens novels, although there was little mention of France, the experience of the War and the change toward the French way of life were given their fullest fictional statement.

Ford's linking of the War with the nineteenth-century heroic values, as well as with the Prussian glorification of power and the state, was stated most explicitly in his two propaganda books, both published in 1915, *When Blood Is Their Argument, An Analysis of Prussian Culture* and *Between St. Dennis and St. George*. These two volumes were written at the suggestion of Ford's political friend, C. F. G. Masterman; and although they were slanted as propaganda, and must be read as such, the books also embodied many of Ford's basic attitudes toward heroism. Their historical accuracy was questionable, but as expressions of a point of view they were quite significant. Early in *When Blood Is Their Argument* Ford stated his thesis that under the auspices of Prussia the standard of culture in Germany had steadily declined, only to be replaced by *Kultur*, a Prussian nationalistic expression marked by a reduction of all art and learning to a narrow specialization directed toward the aggrandizement of the state.[1] Thus Germany had committed for Ford the capital offense: art had been made subordinate to a distorting heroism. There were, Ford went on to say, two Germanies, divided by a line running from the mouth of the Elbe to a spot just north of Dresden. "Prussian *Kultur* comes almost exclusively from the north and east of that line," but it had gradually come to dominate nearly all of Germany.[2] And this *Kultur* entailed a perverse subordination of nearly all humane activity to the ideal of the state. Prussianism is therefore a "monomania," and, Ford went on to say, "if Prussia wins the present struggle . . . every inhabitant of the whole world will have of necessity to become a monomaniac instead of a reasonable human being."[3] The advent of Prussianism in Germany marked the advent of the doctrine "that the object of the state is to wage war."[4] To this aim all else was to succumb, because the state was the embodiment of the grandest heroic ideals.

As an illustration of the "astounding" Prussian nationalism Ford quoted a statement by the historian, Heinrich von Treitschke:

> I have never in my life given one thought to my duties to society. I never in my life by so much as one single thought neglected to consider my duty to the Prussian state.

And Ford commented that while "Amongst Anglo-Saxon races . . . the State is almost universally regarded as a necessary evil," for the Germans it "is the be-all and end-all of human existence."[5] Prussianism was, for Ford, the expression of an "embittered population whose cultural high-

lights are all products of malignity," a "population filled with megalomania by the tradition of 1870 and the writings of Richard Wagner; inspired to a religion of materialism and egotism by misreading the writings of Friedrich Nietzsche," a "population without rest, without joy, without ease, and without any ceasing of the passion for money." These people, "whose traditions of discipline are such that they can seriously style the military serfdom of a Teutonic Bankgenossen the highest ideal of liberty," were "preached to by the entire state," up to 1914, "that the only means of getting rich is waging war."[6] Under the influence, then, of Prussia, "the way of the sword," which was "the way of Prussia," had come to dominate Germany, and the First World War was for Ford an opportunity to prevent the Prussian way of life from overcoming the entire world.[7]

In his first volume of propaganda, Ford referred to himself as "a special pleader" for French culture, which he identified with "altruism . . . constitutionalism, and . . . such forms of art and learning as promote a sympathetic comprehension of my fellow-men."[8] France had already come to represent for the author a way of life that offered an alternative to both the grandiose heroism of Germany and the fumbling self-interest of his own country. The nation to the south came to stand for a decent sense of human limitations, as well as respect for the arts and an altruism that was based on "a sympathetic comprehension" between individuals. World War I posed for all possible survivors a crucial choice:

> We have in fact to decide whether our children and our children's children shall be monomaniacs or graceful and all-round beings; we have to plump for professional amateurism in politics, the arts, the universities and every department of life. We have to decide whether the future of the race shall be that of organized, materialist egoism, or that of what I would call the all-round sportsmanship of altruistic culture. That question at least we can decide, whether we are at home or in the trenches in Flanders, and that question too is the most portentous that has been propounded to us by the year 1914. . . .[9]

The War for Ford was not an effort to salvage England in its present form. It was a crisis under which the English might become aware of the alternatives of Prussian egoism and French altruism, of Prussian didacticism and the French respect for art in itself. England, with its strong sense of decorum and ethical moderation, stood somewhat between the two poles, and its participation in the War would be especially justified if it chose for its future the way of France.

The differences between the cultures of England, France and Germany were drawn even more strongly in Ford's second volume of propaganda, *Between St. Dennis and St. George*. Ford began by discrediting the anti-

war efforts of the British Left, a faction that still seemed to him essentially childish and dishonest. Men such as Bernard Shaw and Bertrand Russell, Ford argued, used in their statements against the war effort the methods of "intellectual fictionists." The writers of the Left, he went on, were "sufficiently acquainted with the defects of the English governmental system, which, being a human organisation, has defects enough. But of the working of the German organisation or of the disadvantages of German life their ignorance is as profound as it is avowed." In his pamphlet, "Common Sense About the War," Shaw had presented "ten or fifteen instances of militarist or semi-militarist authors and organisations of this country. In the course of this work," Ford countered, "I present Mr. Shaw, in return, with one hundred German utterances." Thus Ford hoped quantitatively to refute Shaw's main thesis that the British and the Germans were both in practice equally militaristic. Ford dismissed such arguments from the Left as responses to "the force of party exigencies."[10]

But it was not only the current British Left that leaned too sympathetically toward Prussianism. In his line by line refutation of Shaw's pamphlet, which was added as an appendix to *Between St. Dennis and St. George*, Ford accused the Great Victorians, such as Mill, Carlyle, Spencer, George Eliot and George Henry Lewes, of "lickspittle toadying to Prussian Materialism, Prussian Philologie, and Prussianism in general." He found this tendency to reach its "culmination in Mr. Shaw's pamphlet."[11] Ford's harsh indictment of these figures as even precursory Prussian apologists was without a doubt inaccurate, but he built his case on the same qualities of abstract moralizing and evasion for which he had always condemned the Victorians. Some, such as Carlyle, had certainly voiced ideas which could have degenerated into Prussian political heroism; but Ford's basic point, in his discussion of Shaw's pamphlet, was that the Victorians, by their evasion of reality, had allowed that sickness of which the War was but the worst and final manifestation to grow far too severe.

Despite the link between Prussianism and the Great Victorians, England was distinguished from Germany for Ford by a much smaller degree of bellicosity. In fact, "the English were unmartial to a degree that rendered them a danger to peace, whilst the Germans were martial to a degree that rendered them absolutely ridiculous."[12] In comparison to Prussian heroics, Ford viewed the English sense of propriety as a desirable thing. It offered a *modus vivendi* which, while it discouraged profound contacts between men, at least created an atmosphere in which life might "run smoothly in all such affairs as are suited for the smooth running of life."[13] English "correctness of attitude" furnished a means of existing harmoniously from day to day, and as such provided a partially satisfactory alternative to the inflated idealism of the Germans. With all its

reticence and false responsibility, the English code of behavior was still preferable to the ringing military rhetoric which Ford saw as guiding German behavior.

Comparing the attitude toward war of the three major powers, Ford concluded that "the Englishman ignored war, did not give a thought to its existence or to what it would mean if it came into existence," while "the German desired war . . . and . . . the Frenchman dreaded and detested war whilst acknowledging it to be a sad necessity so long as central Europe remained in the hands of its present rulers."[14] Although Ford now modified the earlier position of *When Blood is Their Argument* by distinguishing the relatively peaceful German people from their bellicose rulers, he still viewed Germany as a serious threat to the entire world.[15] And this threat, he felt, had to be countered by an extension of the French attitude, which embodied the most effective synthesis of the ideal and everyday.

Reality necessitated that Prussianism be fought on its own terms; and these terms were military, since until they were proven wrong the Prussians would accept no other.[16] For the Germans, unlike the English, saw political issues

> in terms of blood, cataclysm, and irremediable disappearance. If Mr. Asquith had fallen in 1913 there would have been no particular reason why he should not be back in power, or at any rate leading the party in the House of Lords, in 1920. . . . But if William II had fallen in 1913, the House of Hohenzollern, the whole Hohenzollern tradition, the whole Hohenzollern race might well be expected to disappear for ever in a cloud of obloquy that would be enhanced by the writings of State-paid professors to all eternity.

World War I may well have begun after "the leaders of the German Imperial and the Prussian Royal State" resolved for themselves, with a sense of their imminent historical oblivion, that " 'If we cannot reign in the memory along with Marcus Aurelius and Constantine let us at least be remembered as are Attila and Genghis Kahn.' "[17] A culture that glorifies the state in times of success, may well react to the failures of the state with a sense of catastrophe and a clamorous heroism in which all restraint is forgotten. For the imaginative German

> war remained something mediaeval or classical—a matter of cleanness, of sharp spears, of nudity, of shining swords, of shining armour, of shining and mailed fists, of heroisms and of all the desirables . . . In France at least they had realized that the days of individual glory were over . . . I never heard a French officer speak of any chance of glory in war. It would just be bureaucratic promotion, ceaseless patience, and endless strain on the nerves.[18]

The French sense of limitation, of anti-heroism, was in marked contrast to the qualities of Prussianism. And, foreshadowing his idea of the "small producer," Ford contended, even as early as the war years, that "the French farmer . . . the small handicraftsman . . . and the small trader," who "do not expect vast things of life" and "do not strive after the immense fortunes of the modern industrial system . . . will have saved Europe, if Europe is to be saved."[19]

The sense of a more clearly circumscribed, more private existence, which was the basis for the life-style of the limited hero, came for Ford to be centered more and more in France, particularly in the portion around Provence. But the author's strong sense of affinity with this nation caused him to fall occasionally into the very chauvinism for which he condemned others. During the Dreyfus Affair, as Ford later remembered it in *Between St. Dennis and St. George*, his reaction had been determined by a sense of violated national tradition. He recalled that although during the trial at Rennes he could sense in Dreyfus "a certain radiance of tears and suffering" and "the extreme toughness of a low vitality," he "began to see a frame of mind in which it was possible to imagine that, from that figure, a radiance greater, softer, and more nearly divine might have proceeded had he endured those tortures in silence and had he taken the Heavenly Powers alone, his crown of martyrdom." Ford had sensed at the trial "that the army might still be a sacred thing to France," and at that time and place, the dishonoring of that "sacred body," by an individual insisting on his private rehabilitation seemed, "at least at Rennes, a questionable proceeding. In that ancient part of the world one was too much surrounded by evidence of 'les glories de la France' to let anything that could even by implication besmirch these glories seem other than questionable."[20]

This vestige chauvinism is, however, less significant than its subject. Ford glorified the French nation because it represented to him an idealism and a way of life wholly different from that which he saw as dominant in the Western European world. Ford always acknowledged the need for an idealism to overcome the contemporary sense of chaos, but this idealism had to be grounded in realities and based on a sense of limitation, both of itself and of mankind in general. It was through the recognition of this need that Ford evolved the figure of the limited hero, and the strong espousal of the French way of life. And in this vein, he concluded at the end of *Between St. Dennis and St. George* that "if in the world from now on, there is to be any of the pleasantness that we loved, any of the virtues that we have held made men and women gracious, the cause of France, which is our cause, must prevail."[21] This note of urgency was to inspire nearly all of Ford's writing after the War. The propaganda books, in which the attitude toward France was given its first major statement, were clearly political efforts. But Ford could not create even a piece of

commissioned propaganda without injecting something of his own basic attitudes. And it was decidedly to the author's credit that these two volumes, despite their frequent name-calling and over-simplification, were still controlled by less transitory Fordian attitudes. Their explicit statements of both the anti-heroic mood and the ideals of French culture are a cogent introduction to the important work that was to come.

The War itself was for Ford a result of both the heroism that had infected so much of Europe and the moral and political confusion that had been left by its waning. But the mood of the War for the soldier in the trenches seemed to Ford definitely unheroic, and this same realization became for some of his fictional heroes the final negation of their public role. The War invalidated a useless heroism, but left nothing to replace it; and consequently the need for a new way of life, and the recognition of this need, became even more pressing than it would have been, had the old order been able simply to burn itself out. Ford attempted to render the unheroic nature of the War in two ways: by indicating the way in which the fighting was an extension of civilian difficulties; and by showing how the persistent civilian ineptitude only hindered and prolonged the war effort. Discussing his own method of depicting war, Ford said that "many novelists have treated of the late War in terms solely of the War: in terms of pip squeaks, trench coats, wire aprons, shells, mud, dust, and sending the bayonet home with a grunt.... But," he added, "had you taken part actually in those hostilities, you would know how infinitely little part the actual fighting itself took in your mentality.... You were there, but great shafts of thought from the outside, distant and unattainable world infinitely for the greater part occupied your mind."[22] The persistent and haunting intrusion of civilian and domestic problems and their demoralizing effect on the men at the front became dominant themes in the Tietjens novels; so that it was clear by a certain point that Tietjens had to resolve his problems not so much by winning the War as by reshaping his personal life.

Because he saw the fighting men as victims of civilian self-interest on both sides, the War also crystallized Ford's attitude toward the politician. He quickly noted the discrepancy between reality and political rhetoric and thereby came to see the politician as a direct descendant of the Victorian hero. With the advent of German Fascism in the 1930's, and the ominous sense of another impending war, Ford's hatred of the politician became at times vehement; but even in *Between St. Dennis and St. George* he remarked that "Party politics are a great curse, and secret diplomacy may be responsible for much evil." And, he added, "I do not think that an ideal state, a sort of international kissing-kindness land, would arise if Mr. Shaw, Mr. Brailsford, and Dr. Liebknecht, and, let us say, Mr. Upton Sinclair, were the dictators of the world. Their hearts might well be full of idealisms, but their practices would be inevitably the

self-stultificatory practices of every other committee the world has ever seen."²³ And in November, 1923, in an introductory manifesto for the *transatlantic review*, Ford as editor declared:

> The politics will be those of its editor who has no party leanings save toward those of a Tory kind so fantastically old-fashioned as to see no salvation save in the feudal system as practiced in the fourteenth century—or in such Communism as may prevail a thousand years hence.²⁴

In the same journal, in January, 1924, Ford stated "that every artist should be—or should at least label himself—an English Tory, if only to escape the inevitable job of writing propaganda. For the Tory party will never ask any man of sense to write for it." The low esteem in which Tories held "the man of letters" provided for the writer "an admirable arrangement; for the man of sense or of intellect will never concern himself, if he be wise, with matters of precedence or of party."²⁵ As for the British Left, in 1924 Ford found it marked by hypocrisy. The Left, he commented,

> bolsters its position in a nation that even yet abhors the thought of war by the assertion of its detestations of the shedding of blood. So did the pre-war Prussian government; but like the Prussian government, the British Left has for panaceas the partition of Poland, the absolute subjection of Westphalia and the Rhine to Prussia, and the leaving of the territories to the south of Prussia right down to the Mediterranean defenceless and at the mercy of their predatory neighbors! After a hundred and eight years, they are perfecting what Metternich left unfinished.

For Ford, the Left committed its greatest sin, in gearing its social programs toward "the preservation of the present industrial system in status quo." Not bothering to ask himself what problems within this system needed solution, he went on to contend that the major effect of the Left's program was the maintenance of "the great industrial cities" and of "the immense population of wage slaves"; and he added disparagingly that "these last are the 'constituents' of our Left leaders."²⁶ In the *transatlantic review* for March, 1924, Ford stated explicitly that the magazine would support neither party, since the conservatives represented "nothing that was conservative except the so-called conservative banking interests" while the Laborites under Ramsay Macdonald represented nothing but the encouragement of the northern industrial system at the expense and possible plunder of the lands to the south.²⁷ More and more Ford found himself pitting the concepts of the limited hero and the French way of life against an encroaching political and industrial climate. Feeling alienated from England and the modern industrial world, he be-

came increasingly anti-nationalistic. He saw nationalism, a "silly nagging between nations," as simply a "game" of the "politicians and Finance and Big Business and the Publicists."[28] And viewing himself as "not much of a patriot," he added, "I think it is a man's duty if need be to fight for his country and then to forget all about it."[29] This adverse reaction to politics and politicians may have been encouraged by Ford's post-War experience with the Lloyd George Government. In the autobiographical volume, *It Was the Nightingale*, he relates how upon his return to England after the War he was denied a passport to France. The denial stemmed from a disagreement with Lloyd George over what territory should be given to France at the Congress of Versailles. Confined by the government's action to England, Ford felt himself to be "A queer, paradoxical rat-trap." He found it "utterly detestable that infinitely dirty little squirts of civilians should have the power to interfere with the movements of other civilians or the military." He found in post-War London a sense of formlessness:

> Now it was as if some of the darkness of nights of air-raids still hung in the shadows of the enormous city. Standing on the hill that is high above that world of streets one had the sense that vast disaster stretched into those caverns of blackness. A social system had crumbled. Recklessness had taken the place of insouciance. In the old days we had seemed to have ourselves and our destinies well in hand. Now we were drifting towards a weir.[30]

Ford spent the years from 1919 to 1922 in Sussex as a "Small Producer." Finally in 1922 he was able to move south to France, and when in 1923 the British Government, under Prime Minister Baldwin, abolished the post of Historical Advisor to the Foreign Office, Ford, feeling that too strong a break with tradition had been made, placed himself in voluntary self-exile. "A country whose Foreign Office lacks Historical Advice," is, he believed, "no country for poets—or for anybody else!" And in *It Was the Nightingale* Ford recalled that "From that day I began to feel that I had no country and have gone on feeling more and more convinced that I have none—or that my only country is that invisible one that is known as the kingdom of letters."[31] He no longer thought of himself as an Englishman, or even a Frenchman, but as an artist and a "Small Producer." In the *transatlantic review* he called upon all artists to meet together, regardless of geographical boundaries, to "abandon the consideration of Chamber Politics and turn to those of the world," and to consider only "to what extent Dostoevsky unites peoples or how largely Stendahl is a Separatist." The artist needed to separate himself from his society: "In the cosmopolitan tawdriness of Riviera hotels we shall drift together, abandoning our lay fellow-countrymen who are so infinitely alien, and similarly we shall drift together on vast railway platforms, in

the saloons of liners, the land that is without frontiers travelling with us. This is the real Utopia!"[32]

The artist, Ford had come to realize, must be an outsider, particularly in countries whose culture was dominated by the middle-class. There the painter or the writer "must needs feel a foreigner and lonely. He must have the feeling that not one soul of all those thousands would understand one word of what he was talking of if he really talked of the things that occupied his mind." If the middle-class really knew what the artist was thinking of, "they would tear" him "to pieces on the instant—precisely as a foreigner. That is the same all over the world; but it is at its worst in Anglo-Saxondom."[33] The artist thus occupied the paradoxical position of being an alien in a world that he alone could save, not by preaching, but by the example of his art and his life.

In the world of the First World War and its aftermath, the politician became for Ford a new symbol of all the hypocrisy, egoism and verbalization that was rampant everywhere. The political hero not only veiled social corruption with his rhetoric, but also created the very corruption that was being veiled. The beginnings of this view had been evident in Ford's pre-War novel. Figures such as Churchill of *The Inheritors*, Count Macdonald of *The New Humpty-Dumpty*, and Mr. Blood of *Mr. Fleight*. But Churchill was a bewildered vestige of the old order, whereas Count Macdonald and Mr. Blood were both aristocratic cynics. None of these three figures really accepted the new political world as a matter of course. By the time of the War, however, the self-interested politicians of the home office, securely in power, were determining major British policy and doing a clearly inadequate job. It was with their clumsy orders that Tietjens so frequently had to cope. Ford's growing dislike of the politician was even more strongly expressed in the books of the 1930's. With increasing power in his hands, and less and less questioning of his rhetoric, the political hero had by then turned into the nightmare of a Hitler or a Franco, blatantly putting all dissenters "up against a wall." The unreality of monomania had become the bitter actuality and politics was no longer merely ineffectual, but brutal as well.

One of Ford's minor novels of the early post-War decade, *The Marsden Case, A Romance*, written in 1923, is interesting in that it makes a specific connection between the political figure and the earlier Victorian hero, and thereby ties Ford's war novels to his earlier work. Lord Marsden the father of the central character, is a politician who deserts England during the Victorian breakdown to go to Germany, where he kills himself on the outbreak of the War. The novel takes place during and just after the War, and the psychological shock of that event is always and often explicitly in the background. But the focus is on the sickness of the civilians, with their want of direction, their suspicions, and their frequently predatory behavior. Like *Parade's End*, *The Marsden Case* con-

nects the War with this debased society, but here, through the figure of Lord Marsden, the society is traced back to the Victorians. Yet in spite of this important connection, *The Marsden Case* never becomes a major novel, and at times it is barely readable. Ford lapses into his worst fault, that of relying far too heavily on plot contrivance, and in this novel the plot is so complex that it seems at times to become inadvertantly grotesque. The situation is so special that its larger significance is often lost; and the narrator, a writer who becomes accidentally acquainted with George Marsden, the novel's hero, seldom makes clear, save for a few general references to the world condition, his reasons for telling the Marsden story.

The novel's overwrought plot has two major threads. First, there is the attempt by George's sister, Marie Elizabeth, to establish her claim to the Marsden family peerage, against the wishes of both her father and George, who is acting with knowledge of his father's wishes. Their father, of course, wants to conceal the fact that he has abandoned England. This part of the plot underscores the lack of identity which the major characters feel in their confused world. The second thread of the plot, on the other hand, overshadows the first in the final half of the book. Here, the emphasis is on the difficulties that George experiences during the War, when he is suspected of being a German spy. The suspicion had arisen after George, who had been searching for his father in Germany when the War had begun, was taken prisoner, and had been freed through the help of the poet-professor Curtius, a friend of Lord Marsden and at the time an ominous looking Prussian officer. The intercession of Curtius had given some people cause to question George's loyalty, and he is plagued by this suspicion through a good part of the novel. The book's overall failure stems from the poor integration of these two themes. Each theme is buttressed with further complications, and each is told with a mixture of flashback and present incident, so that rather than complimenting each other, the two themes vie for attention, while their connection remains ambiguous. The confusion is only enhanced at the close when, with a sudden jump forward in time, the situation is resolved by a completely unexpected happy ending.

The attempt by Marie Elizabeth to establish her claim to the family peerage provides the opening for a picture of Lord Marsden, and thus allows Ford to develop the connection between the politicians and the Victorian hero. Lord Marsden is a symbol of the Victorian betrayal of society, the betrayal in which the moralizers went on voicing their abstractions, and in effect detached themselves from the world. Marsden had been Postmaster General in the Gladstone Administration when a fight developed between the Whig and Radical factions of Gladstone's party. It had become necessary to sacrifice someone in order to preserve at least a semblance of peace and the Prime Minister had chosen to dismiss

his Postmaster General. The papers had made a scandal of the affair and Marsden, who had taken the action very badly, left England never to be heard from again.[34] He had simply evaded his family and his country until both had reached the state of confusion in which we see them in the novel. At the outbreak of the War between England and Germany, and just at the time that George is looking for him, Lord Marsden kills himself and thus commits his final evasion.

It is while George is in Germany that he is thrown into the situation which later leads to the ridiculous accusation that he is a spy. At the start of the War, George is imprisoned by the German Government, but soon thereafter Professor Curtius comes to announce that he has managed to obtain George's release. The picture of the poet in full Prussian dress is a dramatic reminder of the changes brought about by the War and of the German militarism which Ford held responsible. Curtius, now called "Upper-Lieutenant Professor Doctor Geheimrath," is very formal and his appearance is most foreboding: "He wore a very long cape of light gray with a dark blue high collar and a great gilt-spiked helmet. It gave George a disagreeable feeling. He was used to officials who were also of course military officers; but these were usually in *deshabille*, obese, spectacled, and engrossed in papers. This was the murderous Prussian in the nail-new spick and spanness of butchery."[35] George is allowed to return to England, but it is an England that becomes so unpleasant that he is finally driven to attempt suicide.

The Marsden Case, although far too intricate and contrived in plot, does contain a few notable scenes and characters, through which the sense of the Victorian betrayal and the sickness of the War period is conveyed. But Ford subtitled the novel, "*A Romance*," and he apparently felt duty bound to give it a happy ending. Thus at the end we see George, years later, at a European hotel. He has married, and he and his wife are representing England at a conference to settle certain boundaries. The narrator is struck by George's self-possession, a quality which has never been developed in the novel, and remarks that "had that young man not been so self-possessed, so every inch an Earl, that poor little fairy tale would never have found its earthly, so fortunate close."[36] This "fairy tale" ending bears little relation to the rest of the novel. And it conflicts noticeably with the book's far more significant linking of the Marsden case with the overall world condition. The narrator comments early in the novel on the madness of the world during the War period:

> The world, I think, was mad then. I don't know if you remember the season of 1914, in London and the world over. It comes back to me as a period of outcries, smashings, the noises of broken glass falling to the ground and physical violences. An accursed year! The whole tone of personal contacts was strained, tense—mad!

Later he states explicitly a theme, which although important to *The Marsden Case*, was not to receive full development until the *Parade's End* tetralogy—the theme that the most painful fact for the soldier on the battlefront is the stubborn persistence, even there, of the problems of his life at home. "Wars are very terrible things," the narrator admits,

> But what is dreadful is that the world goes on and people go on being stupidly cruel—in the old ways and all the time. . . . There is that never ceasing waiting about; and the cold; and the long depressions. Now and then there is a terrible noise—wearing, lasting for days. And some pain. All that is bearable. But what is desolating, what is beyond everything hateful, is that, round your transport tent, the old evils, the old heartbreaks, and the old cruelties are unceasingly at work. And that is what you have to go back to.

If the leaders of the country and the intelligentsia knew what conditions were really like at the front, the narrator concludes, they would no longer think of war as a vehicle for their own heroic aims. "There are other fields in which they may gain glory. I permit myself to say so much."[37] This theme Ford was to develop even more fully in the Tietjens series. The incessant presence on the battlefront of "the old evils" plays upon Tietjens and his men; and Tietjens' difficulty, in the form of Sylvia, his wife, even follows him to the base camp, where she becomes the cause of an ensuing scandal. *The Marsden Case* contains many of Ford's recurrent themes—the betrayal of society by the Victorian hero, German military heroism, and the interplay of chaos and ineptitude on both the war and home fronts—but they are crowded together into a far too erratic and eccentric plot. As Paul Wiley remarks, the elements of the plot are too specialized; the novel loses its sense of historical relevance by coming to seem confined to a legal controversy, and the hero, because he is so strongly involved in the private history of his father's betrayal, lacks the symbolic force with which Ford was able to endow the hero of *Parade's End*.[38]

The sense of historical relevance was the very thing Ford sought for as he conceived the Tietjens novels. There was, following the War, a gradual shift in Ford's conception of the artist's role. It was no longer quite enough that he be a good craftsman, and an accurate observer of whatever he portrayed. These qualities were still basic to any good artist, but his rendering, as Ford now saw it, also had to have significance for its time. The artist for Ford was becoming not only a craftsman but an historical recorder. Two events lay behind this shift in emphasis: the end of the War and the death of Marcel Proust.

At the start of the War, Ford had still seen art as valuable in itself, whether or not it bore any relevance to social issues. The murder of Archduke Ferdinand at Serajevo did not worry him. He believed that the

War could easily be stopped, and he was much more interested in the appearance of the magazine installments of Joyce's new novel, *A Portrait of the Artist as a Young Man*.[39] Yet even before the War, there had been a partial recognition of the value of art as a counterforce to social decay. In *The Critical Attitude*, a 1911 reprint of earlier essays from the *English Review*, Ford had written of Flaubert's *L'Education Sentimentale* that nothing was more true than the words of its author that had his country read the book, "she would have been spared the horrors of the Franco-Prussian war." France, "during the period before 1870," had gotten into a "happy-go-lucky frame of mind that has always existed in England." Flaubert had depicted this frame of mind "so exactly," that if France had "set itself seriously to the task of reading and pondering upon it, undoubtedly some tightening up of the national character must have taken place."[40] Ford later cited *L'Education Sentimentale* as a strong influence on the Tietjens novels, and this early comment shows that the change in his view of the artist's task was not a sudden one. Nevertheless, there was an evident shift in Ford's work after the War, from the attitude of detached historian of Victorian society "to that of analyst of the ills of Western civilization and proponent of remedies."[41]

This modification of his attitude was augmented by the news of Proust's death in 1922. In *It Was the Nightingale*, Ford recalled how upon hearing this news, he "wanted the novelist to appear in his really proud position as historian of his own time," and he added, "Proust being dead I could see no one who was doing that."[42] The shift in emphasis, for it was a shift rather than a full change, was marked by a broadening of the sense of social purpose. At this stage of his career, Ford's views on the technique of the novel remained pretty much the same, and as E. V. Walter notes, one of the accomplishments of the Tietjens novels was their demonstration of the fact that "the well-made novel and the political novel are not mutually exclusive genres."[43] Many of the techniques employed in *The Good Soldier* were also used by Ford in his tetralogy, but they were worked into a context that seemed by comparison far less introverted. The Tietjens novels did not stop at the presentation of a baffled consciousness, turning progressively inward upon itself. However important the rendering of such a paralyzed awareness may have been to *The Good Soldier*, it no longer seemed to Ford quite enough. As his sense of a dilemma in the post-War world began to grow, the novelist felt a need to propose an alternative hero as well as to render his ineffectual predecessor. An answer had to be found that would be valid for a large part of this world; and it was especially important, just because of the pressing nature of the problem, that this answer be implied through the full dispassionate persuasiveness of the novel, and not be distorted by didactic exhortation. The Tietjens novels were Ford's attempt to create a work of explicit social relevance. Here, although the focus remained on a

small group of people, the social context was considerably enlarged, and the reconstruction of a hero along the lines of Ford's suggested answer was imaginatively conveyed. And always the relationship of Tietjens' growth and self-definition to the rest of his society was made quite clear. It was not a question of Ford becoming a crudely didactic novelist, but rather of his coming to feel that his renderings must have greater relevance for a world that needed to be shown more and more of itself and its alternatives, if it was to survive.

As an "historian of his own time," Ford decided to write the Tietjens novels with a specific purpose in mind, despite the fact that he confessed as late as 1933 to having "the greatest contempt for novels written with a purpose." When he sat down to begin the Tietjens series he "sinned against" his "gods to the extent of saying that" he "was going . . . to future wars." And he added that if the world could see war not in terms of horror, death, or self-sacrifice, but of worry, "if the world could be got to see war from that angle there would be no more wars."[44] By reducing war to the level of the non-heroic by divesting it of all its glory so that only the anguished reality of boredom and the constant worry would be left, Ford hoped to eliminate not only the ceremonious mythology, but war itself. The Tietjens novels have of course other themes: there is the very central growth of Tietjens himself from a traditional aristocrat to a limited hero; there is the breakdown of the entire society, of which the War is only one manifestation; and there is the relationship between war and sexual maladjustment as a social phenomenon. But the War was a cataclysmic sign of the larger and underlying social collapse, and it was also a more tangible threat. By attempting to eliminate this threat, and by constantly showing its relation to civilian problems, Ford hoped that he could help bring about a condition in which the problems responsible for the social collapse might also eventually be solved.

The initial circumstances of the Tietjens story, Christopher's marriage to Sylvia, was derived by Ford from a story told to him by his friend, Arthur Marwood, and from the character of Marwood himself. The novelist recalled how he and Marwood were once in a train, "going back to our cottages after a hard week over manuscripts in the office of the *English Review*." Marwood had told him of a man who had picked up a woman on a train between Paris and Calais. She later persuaded this man that he had made her pregnant, but after their marriage he had discovered that the child might be another man's. "There was no real knowing." The man would not divorce the woman out of a sense of decency, while she, in turn, held on to the marriage because of her Roman Catholicism.[45] The similarity to the story of Tietjens and Sylvia is evident, although Ford of course greatly complicated both characters. In Marwood's story, the man had eventually fallen in love with another woman, but his wife had returned, and he had deteriorated to alcoholism and eventual suicide.

A NEW BEGINNING

Ford's major alteration of this part of the story was that unlike either the unfortunate man or Ashburnham in *The Good Soldier*, Tietjens does not deteriorate and finally kill himself, but goes on to construct a wholly new way of life.[46]

The character of Marwood, on whom Tietjens was partly modelled, had been marked for Ford by a

> knowledge of the world's circumstances ... so vast and deep that, as it were, to carry on his consciousness through the years seemed hardly to present any difficulties.... There he was, large—'an elephant built out of meal sacks.' Deliberate, slow in movement and extraordinarily passionate—with an abiding passion for the sort of truth that makes for intellectual accuracy in the public service. It was a fascinating task to find him a posthumous career.[47]

Marwood had, moreover, "the clear eighteenth-century English mind which had disappeared from the earth, leaving the earth very much the poorer. It was not merely that his mind was encyclopaedic, it was that his information was all arranged."[48] He was possessed of the old Tory sense of paternalistic responsibility, and this was reflected in the scheme of national insurance which he proposed in the first two numbers of the *English Review*. Goldring quotes Ford as remarking that as "a Tory of the landowning class," Marwood "had a special distrust of all employers of labour and a special affection for labour as individual—if not for the working classes in the mass.... He used to assert that such a scheme was the only thing that would save Western civilization from inevitable communism."[49] But Ford, despite his strong admiration for Marwood, could not make his fictional hero a mere carbon copy, if for no other reason than that the two men lived under radically different historical conditions.

Tietjens had to be given more dimension; he had to acquire fictional interest through an internal complexity of his own. Particularly, he was to have one dimension that Marwood, as Ford recalled him, did not have. Tietjens would have to adapt to a new world, and in order to ready him for this change Ford had to reduce the heroic qualities of his major character. Ford himself makes his intention clear:

> I was in no mood for the heroic. My character would be deprived of any glory. He was to be just enough of a man of action to get into the trenches and to do what he was told. But he was to be too essentially critical to initiate any daring stories. Indeed his activities were to be most marked in the realm of criticism.

If he had any heroic traits, they were to stem not from actions, but from the critical faculty, for the proposed character had to be aware of and to

withstand the constant mismanagement of war policy, all the way from Whitehall to brigade headquarters. Tietjens was not to be a mere gentleman, but was to represent the old English Ruling Class, made up of people who were "distinguished by being authoritative, cynical, instructed in the ways of mankind."[50] Tietjens' dignity came from awareness and stamina, and not from any public display of glory or responsibility. And as he grew toward the role of the limited hero, in which his awareness was a decisive asset, he moved further and further away from the glory that would have been for him only a hindrance. He was to emerge from the old ruling class into a new way of life, a way of life in which Ford hoped that Tietjens would eventually rule by example.

As in the cases of Dowell and Ashburnham in *The Good Soldier*, critical interpretation of Tietjens has hinged on the degree and nature of his heroic traits. The majority of critics regard the hero of *Parade's End* as the embodiment of nearly all Fordian virtues, but such an uncomplicated view is hardly in accord with Ford's tendency in his major novels toward the creation of persons with at least dual characteristics. Too favorable an impression of Tietjens would also seem to rule out the possibility of progression during the course of the four books, and without progression such length would hardly seem justified. Certainly, however, even the Tietjens of the first book is closer to Ford's ideal man than any of Ford's earlier heroes, and he is at this point the aristocratic hero presented in Ford's most sympathetic light. Thus Robie Macauley can find his character to be "synonymous with the character of an ordered, bounded, harmonious past. . . . He is, in fact, 'the last English Tory.' Mirrored in this 'clear eighteenth-century mind,' the world is an equable and logical mechanism in which God, Man, and Nature have a balanced relationship. It is not specifically an English view; it has belonged to every Western nation."[51] Meixner points out that Tietjens "embodies Ford's own essential standard of values," and also that he is "conceived in broad, heroic proportions. Although like the earlier creations he is essentially passive, a stoical adherent to his code, unlike the great majority of his predecessors Tietjens reveals by his actions that he can be effective when circumstances warrant it."[52] J. J. Firebaugh comments on Tietjens' concern for "the men serving under him," and his identification of "their problems with his in a self-sacrificial manner," and Firebaugh attempts through these qualities to link Tietjens to a pastoral tradition, defined by William Empson, in which the "man of birth" descends into "the lower ranks, there to learn how better to rule, and if that descent can further be identified with the idea of the sacrificial god dying for his people, that they—and he—may be born again, we then see Tietjens performing the functions of aristocratic defender and of sacrificial god."[53] All these critics fall short by seeing Tietjens as a far more static figure than the one drawn by Ford. They fail to call attention to his inner conflicts or to his

crucial change. Ford's own claim that he wished to make this particular hero unheroic is apparently forgotten. And Tietjens in the novels is far too human to acquire the characteristics of a mythic god-figure. Cassell, although he notes that Tietjens' world is far from static and that it therefore calls forth a change in Tietjens himself, still emphasizes the hero of *Parade's End* as "the culmination and prototype of Ford's gentleman of honor," and does not show how this honor becomes for Tietjens something of a hindrance that must be overcome.[54]

With a different emphasis, Melvin Seiden, in a highly provocative article, calls attention to the element of anti-heroic comedy in the Tietjens novels. He contends that "Ford is describing a special English brand of corrupting romanticism, a kind of male Boverism. . . . But," he adds,

> we are not forced to choose between two incompatible judgements to Tietjens' character; he is not either a long-suffering and saintly man or a fool. For clearly he is both. It is one of Ford's greatest achievements to have made us feel, as Sylvia does, that Tietjens' paradoxical virtue *is* intolerable, and yet to have done this without in the least mitigating her viciousness or suggesting that Tietjens deserves the calumny he received from her or the world.

But Seiden becomes too insistent on the theme of Tietjens' comic qualities. He sees Tietjens as "the innocent amid vice . . . selfless, unlibidinous, filially pious, almost passionately paternal . . . stinking of sanctity and yet a man of the world, a Colonel Blimp who comes trailing clouds of glory, who in fact—positively acts (as it seems to others) as if he were lamb of God!" Seiden goes on to suggest that Tietjens throughout the novels is conceived in "a tight and abrasive co-mingling of moral and emotional antinomies," and that his new heroism emerges out of "a sublimity inhering in the ridiculous."[55]

Actually Tietjens is both the culmination of the aristocratic hero, and the first of his limited counterparts, and particularly in the early part of the series he has all the virtues and faults of his initial position. But Tietjens is seldom comic, and he is certainly not an "innocent." Even his early decision to take Sylvia back is made not from ignorance, but out of a sense of duty. Tietjens' major fault is that of typical aristocratic ineffectiveness in dealing with emotions, but even in the early sections of the work he is far more capable of decisive and specific action under emotional stress than is a George Moffat or a Robert Grimshaw. And Ford further complicates the picture both by taking us inside Tietjens' mind and showing his awareness, and by showing us the external pressures to which Tietjens is constantly subject. There is a partial comic irony in some of the early scenes, in which we become aware of what Tietjens fails to do, but Tietjens at his most ineffective never approaches the level of Seiden's "ridiculous." Moreover, Seiden, like the other critics, largely

overlooks the factor of progression—a factor that is essential to the four novels. Tietjens undergoes a decisive change, but this change is hardly abrupt or sudden; and its gradualness accounts for a good part of the structure of the novels.

Ford's strongest accomplishment in *Parade's End* is the way in which he controls the double perspective through which Tietjens is seen; and recognition of this device would seem to overrule Meixner's objections that the three final novels are "inferior" appendices to *Some Do Not*.[56] In the early parts of the tetralogy, the hero, as admirable as he is, is seen with a recurrent irony. Even the crucial scene at the end of *Some Do Not* in which Tietjens and Valentine Wannop decide not to become lover and mistress is viewed with a double attitude. But as the story progresses through the rest of the novels, and as Tietjens is subject to greater trials, all the while becoming more and more resolute, the double perspective diminishes, and the limited hero gradually emerges. Events such as Tietjens' reunion with Valentine on Armistice Day, in *A Man Could Stand Up*, recall previous situations, such as their decision, in *Some Do Not*, not to consummate their love. If Ford had stopped at the first novel, Tietjens would remain only slightly more admirable than Ashburnham. With the addition of the other three, he rises far above both "the good soldier" and Ford's other early heroes. In fact, by the final novel, *The Last Post*, Tietjens has become so much the embodiment of Fordian virtues that Ford need say little more about him. The focus of the novel is therefore shifted to his brother, Mark, who represents the dying old order. Tietjens stands, by way of contrast, in the background, and his own assertion of a new identity is able to inspire the others by the end of the book to at least a sense of partial resolution.

One of the qualities of the last three books which bothers Meixner is the noticeable change in technique. While *Some Do Not* is basically a rendering of significant incidents, the other three novels rely much less on external action and much more on that within the characters' minds as rendered through internal monologues. These monologues may not provide as great a degree of overt drama as is found in the first novel, but the techniques of *No More Parades*, *A Man Could Stand Up*, and *The Last Post* seem particularly apt, since they underline a thematic shift toward a more internal focus. As Tietjens becomes more of a limited hero, his social context becomes increasingly less formative. It is through the context and the action of his own mind that he achieves the self-consciousness that is a prerequisite to his new role. The plot of the novel thus centers on the growth of Tietjens' mind, and the change in his attitudes; and the drama is in the progression itself.

Tietjens' difficulties and position before the War are depicted in *Some Do Not*, the first novel of the tetralogy. The certainty by which Christopher is marked in the opening scene, as he sits in the railway carriage with

his friend, Macmaster, is quickly countered by the details of his difficulties with his wife. In addition to his private dilemma, Tietjens must also cope with a society that no longer accepts the traditional values for which he stands. He is gradually ostracized, partly out of jealousy, by the members of his own class, and particularly by its newer entrants. And the older forms of authority, exemplified by the Reverend Duchemin who goes mad, are quickly falling apart. Duchemin, who in his madness carries echoes of Reverend Brede in *The Benefactor*, is in fact ironically replaced in Mrs. Duchemin's affections by Macmaster himself, who completes his social rise by having an affair with and eventually marrying the wife of the deranged clergyman. Tietjens is faced in this novel with a social context quite similar to that in which previous Fordian heroes found themselves. It is still, in Part I, the world before the War, and the tensions of Part II are largely pre-War tensions. The question is one of how Tietjens will face this transitional world, and Ford maintains a constant double view on the issue. On the one hand, Tietjens is far more aware of what is happening than was Ashburnham in *The Good Soldier*, and during the breakdown he fully lives up to his traditional values. But on the other, these values are not wholly relevant in coping with new situations, and if Tietjens did not go beyond them, he would remain simply another ineffectual Fordian hero.

The double view is most evident in Tietjens' relationship with Sylvia. Her criticisms of his exaggerated virtue are justified on one level, since Tietjens is unable to give her the emotional support that she needs. But although Ford later complicates Sylvia's response, he first calls attention to her cruelty in order to mitigate strongly Tietjens' lack of a really free response. Christopher may be incapable of coping emotionally with Sylvia, but with her own admitted cruelty, meeting her needs is no easy task. The double view of Tietjens is intensified by the fact that he frequently questions his own position. Ford delves sufficiently into Christopher's mind, particularly in the development of his growing affection for Valentine, to make us see the doubts that underlie his partial ineffectiveness. The signs of Tietjens' inner conflicts also prepare us for the much stronger internalization of focus that will follow in the next two novels. Throughout *Some Do Not* there are small indications of a new self-assertion of Tietjens' part, and again these center around his relationship with Valentine. But at the end, in the final scene where the two lovers "do not," the double view again asserts itself through an incident shaded with irony.

The first part of the novel focuses on the social breakdown, and concludes with the first real communication between Tietjens and Valentine, the scene in which they ride all night together in her Mother's dog-cart. The opening scene in the railway carriage sets in a short space the mood of Tietjens' early world:

The two young men—they were of the English public official class—
set in the perfectly appointed railway carriage. The leather straps to
the windows were of virgin newness; the mirrors beneath the new
luggage racks immaculate as if they had reflected very little; the
bulging upholstery in its luxuriant, regulated curves was scarlet and
yellow in an intricate, minute dragon pattern, the design of a geome-
trician in Cologne. The compartment smelt faintly, hygienically of
admirable varnish; the train ran as smoothly—Tietjens remembered
thinking—as British gilt-edged securities. It traveled fast; yet had it
swayed or jolted over the rail joints, except at the curve before
Tunbridge or over the points at Ashford where the eccentricities are
expected and allowed for, Macmaster, Tietjens felt certain, would
have written to the company. Perhaps he would even have written to
the *Times*.

Tietjens is the young, established aristocrat, and Macmaster is a friend
whom Tietjens has helped in his rise, and who will later surpass Tietjens.
Macmaster represents the new opportunistic class; although in all fairness
it should be pointed out that he later vows loyalty to Tietjens and Valentine against the wishes of his own wife. The world of the two young men
is one of correctness and certainty. Macmaster, carefully conscious of his
goals and his appearance, is immaculately dressed, whereas Tietjens, still
secure in his position, has forgotten the color of his own tie.[57] But, as
Robie Macauley recognizes, this train "is not running from London to
Rye as they think, but from the past into the future, and ahead of them,
in their one-way journey is a chaotic country of ripped battlefields and
disordered towns"; and "somewhere, beyond some bridge or tunnel, the
tracks themselves will finally disappear into the dry sands of the wasteland."[58]

The situation with Sylvia is quickly established. She has run off to
Europe with a lover, Perowne, who will later in *No More Parades* be
partly responsible for the scandal in which Tietjens is involved at the
front. But she has notified her husband that she wishes to return, and
Tietjens admits to Macmaster that he will take her back on principle,
although he "shall take three days to think out the details." He represses
his feelings about the matter, so that to Macmaster he seems to have none;
but he has filled himself with brandy "to keep him from shivering."
Christopher does not reveal his feelings for two reasons; first, as he "saw
the world, you didn't talk," and secondly, "his wife's flight had left him
almost completely without emotions that he could realize, and he had not
spoken more than twenty words at most about the event."

Ford is able to indicate some of Tietjens' inner torment, but his hero's
outer motivations are essentially those of duty. Tietjens tells his father
that he will not press for divorce because "No one but a blackguard
would ever submit a woman to the ordeal of divorce."[59] He claims "to

stand for monogomy and chastity. And for not talking about it. Of course if a man who's a man wants to have a woman he has her. And again, no talking about it."⁶⁰ But even Christopher's sense of duty toward Sylvia is partially motivated by a sense of guilt over the fact that "he had had physical contact with this woman before he married her," so that Sylvia had gotten him to marry her by hinting that she was with his child. Before leaving on her latest escapade with Perowne, however, Sylvia had planted in Tietjens' mind the idea that the child might have been by Drake, a previous lover; and Sylvia's mother admits to Father Consett, the priest who even after his death will remain in Sylvia's mind as a sign of conscience, that the child is "probably Drake's."⁶¹

Ford in this same early scene shows Sylvia herself talking with Consett, and she articulates here many of the feelings that she will reiterate throughout the four novels. Her hatred for her husband, she explains, is compounded of her own boredom at Tietjens' predictability and her resentment at his sense of duty and decency. His very virtues remind her of her own imperfections and she wants "to stick a knife into him." She tells Consett that Tietjens is "so formal he can't do without all the conventions there are and so truthful he can't use half of them." The priest asks her why, if she knows her husband so well, she "can't get on with him better," but Sylvia only reasserts her boredom and her desire to "torment that man," even if she has to corrupt "the child."⁶² Sylvia senses her husband's paradoxical character, his conventionality and his truthfulness. But his lack of emotional response prods her own insecurity. Macauley comments that Sylvia feels a real terror at the idea of her husband. The intolerable fact to her is that he is sane," and the same fear and resentment of Tietjens lies behind his mistreatment by the other characters as well. "To their jumbled and neurotic lives he stands as a reproach, and they must destroy him if possible."⁶³

This neurotic and insecure society soon begins to ostracize Tietjens, and for the first time in the book, the hero is seen with Ford's full sympathy. Rumors begin about Tietjens' interest in Valentine Wannop before that interest has even begun to materialize. General Campion, Tietjens' godfather, questions Christopher about the relationship, and reveals that the rumor has been pushed by Paul Sandbach, Campion's brother-in-law and one of the newly rich, who has a strong dislike for Tietjens. Revealingly, Sandbach himself is "a flagrantly unfaithful husband." Despite the General's accusing questions, however, Tietjens does not try to defend himself. He knows "that, had he really tried, he could have made the General believe him. But he had behaved rightly. It was better for a boy to have a rip of a father than a whore for a mother."⁶⁴ Tietjens acts out of a sense of duty, but again by taking us inside his mind and showing his motivations, Ford is able to present Tietjens' choice in a more sympathetic light. Tietjens begins, even in *Some Do Not*, to make a

conscious break with his society. He senses its sickness, and he early states the connections between this sickness and the possibility of war. "War ... is inevitable," he tells Macmaster, "and with this country plumb centre in the middle of it. Simply because you fellows are such damn hypocrites. There's not a country in the world that trusts us. We're always, as it were, committing adultery ... with the name of heaven on our lips."[65] With the breakdown of values, as Macauley suggests, "the traditional modes of relationship among people had disappeared and there were no new ones to take the place." War was "simply a dramatic heightening of this process of ruin."[66] Tietjens' defiance of this confused society is not limited, however, to words. Once, on a golf course, he had seen two suffragettes being chased by "two city men, flushed with triumph and panting,". Tietjens had stopped the men forcefully, roaring "at the top of his voice: 'You infernal swine. I'll knock your head off if you move.'" Later we learn that one of the suffragettes had been Valentine, and also that the night of the golf-course incident Mr. Sandbach and more than half-a-dozen young compatriots "had gone scouring the country lanes, mounted on motor bicycles and armed with loaded canes (. . .) for Suffragettes! Every woman they had come across in the darkness they had stopped, abused, threatened with their loaded canes and subjected to cross-examination. The countryside was up in arms."[67]

Tietjens is quickly differentiated from the callousness of such men in both his private and social attitudes. After the breakfast at the Duchemins, during which the Reverend Duchemin has a fit and begins to "shout obscenities" at the other guests, and during which Edith Ethel Duchemin and Macmaster feel their attraction for each other, Tietjens is walking with Valentine. His feelings are mixed, for he thinks first that he is "as badly off" as Mrs. Duchemin: "Sylvia's as bad as Duchemin." But then he feels guilty for walking with Valentine, whom he is sure is "virtuous" and has a "virginal cockiness."[68] Again, Ford builds sympathy for Tietjens by showing his inner doubts. His brand of Tory paternalism also sets Tietjens above the other men of his class. He feels that every working-man should "have a minute of four hundred a year and every beastly manufacturer who wanted to pay less" should "be hung. That it appeared was the High Toryism of Tietjens as it was the extreme Radicalism of the Extreme Left of the Left."[69] The equation of High Toryism with the far Left is interesting in that it both distinguishes Tietjens from the more mercenary tendencies of his society and suggests that while Ford could not regard the political Left as a panacea, he was in sympathy with many of its aims. The equation is another instance of the way in which Tietjens begins to achieve definition apart from his world, thereby moving closer to his final role of limited hero.

In the climactic dog-cart scene of Part I, Tietjens is given further self-definition. For a short time he is able to respond to Valentine on a specific

A NEW BEGINNING

emotional level. He and Valentine have helped one of Valentine's suffragette friends to find refuge, and they drive back through a warm and mist-ridden night. The scene is wrought in a rhythmic language that suggests erotic joy, and yet there is no indication of any physical contact, only a strong, mutual and hardly-verbalized emotion. Tietjens begins to feel a respect and concern for Valentine, because of her "having the constructive desire and knowing how to set about it." He begins to think in terms of bucking convention in order to be with her. Valentine, whose attitude toward Tietjens is still a mixture of mockery and admiration, regards the ride as "the first holiday I've had in four solid months," and she succeeds in getting them lost. The scene crescendos: "They agreed that they had no responsibilities, and after that went on for unmeasured hours in silence; the mist growing, but very gradually more luminous (. . .). Once or twice at a rise in the road they saw again the stars and the moon, but mistily. On the fourth occasion they had emerged into the silver lake; like mermen rising to the surface of a tropical sea." For a moment, "Tietjens almost kissed her. Almost. An all but irresistible impulse."

During the ride, Tietjens begins to identify himself as an artist. He remarks to himself that the mist "was, perhaps, no longer silver: if you looked at it with the eye of the artist (. . .). With the exact eye! . . . . The exact eye: exact observation; it was a man's work. The only work for a man. Why, then, were artists soft, effeminate, not men at all; whilst the army officer, who had the inexact mind of the schoolteacher, was a manly man? Quite a manly man, until he became an old woman!"[70] Tietjens in the course of this scene acquires a new and very favorable dimension, and this dimension remains in our mind as we see him revert suddenly to his old role of duty, but in a sympathetic manner, and with a specific, decisive act. In the early dawn, the dog-cart comes head-on into General Campion, driving a car he can bearly control, just as he will ally himself with, but never really comprehend, the new social order. Tietjens manages to control the horse so as to avoid a full crash, but the animal is nonetheless badly scraped and wounded by the car. Tietjens, enraged and deeply moved, curses heavily at the General. Then he thinks back to the fact that Sylvia's child is not his, and he begins to doubt his power "to beget children. Clumsy sobs shook him. It was the dreadful injury to the horse which had finished him. He felt as if the responsibility were his. The poor beast had trusted him and he had smashed it up. Miss Wannop had her arms over his shoulder." Christopher sends Valentine home, and stays with the horse until the doctor arrives, for as the carriage driver who takes Valentine home remarks, Tietjens is "Always the gentleman (. . .) a merciful man is merciful also to his beast," and in the final analysis "Some do and some (. . .) do not."[71]

The title phrase is used again at the close of Part II, when Tietjens and Valentine decide not to become lover and mistress before Tietjens' return

to the front. And in both cases, Tietjens' sense of responsibility is seen with a double view. Each time, it holds him slightly away from Valentine, but each time his being one of the few who "do not" differentiates him from an upper-class whose members spend their time attacking suffragettes on dark roads and driving cars that they cannot control.

The second part of *Some Do Not* develops the relationship between Tietjens and Sylvia, and comes to a climax with Tietjens' and Valentine's decision not to consummate their love. The latter relationship contrasts with Tietjens' passionless marriage that he and Valentine deny themselves partly out of an almost shy hesitation that indicates mutual respect. There are echoes of previous encounters between Fordian heroes and their women, but the overtones in this case are far less ironic. Part II begins with a major time shift. It is the third year of the War; Tietjens has been to the front, and through shell shock has suffered a loss of memory. He is home on leave, and he and Sylvia are discussing the future of their relationship and of their child. The loss of memory, since it had been one of Tietjens' most active faculties, is, as E. V. Walter suggests, especially significant. It is actually a loss of the past, and shows the destructive effect of the War on tradition.[72] Sylvia is in another rage at Tietjens, and she flings a plate of food at his head, all the while screaming at him of her boredom and needling him about Edith Ethel, whom she supposes to be his mistress, and who is now Mrs. Macmaster "over six months." But because of another rumor she also suspects Valentine.

Sylvia's major characteristic in this scene is her desire to be punished. She still resents her husband strongly for his dispassionate reaction, even though she suspects him of affairs and no longer regards him as quite as perfect. She recalls how she had married Tietjens during her affair with Drake, "in a scare that had been as much her mother's as her own," and her attitude toward her husband in the present scene is compounded of guilt, resentment at not receiving the attention of punishment for her cruelty, and a generally compulsive need to draw from Tietjens some recognition of herself. She says to Christopher in desperation:

> If you had once in our lives said to me: 'You whore! You bitch! You killed my mother. May you rot in hell for it (. . . .)' If you'd only once said something like it (. . .) about the child! About Perowne! (. . .) you might have done something to bring us together. . . . But in the name of the Almighty, how could any woman live beside you (. . . .) and be forever forgiven? Oh no: not forgiven; ignored! (. . .) Well, be proud when you die because of your honour. But, God, you be humble about (. . .) your errors in judgement. . . . Don't you know, Christopher Tietjens, that there is only one man from whom a woman could take '*Neither I condemn thee*' and not hate him more than she hates the fiend! (. . .)

Tietjens can only bring himself to answer this confrontation with what he knows to be a lie, that he believes her to be "a good woman. One that never did a dishonourable thing." Sylvia recoils from this subterfuge, but Tietjens only adds, "I daresay you have ruined me. That's nothing to me. I am completely indifferent. . . . I don't care. I can't help it. Those are—those *should* be—the conditions of life amongst decent people."[73]

Finally the husband and wife come around to discussing the future of their child. Tietjens tells Sylvia that he has spent a good deal of money tracing her movements with Drake, and found that Sylvia's former lover cannot be the father of the child. This question of parentage is raised throughout the novels, but is never settled with certainty, so that it suggests a larger uncertainty toward traditional roles. Tietjens also agrees to raise the child a Catholic and make him heir to Groby, the family estate. He says that he will be happy to think of the boy in the hands of Father Consett, "the best man I ever met and one of the most intelligent," but Sylvia informs him that Consett has been hung in the Easter Rebellion.[74] The Priest remains, however, a symbol of the good in Sylvia's conscience, and he is one of the major devices that Ford used to present Sylvia as a partially sympathetic character. She might have been a simple "bitch," as she is later called by Christopher's brother, Mark, but Ford moves constantly behind her overt behavior to show the conflict between the side of her that worships Father Consett and the side that wants to torment her husband. As a highly emotional woman, it is difficult for Sylvia to resolve the problem on a purely spiritual plane; for she is in need of an emotional response that her husband cannot give her, partly because she herself has killed any such response in him. Nonetheless, Tietjens appears at his weakest when he replies to Sylvia's desperate attempts at recognition with protestations of his own indifference. By presenting Sylvia in a double light, Ford is better able to draw his double picture of Tietjens, and to establish a telling contrast between his hero's responses to Sylvia and those he makes, particularly in the third novel, to Valentine Wannop.

Society's ostracizing of Tietjens continues to plague him through the war years. Just before he is to return to the front, Christopher learns that his bank has dishonored one of his checks, simply because of a seeming overdraw and the hostility of one of the bank officials. Shortly thereafter, Tietjens is visited by Mark. The older brother recalls how, along with their father, he had once asked his own roommate, the slyly malicious Ruggles to inquire into Christopher's place in "the great book" of social status. Ruggles had informed the senior Tietjens of all the circulating rumors—that Christopher's wife had been with child when he had married her, that he "was suspected in high places of being a French agent," and that he held this post "in order to obtain money for Miss Wannop,

by whom he had had a child, and to maintain Macmaster and Mrs. Duchemin on a scale unsuited to their means, Mrs. Duchemin being his mistress." Christopher's father "believed implicitly in the great book," and the day after Ruggles' visit, he was found dead. As with the question of Sylvia's child, however, Ford lets the details of the senior Tietjens' death remain ambiguous, so that it is never clearly established as suicide or accident.[75] This ambiguity creates another dilemma of definition for Christopher, as he does not know where his guilt lies, or if he is guilty at all.

As the novel progresses, Christopher begins to define himself more and more through his feelings for Valentine, so that as he and Mark walk to the War Office, Christopher decides to make Valentine his mistress. The growing confidence in his relationship to the girl gives Tietjens the courage to refuse Mark's offer of money to patch up the supposedly overdrawn bank account. When Mark discovers that the bank was wrong, and that it had erred because one of the officials had desired to discredit Christopher, he can only exclaim, "This is the last of England." The growing meaningfulness of Valentine to himself also enables Christopher to meet a direct emotional crisis with the girl and comfort her. Just as Christopher and Mark approach the War Office, they meet Valentine, who immediately asks Christopher if he is "the father of the child" that Edith Ethel "was going to have," and adds, "your wife says you were." Tietjens makes "his last effort of the afternoon," and replies, "Damn it all. How could you ask such a tomfool question? *You!* I took you to be an intelligent person. The only intelligent person I know. Don't you *know* me?" Valentine then asks if Sylvia is not a truthful person, and Christopher answers, "What she says she believes. But she only believes what she wants to for the moment. If you call that truthful, she's truthful. I've nothing against her." And he adds to himself, "I'm not going to appeal to her by damning my wife." Valentine begins to cry, and Christopher leaves her with Mark, while he himself hurries into the War Office, with a sense that if he does not soon meet a simple bureaucrat "who would have fish-like eyes and would ask the sort of questions that fishes ask in tanks, he, too, must break down and cry."[76]

Tietjens is very much in control of this situation. He is able to perceive Valentine's needs, and at the same time to assert his own. He is also able to recognize, and to an extent to admit, the emotional turmoil within himself. Christopher's response during the incident has the further advantage of placing Valentine and himself in a favorable light with Mark, so that the older brother expresses his approval to Valentine while Christopher is inside. "It was the first moment of the lifting of strain that she had known since the day before the Germans crossed the Belgian frontier near a place Gemmenich."[77]

Valentine herself must grow before she can fully commit herself to

A NEW BEGINNING

Tietjens. She must acquire a greater personal sense of the social breakdown, and she does so through the experience of disillusion with Edith Ethel. Valentine recalls the scene: "By the light of candles in tall silver sticks, against oak panneling," that is, against all the symbols of tradition, Mrs. Duchemin "had seemed like a mad block of marble, with strong, dark eyes, and mad hair. She had exclaimed in a voice as hard as a machine's: 'How do you get rid of a baby? You've been a servant. You ought to know!'" This incident, Ford comments, "had been the great shock, the turning point of Valentine Wannop's life." She had early in her life "learned to do without, and the world as she saw it was a place of renunciations, of high endeavor and sacrifice," or, that is to say, of abstract responsibility. Even the passion of Macmaster and Edith Ethel had seemed to her "beautiful." But with Edith Ethel's question disillusion had cut her like a sharp nail. "What then," she had asked herself, "were tall candles in silver sticks for?" And the next day, the War had begun. The disillusioning had really been a good thing for Valentine. It had made Tietjens seem more real, "less of an inclination . . . He had seemed to grow less infallible. A man with doubts is more of a man, with eyes, hands, and the need for food and for buttons to be sewn on."[78]

The disillusionment had also given Valentine a sense of man's double nature, and of the significance of personal triumphs over contradictory tendencies, that could be a key to the novel's view of Tietjens himself:

> And Valentine knew that Edith Ethel really loved beauty, circumspection, urbanity. But also, as Valentine Wannop saw it, humanity has these doublings of strong natures. . . . Edith Ethel must break down into physical sexualities—and into shrieked coarsenesses of fishwives. How else, indeed, do we have saints? Surely, alone, by the ultimate victory of the one tendency over the other![79]

It is almost as if both Tietjens and Valentine must undergo an initiation of disillusionment before they can be ready for each other. Each must have his world of appearance shattered—Tietjens, that of convention and Valentine, that of renunciation, high endeavor, and sacrifice—before they can commit themselves to the small and everyday reality of each other's doubts and feelings. The collapse of their society and the experience of the War are for the lovers a kind of initiation rite, with the crucial difference that in place of an ordered ritual to sanction a new phase of their lives, they experience only chaos and must move on to reconstruct themselves.

The closeness between Tietjens and Valentine continues to grow. Tietjens is able to assuage Valentine's pacifist doubts about his military service by telling her that he too is a "conscientious objector." He goes on to explain, "My conscience won't let me continue any longer with these fellows. . . . So I've a great bulking body! I'll admit I'm probably

not much good. But I've nothing to live for; what I stand for isn't any more in this world." His admission of his doubts to Valentine not only sets Tietjens further above "these fellows"; it is also, as he tells her, an attempt to bring them closer, "to see where . . . similarities come in," so that they can grow more fully to "respect" each other.[80] Yet in spite of this deepening intimacy, Tietjens and Valentine find that they cannot bring themselves to become lover and mistress. Various circumstances and their basic natures circumvent their intent. They had had, as Tietjens recalls to himself, on their appointed night to take care of Valentine's brother, "a drunken bluejacket with intermittent legs." And they themselves had too strong a sense of the illicitness of the experience. Valentine had expressed readiness "for anything you ask." And "he had said at some time: 'But obviously (. . . .) Not under *this* roof (. . . .)'" Valentine had given Christopher a piece of parchment with a blessing in Hebrew, and they had parted.[81] The next day Tietjens had gone back to the War.

A gentle irony pervades the final scene: for Tietjens' recognition that they are the sort that "do not" both sets them apart from the crude eroticism of their world and acknowledges the limitations of their own backgrounds. The situation calls to mind similar scenes in Ford's earlier novels, in which the hero refuses a woman who virtually offers herself to him. Given the nature of Tietjens' and Valentine's relationship, a consummation of their love would not have been immoral, but it would have been against their background and nature. They are able to talk about their reticence of passion by their ability to recognize their own inhibitions, the irony of the situation is made gentle, and the two lovers are able to build on their relationship. Tietjens will undergo additional war experiences, and Valentine will commit herself to the point where she will no longer fear that Tietjens, on the night that he had refused her offer of herself, had rejected her personally. When they are reunited after the War, their definition of themselves and their response to each other will be considerably stronger.

No More Parades, the second novel of the tetralogy, focuses on the War itself, and continues the pattern of initiation by subjecting Tietjens to a series of demanding trials. There is no glory, only a worsening of Tietjens' personal situation, and an explicit linking of the War with the general moral collapse. Tietjens, as commander of a base camp, is caught in numerous difficulties, most of which are caused by Sylvia, who has followed him to the front. But he experiences not so much his own individual nemesis, as a small fragment of the overall condition. The troubles of his men parallel his own, and like his they have civilian origins. After a major scandal involving himself, Sylvia, and one of her previous lovers, Tietjens is sent by General Campion up the line. But all the while that Ford shows his hero bearing the brunt of disapproval by the old order, he also increases our admiration for Tietjens by continu-

ously having him survive his trials with integrity. His values are tested to the point where they become, by their very survival, much more than rhetoric. The sort of appearances that Tietjens had advocated in his views on marital fidelity in *Some Do Not* are gradually replaced by a hard-won reality of values which places Tietjens far above those who condemn him.

Before he is ready to assume his new role, Tietjens must first undergo the major trials which prepare him for the change. The War becomes a continuation of the initiation to which he has been subjected by the breakdown of his world. This initiation, which lies behind the structure of *No More Parades*, has three parts. In the first, Tietjens is confronted with problems which his men face and which parallel his own. Lieutenant McKechnie, for example, is a lunatic remnant of a once brave officer and classical scholar. His troubles with his wife are a wildly exaggerated version of Tietjens' own difficulties, and the mad Lieutenant gets to the point where he hears the sound of shelling inside his brain. The second part focuses on Sylvia, who involves her husband in the book's climactic scandal. She is still seen with a strong double view, as is Tietjens himself, so that the problem of good and evil, of right and wrong choices, is deliberately made by Ford to seem highly complex. Finally, in the third part, Tietjens is sent up the front by Campion, to almost certain death. This is the worst of his trials, but we sense that if he survives it, he will have emerged a much stronger figure. For already, Ford's sympathy is increasingly on his side, and he is seen as a man of intelligence who is wasted through the narrow vision of his superiors. Ford voices this view in a biblical proverb which serves as the novel's epigram:

> For two things my heart is grieved:
> A man of war that suffereth from poverty
> and men of intelligence
> that are counted as refuse.[82]

Thus, although the focus of this novel is on Tietjens' inner trials and his strengths and weaknesses, a strong criticism of the society that can impose such trials upon him and then, by sending him up the front lines, virtually throw him away is constantly implied. Tietjens' success in these trials will, moreover, be irrelevant in the eyes of this society; and he will have to reconstruct his life on private terms, so that his triumphs do not wane to bitter ironies.

The unheroic nature of the War is established almost at the outset. Tietjens sees the War as a time of "Intense dejection, endless follies, endless villainies," and he sees "all" his "men given into the hands of the most cynically care-free intriguers in long corridors who made plots that harrowed the hearts of the world." The base is constantly being shelled by air-raids, and Tietjens feels that "to pack a million and half of men

into and round that small town was like baiting a trap for rats with a chunk of rotten meat." Their defenses "were . . . a made joke," and "The Hun planes could smell them from a hundred miles away." The theme of civilian stupidity, in contrast to the "ocean of mental suffering" of the men on the front is constantly emphasized. Tietjens feels a "heavy depression" that "These immense sacrifices . . . were all undergone to further the private vanities of men who amidst these hugenesses of landscapes and forces appeared pigmies! It was the worries of all these wet millions in mud-brown that worried him. They could die, they could be massacred by a quarter million, in shambles. But that they should be massacred without jauntiness, without confidence, with depressed brows, without parade," that is what eats at their commander constantly.[83] Tietjens quickly realizes that the glory of war is gone and that *"There will be no more parades. . . .* There won't, there damn well won't. No more Hope, no more Glory, no more parades for you and me any more. Nor for the country (. . .) nor for the world, I dare say."[84] The war experience, along with this realization, represents, as Robie Macauley points out, "Tietjens' dark night." Tietjens is able to retain his own sanity throughout the ordeal only by remaining aware at all times of the distinction between himself and "the total breakup."[85] This distinction will be important also, as part of Tietjens' new definition of himself.

The sense of "the total breakup" imposes itself on Tietjens in many ways. His aristocratic concept of God as "a great English landowner, benevolently awful, a colossal duke who never left his study and was thus invisible, but knowing all about the estate down to the last hind at the home farm and the last oak," undergoes considerable change, and Tietjens is now forced to admit to himself that "It was probably done with. . . . There would be no more parades of that sort," and that God has no doubt become "A Real Estate Agent with Marxist views."[86] Along with the falling apart of his once-ordered world, Tietjens feels strongly the problems of his men, which are as much a part of the overall breakdown as his own. The most fully-developed instance of this is his guilt over the death of O Nine Morgan, a Welshman in his company to whom Tietjens had refused permission for a leave. The refusal was based upon a request from the police that Morgan not be allowed to come home because "his wife had taken up with the prize-fighter Red Evans Williams of Castell Coch." If he had given the fellow leave the prize-fighter would have "smashed him to bits." But Morgan had been hit by a shell, during the time when he might have been on leave, and Tietjens feels that his refusal was in some way responsible for Morgan's death. He tells Morgan's mate, "If I had given him leave . . . he would not be dead now." And the soldier, One Seven Thomas, answers, "No surely not . . . but it is all one. Evans of Castell Coch would surely to goodness have killed him." But in spite of Thomas' assertion that Tietjens is "a good captain," the image of

"O Nine Morgan's eyes looking at him with a sort of wonder, as they had looked when he had refused the fellow his leave," continue to haunt Tietjens during the moments of crisis, such as the time when Campion's aide, "that insignificant ass Levin," probes at the General's request into Tietjens' "private relations with his wife."[87]

This history of O Nine Morgan, as well as Tietjens' own difficulties with Sylvia, emphasizes the point which Ford later made in *It Was the Nightingale* that "what preyed on the mind of the majority of not professionally military men who went through it was what was happening at home."[88] And "what was happening at home" was simply the large sickness that lay behind the death of an O Nine Morgan at the front.

The responsibility which Tietjens feels for the dead Welsh soldier indicates another of the qualities which he brings to his role as office—his basic sympathy. This sympathy, as Tietjens admits to himself when, against his better judgement, he grants a soldier a pass to bid goodbye to his mother, is encouraged by the thought of Valentine: "He ought to turn the man down at once. He was pervaded by a sense of her being. It was imbecile. Yet it was so."[89] His sympathy extends beyond the men to their animals. Even when he is told by Campion that he is "going up the line next week," Tietjens becomes concerned over the fact that the horses are being kept cold as part of a new training method called "hardening."[90] Tietjens' reaction here, at the end of Part I, parallels that at the end of Part II, when, after the long interview with Campion which results in his being sent up the lines, he finds satisfaction in inspecting the cook houses; and it is also similar to his concern for his horse at the close of the dog-cart scene in *Some Do Not*. Tietjens' sense of responsibility is consistent, and it differs from the false responsibility of a hero such as Edward Ashburnham in that it increases under conditions of adversity and stress, whereas Ashburnham's responsibility under similar conditions simply became vestigial. But before he becomes a limited hero, Tietjens must learn to supplement his sense of responsibility with the ability to express to Valentine the emotional commitment which he feels for her, and which will eventually involve their living together without the tie of formal marriage.

But while Tietjens is moving toward a commitment to Valentine, he is still plagued by Sylvia, who is herself torn by intensely conflicting feelings; and Tietjens is unable to respond to her in a way that might resolve the situation. Before he had left, Sylvia had promised to go into a convent; but Tietjens at the camp has seen pictures of her in the papers with groups of laughing young men. He of course resents the implications of these pictures, particularly since he realizes that "Sylvia must have supplied the information." Yet his attitude is mixed, for he recalls to himself the compassion she had once shown when their child had been sick! "She had stood at attention, the corners of her mouth moving a little: the

thermometer going down as you watched it."⁹¹ But Sylvia has followed him to France, and one day she appears just outside the camp. Tietjens' main feeling, upon learning of her arrival, is that his basic sense of privacy has been violated. "And until that afternoon he had imagined that his wife, too, would rather be dead than have her affairs canvassed by the other ranks. But that assumption had to be gone over. Revised." Tietjens had imagined "when he had come out to France . . . that he was cutting loose from this earth. . . . He had imagined Sylvia in her convent and done with." All of this had been an evasion, and the reappearance of Sylvia brings him back to the question of his past and his future.

He decides to write a report to himself, in the unemotional, "exact language" of an army report. He ponders the question of the parentage of Sylvia's child, and concludes that "the matter is debatable." He recalls how when he returned home from his parting night with Valentine, Sylvia had been enraged because she had sensed that Tietjens had not resolved his passion for Miss Wannop by physical consummation. Sylvia had hoped that Tietjens' feelings for Valentine would be purely physical in nature, and that afterwards he would return to her. In her rage, Sylvia had threatened, as Tietjens now recalls, to ruin him in the army, and he adds: "I never spoke. I am damn good at not speaking. She struck me in the face. And went away." He had heard her get into a car, and had thought her off to the convent. Thus Tietjens sets down his reactions, and inadvertently his silent avoidance of Sylvia's feelings. But after making out the report to himself, he begins to hesitate at the idea of self-justification: "Hang it all, he was not justifying himself (. . . .) He had acted perfectly correctly as far as Sylvia was concerned. Not perhaps to Miss Wannop." And then he realizes that "if he, Christopher Tietjens of Groby, had the need to justify himself, what did it stand for to be Christopher Tietjens of Groby? That was the unthinkable thought."⁹² But Tietjens does feel the need to justify himself, significantly to himself, and his sense of privacy has been violated. To be Tietjens of Groby is no longer enough, and the new conditions impose on the old Tory the need for a greater internalization of focus and a stronger definition of self.

Sylvia has followed Tietjens to the front both to attempt to regain his attention and to torment him, and this dual motivation is constantly evident in her thoughts and actions. If Tietjens is unable to satisfy her emotional needs, she has certainly given him little reason to make the effort, and is unable to control sufficiently her own contradictory impulses to give her husband any real encouragement. Even as she sits waiting for Tietjens in the hotel lobby near the front, she is with Major Perowne, the man with whom she had run off to Europe before the War in *Some Do Not*. And Sylvia is unable to resolve her own feelings toward Perowne, so that while she half-discourages him, she half-leads him on, until finally she involves Perowne, Tietjens, and herself in the climactic

A NEW BEGINNING

hotel-room scandal. As Tietjens enters the lobby, Perowne asks Sylvia what he wants, and she replies that "He wants . . . to play the part of Jesus Christ." When she amplifies this comment, it becomes clear that out of her own sense of guilt and unworthiness, Sylvia sees Christopher as playing toward her a Christ-like role of duty and obligation, for she says, "Christopher is playing at being our Lord calling on the woman taken in adultery (. . . .) He's giving me the social backing that his being my husband seems to him to call for." While she is thinking of Christopher, Sylvia's mixed feelings toward him become evident. She prays to Father Consett to "Get our Lady to get me over this (. . . .) It's the ruin of him and the ruin of me," and then she says, "But, oh damn, don't! (. . .) For it's all I have to live for."[93]

At this point, Sylvia appears as a woman who has rebelled out of a fruitless desire to be emotionally dominated. Her rebellion is in part an explicit criticism of Tietjens, although it may be legitimately asked whether Sylvia could ever present to her husband a consistent self to dominate. In the lobby, she continues to think of Father Consett, "hung at the word of a half-mad, half-drunk subaltern, because he had heard the confession of some of the rebels the night before they were taken," and she asks the Priest to "Have mercy on me, for half the time I don't know what I'm doing." She makes a mental pact with the Priest that if during the next ten minutes she should see in the room one man who looks presentable, she will go into retreat in a convent for the rest of her life. The man never appears, and during the ten-minute period Sylvia recalls the hostility with which she had thrashed a white bulldog the night before it died. It had been cold, and "the poor beast had left its kennel to try and be let into the fire (. . . .) and I found it at the door when I came in from a dance without Christopher (. . . .) And got the rhinoceros whip and lashed into it. There's a pleasure in lashing into a naked white beast (. . . .) Obese and silent like Christopher (. . . .) The last stud-white bulldog of that breed (. . . .) As Christopher is the last stud-white hope of the Groby Tory breed."

Shortly afterward, in sharp contrast to this image of hostility, Sylvia recalls, as Tietjens had before, the time their child had been sick. Tietjens "had taken the responsibility, which the village doctor would not face, of himself placing the child in a bath full of split ice." She remembers "him bending, expressionless in the strong lamp-light, with the child in his clumsy arms," and she realizes that "Christopher had been to hell to bring the child back."[94] But with all her mixed impulses, Sylvia finds some sense of resolution in venting her desire to torment Christopher by telling General Campion that her husband is a socialist and "desires . . . to model himself upon our Lord."[95] Her false information helps sway the General to the point where he will eventually send his godson to almost certain death.

Sylvia's inability to resolve sufficiently or indicate her own feelings leads ultimately to the chaotic incident in her room. During her conversation with Major Perowne, she tells him of her desire to be reconciled to her husband, and does not encourage him; yet when Perowne asks to come to her room that evening, she answers ambiguously, "You can come (. . . .) I won't lock my door. But I don't say that you'll get anything (. . . .) or that you'll like what you get (. . . .) That's a fair tip. . . . Take what you get and be damned to you."[96] Later, still in the lobby, Tietjens approaches and asks Sylvia to dance. In her own confusion, this is exactly what she craves, and they have a brief moment of closeness. Christopher asks if they hadn't better talk, and Sylvia invites him to her room.[97] The details of the scene in the room come out gradually, during Tietjens' interrogation by Levin the following morning. Tietjens had been discussing the estate with Sylvia in her room. Perowne had entered, ostensibly looking for the bathroom. Tietjens had flung Perowne out of the room to the floor, just as General O'Hara had appeared. Perowne then told O'Hara that Sylvia had invited him, and accused Tietjens of attempted blackmail. O'Hara, with whom Sylvia had also flirted, had believed Perowne's charges, and Tietjens had angrily threatened to place O'Hara under arrest for drunkenness. O'Hara had subsequently arrested Tietjens for insubordination.[98] In the consequences of this incident, Sylvia's desire to torment her husband is realized, almost unawares, for the final irony lies in the fact that the realization comes out of one of Tietjens' and Sylvia's few moments of intimate communication.

Whereas General Campion reacts to the ensuing scandal by sending Tietjens up the lines, Tietjens' strongest flaw during their interview is his stoicism. For although he had received a permanent base classification as the result of a bad chest, and although Campion admits that he knows "it's probably death to send you up the line," Tietjens does not protest the General's decree, but only thinks of protest and asks himself, "Would, say (. . . .) say, an Anglican saint do it?" Campion raises the question of Tietjens' socialism and Tietjens replies that he had "no policies that did not disappear in the eighteenth-century," and that he is "a Tory of such an extinct type" that he might be mistaken for anything, even a socialist. Moreover, Tietjens refuses to tell Campion that the unfavorable part of the report on himself was filed by Drake, now a major, and quite possibly the father of Sylvia's child. He tells his godfather only that he is "really . . . the English public schoolboy . . . an eighteenth-century product" who thinks that "the vilest of sins is to preach to the headmaster! That's me sir. Other men get over their schooling. . . . I remain adolescent. These things are obsessions with me. Complexes, sir!" Tietjens' dignity here is questionable, and he himself is aware that he is acting without reason; for when Campion asks him why he does not divorce Sylvia and Tietjens replies that he had "no grounds," he thinks to

himself, "Why the devil am I so anxious to shield that whore. It's not reasonable. It's an obsession." The terms of the eighteenth-century school do not hold valid when he has to deal with a godfather and general who during the whole interview has in the back of his mind the possibility of using Groby as a political headquarters should Tietjens be killed at the front.[99]

Tietjens' submission to Campion is part evasion, but it is also an act of resignation. The hero has been subject to so many trials that he falls into a stoic acceptance of the one which shall prove to be final and most decisive. In a sense, he has already gone beyond Campion in his definition of himself, and what the General does to him is irrelevant. Tietjens has already voiced his developing sense of heroism to Levin. It is a heroism based on personal integrity: "success or failure," he says, "have nothing to do with the credit of a story. And a consideration of the virtues of humanity does not omit the other side. If we lose, they win. If success is necessary to your idea of virtue . . . they then provide the success instead of ourselves. But the thing is to be able to stick to the integrity of your character, whatever earthquake sets the home tumbling over your head."[100]

This sense of integrity, of the need to be truthful to oneself, contrasts sharply with the preservation of appearances which Tietjens had once considered as virtuous with regard to marital fidelity. It clearly indicates his changing view of himself and its internal focus prepares him for the change of roles which he is about to undertake. The social remoteness of the battlefield up the line will almost remove the obstruction of men such as Campion, and will thus give Tietjens the opportunity to privately fortify the change and to prepare himself for the life which he and Valentine will undertake together.

With the third novel of the series, *A Man Could Stand Up*, the focus shifts decisively to Tietjens' rebirth as a limited hero. This is the last novel in which Tietjens directly dominates the scene, for in *The Last Post* he will remain in the background until the very end. The idea of standing up signifies the self-sufficiency that is essential to the limited hero's way of life; and the career of George Herbert at Bemerton, with its qualities of faith and serenity, becomes for Tietjens a symbol of this new ideal. But the change is actually centered around his relationship with Valentine. The novel is divided into three parts, and the Tietjens-Valentine relationship frames that section dealing with the War. The middle section, which renders Christopher's thoughts and actions during a day in battle, is reduced in emphasis by this frame structure, and the war scenes function at the same time as a grim reminder behind the Armistice Day scenes of Parts I and III. The second part also has a crucial ironic touch. During the day Christopher performs a heroic act of the conventional style, saving two men from a shelled trench, but this action

only elicits the disapproval of Campion who reprimands him for his muddy uniform. This episode merely underscores the futility of standard heroism in the modern world, and emphasizes the necessity for an alternative role.

Part I of the novel takes place on Armistice Day, and centers on Valentine as she learns of Tietjens' return. She feels in herself a loss of respect for the older symbols of authority: "Was that to be a lasting effect of the cataclysm that had involved the world? The *late* cataclysm! Thank God, since ten minutes ago they could call it the late cataclysm!"[101] Then she receives a phone call from Edith Ethel, and although Lady Macmaster's motives for calling are hardly altruistic—she thinks that Valentine may be useful in persuading Tietjens to cancel a debt, and she will later tell Sylvia of Valentine's and Christopher's meeting—she informs Valentine that Tietjens has returned to his empty rooms at Lincoln's Inn, and that he has asked for her.[102] Tietjens' own request is significant as the beginning of a new commitment, since he has not written Valentine at all during the War. At the thought of going to Tietjens, Valentine is torn by fears. "What," she thinks, "was the coming together that was offered her? Nothing, on the face of it, but being dragged again into that man's intolerable worries as unfortunate machinists are dragged into wheels by belts—and all the flesh is torn off their bones." The imagery suggests that Valentine is afraid that her very self will be devoured, and that part of her fears are of a sexual nature. She wonders whether Tietjens' decision not to sleep with her on the night before he had left again for the front might not have been an insult. Nevertheless, she asks herself, "What *should* keep them apart? (. . .) Middle Class Morality? A pretty gory carnival that had been for the last four years." And she resigns from her job at the school run by her father's friend, Miss Wanostrocht, whom she associates with "the brilliant Victorians" and "Middle Class Morality." It is the beginning of her decision to give herself fully to Tietjens; and together with Tietjens' own asking for her, the beginning of their gradual commitment to each other.[103]

The anti-heroic view of war, which Ford began to develop in *No More Parades*, culminates in Part II of *A Man Could Stand Up*, and is gradually supplanted in emphasis by Tietjens' efforts at personal definition. Just as the war-section lurks behind the armistice, as a reminder of the degree to which the old society had fallen, so the two armistice sections frame the battle scene as an indication that the real problem to be solved is in the civilian world. Throughout Part II, the focus is predominantly internal, and we see a good deal of Tietjens' thought through a long monologue, which takes place during one day of battle. The War, as Tietjens sees it, is an agonized "process of (. . .) eternal waiting (. . .) you hung about and you hung about, you kicked your heels and you kicked your heels."

A NEW BEGINNING

And a day of battle is nothing more for the men than a day of boredom, "during which the Germans would strain themselves (. . .) to kill a couple of Tietjens' men, and Tietjens would exercise all his care in an effort not to have even one casualty." At the end of the day, the men "would have to set to work to repair the trenches in earnest."[104] In this atmosphere of shells and boredom and continuous death, Tietjens fights to preserve his own integrity. His greatest fear is that he might be taken prisoner and lose the final remnants of his privacy.[105]

The act of standing up on a hill becomes the symbol of the integrity which Tietjens and his men attempt to maintain. A sergeant remarks that after the War, when there is no longer any danger of being shelled, a man will be able to "stand up! Take a look around . . . as if he wanted to breathe deep after bein' in a stoopin' posture for a long time."[106] But Tietjens realizes that for himself the mere act of standing up will not be enough. There must be companionship, communication, "someone to talk to." This "passionate desire to go where you could find intellect: rest" draws him to feel a kinship to Eisenstein, a soldier who had been a journalist on an "Extreme Left" newspaper; and through this kinship Tietjens once again establishes a connection between his sort of Toryism and the ideals, if not the policies, of the Left. Tietjens' desire for talk is, however, essentially a desire for Valentine, and is part of his growing commitment to her. He thinks to himself that

> the beastly Huns stood between him and Valentine Wannop. If they would go home he could be sitting talking to her for whole afternoons. That was what a young woman was for. You seduced a young woman in order to be able to finish your talks with her. . . . You can't finish talks at street corners; in museums; in drawing rooms. You mayn't be in the mood when she is in the mood—for the intimate conversation that means the final communion of your souls. You have to wait together—for a week, for a year, for a lifetime, before the final intimate conversation may be attained.

And Tietjens, as he thinks, realizes that he is defining a new self:

> That in effect was love. It struck him as astonishing. The word was so little in his vocabulary (. . . .) Love, ambition, the desire for wealth. They were things he had never known of as existing within him. He had been the Younger Son, loafing, contemptuous, capable, idly contemplating life, but ready to take up the position of Head of the Family if Death so arranged matters. He had been a sort of eternal Second-in-Command.[107]

Tietjens is about to make himself first-in-command, but in a sphere of operations radically different from either Groby or the battlefields up the line.

All the while that he is committing himself to Valentine, Christopher is also committing himself to the way of life that he wants to live with her. He hears one day the key-bugle at dawn, "playing the air 'I know a lady fair and kind,'" and he feels "A sudden waft of pleasure at the seventeenth-century air that the tones give to the landscape." The seventeenth century seems to him "The only satisfactory age in England," and he realizes that although it is impossible to return, "Still, the land remains." Tietjens searches his mind to recall the name of "George Herbert's parish," as if he were searching for a tradition. Then it comes to him: "The name *Bemerton* suddenly came onto his tongue. . . . *Bemerton*, outside Salisbury. . . . He imagined himself standing up on a little hill, a lean contemplative parson, looking at the land sloping down to Salisbury spire. A large, clumsily bound seventeenth-century testament, Greek, beneath his elbow."[108] Later, as Valentine recalls to herself in *The Last Post*, Christopher decided to set as a goal the purchase of a living at Bemerton for his son.[109] In *The March of Literature*, his large one-volume survey and personal interpretation of literary history, Ford himself links together the times of Purcell and Shakespeare, and sees in the England of this age, "a beauty of aspect such as she has never recaptured, but such as placed her for the time on the level of the beautiful civilizations of the past—with Athens and with Arles of the troubadors."[110] And as Tietjens, on the battlefield, thinks back to the England of Herbert and Bemerton parsonage, he decides not to live at Groby: "No more feudal atmosphere! He was going to live, he figured, in a four-room attic flat, on the top of one of the Inns of Court. With Valentine Wannop. *Because* of Valentine Wannop."[111] Tietjens' commitment is now complete, at least in his mind. And although it is not yet realized in actuality, we are convinced that Tietjens' new role is one that he is now ready to assume.

But even after his commitment has been made to himself, Tietjens undergoes one final experience which indicates that the old public heroism is dead and without meaning in a world where even General Campion is impervious to it. A shell hits Tietjens' company, and buries two of his men, Aranjuez and Duckett, in the mud. Tietjens is himself half-buried, but two others quickly pull him out, and through a great exertion of strength and will-power, he is in turn able to save the trapped men. Even while performing this act, however, Tietjens is thinking not of his own heroism, but of Valentine, so that Duckett's face, blackened with mud, looks "as if Valentine Wannop had been reposing in an ash-bin." But just at the heroic moment, General Campion, who is now to become full commander of the entire force, appears; and his only reaction is to reprimand Tietjens for his dirty uniform and lower him to the command of a unit of prisoners.[112] It is especially ironic that an actual act of heroism,

A NEW BEGINNING

such as Tietjens', is not recognized as such because its accidental appearances do not fit the demands of propriety.

By the beginning of Part III both Tietjens and Valentine have reached a state of individual commitment, and conventional heroism and morality have been incontrovertibly repudiated. The two lovers are now ready to commit themselves to each other. The significant element of their response is the way in which each becomes sensitive to the needs of the other. Thus both of them, and noticeably Christopher in contrast to his earlier emotional reticence, grow increasingly sensitive within a specific situational context. This new responsiveness differentiates Tietjens both from his earlier self, and from those Fordian heroes, such as George Moffat and Edward Ashburnham, whom we have seen fail in similar contexts. By the time of the mad armistice-night revel which closes Part III, Valentine feels secure enough in Christopher to sense that they can withstand the chaotic world signified by the drunk and dancing men.

When Christopher and Valentine meet each other at Tietjens' rooms, they each solidify their previous commitments. At first, Tietjens seems to Valentine a large man, "grotesque" and "clumsy," and seemingly "mad." He asks her to wait until he carries out a cabinet that he intends to sell, and Valentine has mixed feelings of sadness, joy and fear. But she quickly convinces herself not to leave, for "This was the most exciting spot on the earth . . . She was going to pass her day beside a madman; her night, too (. . . .) Armistice night! That night would be remembered down unnumbered generations. Whilst one lived that had seen it the question would be asked: What did you do on Armistice night? My beloved is mine and I am his!" And Tietjens on his part speaks on the phone to Mrs. Wannop, who tries to dissuade him from seducing her daughter. He notices Valentine, and he perceives her need for him; "He must," he thinks to himself, "comfort her." Tietjens is no longer indifferent, as he had professed to be toward Sylvia in *Some Do Not*, and his quick perception of Valentine's need is especially meaningful by its implied contrast. Ford at this point comments:

> The war had made a man of him! It had coarsened him and hardened him. There was no other way to look at it. It had made him reach a point at which he could no longer stand unbearable things. At any rate from his equals. . . . And what he wanted he was prepared to take (. . . .) What he had been before, God alone knew. A younger son? A perpetual Second-in-command? Who knew. But today the world changed. Feudalism was finished; its last vestiges were gone. It held no place for him. He was going—he was damn well going!— to make a place in it for (. . .) A man could now stand up on a hill, so he and she could surely get into some hole together.[113]

THE LIMITED HERO

The "small hole" of which Tietjens thinks signifies the willful circumscribing of his life, and thereby evokes a distinct trait of the limited hero. The decisions of both Christopher and Valentine to remain together constitute a crucial reversal of an often climactic Fordian scene; and as if to distinguish this scene from similar ones in other novels, Ford here renders his central character with the double attitude noticeably and entirely removed.

The final mad scene on armistice night pits the remnants of Tietjens' former world against the uncertainty of his new life, and in the midst of the frenetic celebration, Valentine feels a surge of trust in the man with whom she will confront the world of these wounded and shouting men from Tietjens' former company. The uninvited soldiers crowd into Tietjens' flat. The first to be admitted by Valentine is the mad Captain McKechnie, who tells her that General Campion has become Sylvia's lover and that the General had disgraced Tietjens "so that he, Campion, might be less disgustingly disgraced for taking up with his wife." This situation is, however, left ambiguous. Tietjens tells "himself that if he had any proof that Campion had committed adultery with Sylvia, he would kill him." But all he knows with any certainty is that the General is using Groby for political headquarters.[114] In *The Last Post* we learn from the recollection of the event by Mark's wife, Marie-Léonie, that Sylvia herself had appeared that night. She had been told of Valentine's reunion with Christopher by Lady Macmaster. And Valentine recalls, also in the final novel, how Sylvia, dressed in white, appeared and announced that she had cancer, and then had fallen theatrically down the stairs, and how she, Valentine, had felt rage and disbelief.[115] Later that night, the mad revelry begins. It forms the final image of the third novel, an image of a world going around in circles, in which Christopher and Valentine seem by contrast a resolute and stable center:

> They were going round them: yelling in unison:
> 'Over here! Pom Pom Over here! Pom Pom
> That's the word, that's the Word; Over here' (. . . .)
>
>   At least they weren't over there! They were prancing. The whole world round them was yelling and prancing round. They were the centre of unending roaring circles. The man with the eye-glass had stuck a half-crown in his other eye. He was well-meaning. A brother. She had a brother with the V.C. All in the family.
>   Tietjens was stretching out his two hands from the waist. It was incomprehensible. His right hand was behind her back, his left in her right hand. She was frightened. She was amazed. Did you ever! He was swaying slowly. The elephant! They were dancing. Aranjuez was hanging on to the tall woman like a kid on a telegraph pole. The officer who had said he had picked up a little bit of fluff (. . .) well, he had! He had run out and fetched it. It wore white cotton gloves

A NEW BEGINNING

and a flowered hat. It said: 'Ow Now (...) There was a fellow with a
most beautiful voice. He led: better than a gramaphone. Better (....)
 Les petites marionettes, font, font, font (....)
 On an elephant. A dear meal-sack elephant. She was setting out
on (...)[116]

And this novel closes. It remains only for Valentine and her "dear meal-sack elephant" to be placed in the context of both their new life and the post-War period. The establishment of this context is the main task of *The Last Post*.

In the final novel of the Tietjens tetralogy, the focus of the series undergoes a major change. Tietjens is still the central character, but he remains in the background, like an accomplished fact. The overt attention of the book is centered on the other characters, whose thoughts we see through a series of internal monologues. These characters are, however, each linked, in some way to Tietjens' life, and either affect or comment upon it. Tietjens and Valentine, along with Mark and his wife, Marie-Léonie, have gone to live on a small farm, and Tietjens himself has taken up the life of the "Small Producer." He has also, in order to provide for Valentine, become a dealer in old furniture. The burden of the old order has been shifted to Mark, who has intentionally retreated into total silence ever since Armistice Day. During the course of the book, Groby is rented by Sylvia to a member of the commercial aristocracy who destroys its great tree; and the book ends with two reconciliations: that of Sylvia to the overall situation and that of Mark to his God. Both reconciliations suggest the triumph of religious faith, for it is the spirit of Father Consett that finally dominates Sylvia, and Mark feels at the end a very personal sense of God's presence. These two reconciliations bring to the front of the story a theme that has previously appeared only through Sylvia's brief evocations of Father Consett, and they add an additional dimension to the novel's total view.

The novel's technique synthesizes the social and individual concerns of the three previous books, but places emphasis finally on the individual sphere. Its large social focus is similar to that of *Some Do Not*. And yet this very social focus is narrowed by Ford's use of the internal monologue technique of *No More Parades* and *A Man Could Stand Up*. The fact is that the problem of how to live has now become an internal one for all the characters, whether they are ready for the change or not. Through the monologues their various responses are evident, and can be compared to that made by Tietjens himself. By the end, his serenity, along with the self-sufficiency of his new way of life, has the effect of bringing about a partial serenity in the lives of the people who surround him.

The shift of focus in *The Last Post* has both advantages and certain drawbacks. To some extent, the reader's growing empathy with Christopher is disappointed, for in this concluding novel, the development of

Tietjens' consciousness is totally dropped. Moreover, the necessity of becoming involved with entirely new patterns of thought in the internal monologues of the other characters is a bit disconcerting, particularly since a good deal of the new and relatively extraneous material is introduced and must be quickly assimilated. This material Ford uses chiefly to give body to his characters' thoughts. But the book's weakness is also its strength. By the sudden contrast with the previous three books, Ford encourages us to step back from this particular novel, and to bring together our impressions of the tetralogy as a whole. And since the techniques of the fourth novel recall those by which Tietjens is rendered in the second and third, a similarity is suggested, and the attitudes toward Tietjens which Ford has induced can now be applied to the other characters as well. Their partial strengths reflect Christopher's success, and their failings show his strengths by way of contrast. Tietjens becomes an assumed source of stability in a world that is highly uncertain; and since the other characters are also a part of this world, Ford implies that their solution ought to be similar to Christopher's, even if they can succeed only in part.

The Last Post is set in and around a cottage where Christopher and Valentine are living, along with Mark and Marie-Léonie. Nearby is the estate of Lord Fittleworth, where Sylvia and General Campion have settled. Living with them is Sylvia's son, Mark, Jr., whom Sylvia addresses as Michael because of the animosity between Christopher's brother and herself. There is little plot—only enough to give a sense of continuity to the nine interior monologues which constitute the major "action" of the book. These monologues appear in the following order: 1) Mark, 2) Marie-Léonie, 3) Crump, a farmer, 4) Mark, Jr., 5) Mark, 6) Marie-Léonie, 7) Sylvia, 8) Valentine, and 9) Mark. It is Mark who represents the old order for which Christopher once stood, and Mark's culminating expression of faith in his brother is the final recognition by this order of its own demise and of the superiority of Christopher's new way of life.

Robie Macauley, in his introduction to the 1950 and 1961 editions of *Parade's End*, feels that *The Last Post* is a "strangely inconclusive conclusion to the Tietjens story. In form," he says, "it is the oblique of any of the books, the most extreme example of what might be called Ford's 'tangential relevance.' " Macauley then discusses the Dedicatory Letter which Ford addressed to Isabel Patterson, in which he said that he "never should have concluded this chronicle to the stage it has now reached," had it not been for her "stern, contemptuous, and almost virulent insistence on knowing 'what became of Tietjens.' " This letter, Macauley contends, is a "misleading note," and should "Most likely . . . be taken more as a compliment to a literary friend than as exact truth."[117] Macauley raises an interesting question, and his contention is supported by a letter which Goldring quotes Ford as having written to a correspondent, at the time

A NEW BEGINNING

that it was proposed in 1930 to bring the Tietjens books out as a unit. In this letter, the author stated: "I strongly wish to omit *Last Post* from the edition. I do not like the book and have never liked it and always intended to end up with *A Man Could Stand Up*."[118] We are left with two problems: the establishment of Ford's intention; and the evaluation of *The Last Post* as an existing part of the series in its published form. Unfortunately, the proposed 1930 edition of *Parade's End* never appeared, so that we have no way of knowing whether Ford would actually have stopped the inclusion of the final book.

As the matter stands, *The Last Post* is a part of the 1950 edition and, all questions of intention aside, it must be considered as such. The novel would definitely seem to enhance the structure of the total work. It shifts the tone of the four books to one of relative optimism, in accord with the change in Tietjens' self-orientation. Moreover, it allows Ford to render the solution to Tietjens' dilemma in a civilian context, and thereby underlines his view that the War was essentially an extension of the civilian breakdown. The novel also renders through some of its characters the various elements that comprise the early post-War world, of which Tietjens and Valentine must at least be indirect parts. *The Last Post*, with all its disrupting of the reader's focus and expectations, and with all its extraneous detail, still carries Tietjens' change of roles into the civilian world, and is therefore significant in any study of Tietjens as a Fordian hero, and of the nature of his change.

The novel begins with Mark's withdrawal from the world. He speaks to no one, but admits to himself that his condition is willful, even though it has been officially attributed to a seizure. He has remained silent as a protest against both the terms of the Armistice and Christopher's relinquishing of Groby to Sylvia; for Mark has wanted Britain to occupy Germany and his brother to occupy the family estate.[119] In such a manner, all the functions of the old order could have been preserved. Now he lies inert all day, speaking to no one, and being fed by his wife through a syringe. Mark's withdrawal is a final grotesque extension of the British reticence that Ford had criticized in *The Good Soldier*, as well as a final culmination of the ineffectiveness of the old order. At Christopher's request, his brother has recently turned his twenty-year common-law marriage with Marie-Léonie into a legal union, the purpose of which is to protect Groby from falling into Sylvia's inheritance. Since Marie-Léonie is the wife of the elder brother, she will have legal rights to the estate if both Mark and Christopher should die.[120] Now Marie-Léonie feeds and cares for Mark, and all but worships him as a god. Still, in spite of an assumed warmth and affection, their relationship, like the rest of Mark's daily existence, is devoid of any real emotional expression. As he lies in his bed, Mark recalls to himself the bugle call that has given the book its name: "On Armistice Day, they had played the Last Post on the steps of

the church under Marie-Léonie's windows (....) The Last Post! (...) The last of England! He remembered thinking that. He had not by then had the full terms of that surrender, but he had a dose enough of Christopher's stuck piggedness! (...) A full dose!"[121] Once he had learned of the full terms of the Armistice, Mark had decided that "public life had become so discreditable an affair that the only remedy was for the real governing classes to retire altogether from public pursuits. Things in short must become worse before they could grow better."[122] And so he had withdrawn from the post-War world. Unlike his brother, however, Mark has not developed an alternate way of life, but instead has driven himself into a psychosomatic state of willful paralysis that ends, at the close of the book, in his death.

Among the questions Mark ponders are the suicide of his father and the parentage of Sylvia's child. Each of these questions is resolved by Mark to his own satisfaction, but is actually left unresolved for the reader; for in each case, in the fifth and ninth monologues, Mark gives two contradictory answers. Of his father's death, he thinks at first that "There had been no doubt about it when he got there. His father had committed suicide. His father was not the man, unadvisedly, to crawl through a quickenhedge with his gun at full-cock behind him, after rabbits (....) It had been proposed." Yet in the final monologue Mark thinks to himself: "Crawling through a hedge after a rabbit was thinkable. . . . And as for not putting the gun out of action before crawling through the quickset (...) Many good, plucked men had died like that (....) *And Father had grown absent-minded!* (...) just now, he had remembered that father had grown absent-minded. Dad quite obviously did not commit suicide. He wasn't the man to do so."[123] Similarly on the question of the child's parentage, Mark decides in the earlier monologue that "The probability was that he *was* the other fellow's son. That woman would not have trepanned Christopher into the marriage if she hadn't at least thought that she was with child." But again before his death, Mark reverses his position, for "It came to his mind to remember, almost with pain. He had accepted nephew Mark as nephew Mark: a strong slip," but "the boy had the right sort of breeches."[124] In each case Mark contradicts himself, and the parallel contradictions serve to emphasize the limitations of his final resolutions. They are personal, and apply neither for Teitjens nor ourselves, but for Mark alone.

Many critics, however, argue against such an interpretation. Arthur Mizener, in a discussion of the way in which Ford uses the monologues of *The Last Post* to fill in questions of the tetralogy's plot, comments that "in due course we learn that Sylvia's child is really Christopher's" and "that the senior Teitjens was not a suicide."[125] And John A. Meixner, developing his argument that *The Last Post* is an inversion of the whole mood and intent of the first three novels, contends that "all cruel disloca-

tions resolve into order. Christopher's son is self-evidently his own. Christopher's father did not commit suicide."[126] Both these critics place too much stress on Mark's point of view, treating it as if it were applicable to the entire novel. But as we have seen, Mark's is only one of many responses developed in *The Last Post*, and it is a response that is representative of an old order, unable until the very last moment to accept the new. As such, his is a response that can scarcely be regarded as synonymous with Ford's or even Christopher's point of view; for the older brother stands for the very order which both Ford and Tietjens wish to leave behind. Mark's private resolution of the doubts surrounding his father's death and the parentage of Christopher's child are significant essentially for their dramatic value, for they indicate a growing pattern of acceptance and reconciliation that is induced by the increasingly evident validity of Christopher's new mode of life.

The explicit contradictions in Mark's own thoughts on the two areas of doubt, contradictions which remain unnoticed by either of the critics, are simply additional evidence for the dramatic function of these thoughts. There is no indication in the novel itself that Mark's final resolutions should be taken as climactic for anyone but himself. And there is little narrative progress in *The Last Post*, so that nothing but his observation of Christopher's current life intervenes between Mark's differing opinions to cause him to change his mind. It is not the areas in question that are resolved at the novel's end, but Mark's attitude toward them, and by implication toward the younger brother whom he will shortly leave behind. The two questions of the child's parentage and the senior Teitjens' suicide are, furthermore, raised throughout the tetralogy, and each time there is an answer that contradicts previous ones, and which will later itself be contradicted. For example, in *No More Parades*, after he has in the previous novel told Sylvia that the child is undoubtedly his, Tietjens admits to himself that the question of parentage is debatable.[127] Mark's answer is no more certain than that given by his younger brother, and in the case of the child's parentage, he is even less likely to know the truth. His is simply a resolution which signified his coming to terms with Christopher and with the universe before he dies.

If Mark represents the ineffectiveness of the old order, the confusion and restlessness of the new is shown through the brief rendering of Mark, Jr., Sylvia's son, and Mrs. de Bray Pape. Mark, Jr., is sent by Sylvia to spy on Tietjens and Valentine, but he feels little inclination for the task. Instead he asks himself about his uncertain future: "What was to become of him? He had great wealth; terrific temptation would be his. His mother was no guide. His father might have been better." In search of a "guide," he turns to the fashionable radicalism of his university: "Well, there was Marxian-Communism. They all looked to that now, in his set at Cambridge. Monty, the Prime Minister's son with black eyes, Dobles,

Campion's nephew, lean as a rat; Porter, with a pig's snout, but witty as hell. Fat ass!"[128] Although Mark, Jr., is to be the heir of Groby, Sylvia is currently tormenting Christopher by renting the estate to Mrs. de Bray Pape, a comic emissary of the *nouveau-riche*. This woman, wife of "the largest olive oil merchant in the world," tries to construct a past for herself by claiming descent from Madame de Maintenon, "not by blood but by moral addinity." And "She had," as she believes, "authority conferred on her Metempsychosistically. She believed that the soul of Madame de Maintenon, the companion of Louis the Fourteenth, had passed into her."[129] Yet when she encounters an actual symbol of the past, Mrs. de Bray Pape shows it small respect. At her orders, Groby Great Tree is quickly cut down, despite Christopher's flying to York in a last effort to save this symbol of his past. While hauling up the stump, moreover, the woodcutters destroy two-thirds of the old ballroom wall, as well as the schoolroom above it, and Christopher's boyhood bedroom all but disappears. The new tenant has also "pretty well mangled the great dovecoat in creating in it a new power station." Sylvia triumphantly hearing this news, feels her revenge successful: "She had got down Groby Great Tree: that was as nasty a blow as the Tietjenses had had in ten generations."[130]

Sylvia herself is more crudely portrayed in *The Last Post* than she had been in the earlier novels. Until her final reconciliation to the fact of Valentine's and Christopher's relationship, she is seen pretty much as the bitter woman intent on revenge; and her reaction to events such as the cutting down of Groby Great Tree is largely melodramatic. She is first seen in the novel in conversation with General Campion, and she asks him if pending a divorce from Christopher, he will marry her. Campion exclaims, "Good God, no," and then adds that a man cannot marry his godson's wife. Sylvia has not been Campion's mistress, but their relationship would seem to be more than one of political convenience. It is strange that although Campion had intended to use Groby for his campaign headquarters, he has acquiesced in her rental of the estate, and is now living, along with Sylvia, at Lord Fittlesworth's. Campion himself is another example, similar to Lord Marsden in *The Marsden Case*, of the connection which Ford made between the hero of the old order and the politician, although admittedly in Campion's case the two roles are not simultaneous. The General has designs on a post in India, and Sylvia wants to marry him in order that she may relieve her boredom by following him to the East. She pictures herself as an Indian Cleopatra, with "a lover gasping at her feet, exclaiming, 'I am dying, India, dying.'" Her former view of Tietjens as dully conventional has not altered considerably but she has slowly readied herself to accept his situation by deciding that "It is, in the end—the function of God and the invisible Powers to see that a good man shall eventually be permitted to settle down to a

A NEW BEGINNING

stuffy domestic life (. . .) even to chaffering over old furniture. . . . God is probably—and—very rightly—on the side of the stuffy domesticities. Otherwise the world could not continue—the children would not be healthy. And certainly God desired the production of large crops of healthy children."[131]

One of Sylvia's difficulties is that, in her precarious faith, she cannot conceive of a God who is more than restrictive or stuffily domestic. She cannot, that is, conceive of a type of emotional expressiveness that is neither self-indulgent nor stuffy, but that in itself has an element of spirituality, and represents a means of religious aspiration. Sylvia, as is even evident in her inner tension between the spirit of Father Consett and the desire to torment Christopher, is emotionally and morally confused, and part of this confusion stems from her tendency to fix her ideas of God and of passion at two different poles. She cannot find the synthesis through which she might once have given Christopher the encouragement to respond with the more open side of himself.

In this post-War climate of moral confusion and comic aristocrats, Tietjens must operate and remain a stable force. His major stability is gained, of course, through his full commitment to Valentine, and his life is now defined by the specific emotional involvement. By relinquishing Groby and living in his small cottage, he has cut his ties with the broken past and become a "Small Producer." His self-sufficiency is bolstered by his entry into the antique furniture business. By dealing in old furniture, Christopher also maintains a small tie with tradition, and he becomes the person for whom others receive the small relics of the tradition that the second-hand chairs and tables represent. Ford is suggesting here, and by the details of Christopher's new life in general, that the nature of his change is a major but not a radical one. It is an attempt to conserve the best of the traditional values in a world where they no longer have an institutional context, and where, therefore, the limited hero must create his own milieu. And Christopher's achieved stability becomes the suggestive force behind the series of reconciliations, which together add the dimension of faith on which the novel concludes.

Mark is moved directly by Christopher, whereas Sylvia is moved indirectly by a recognition of the reality of her husband's achievement, and directly by the spirit of Father Consett. Sylvia's change of attitude is the more sudden of the two, but part of its abruptness can be accounted for by her own polarities of character. Just after her sense of triumph over the cutting of Groby Great Tree, Sylvia is once again overcome by her guilt and a sense of Father Consett's presence;

> At any rate, up over the landscape, the hills, the sky, she felt the shadow of Father Consett, the arms extended as if in a great cruciform. . . . She was aware that God—or perhaps it was Father Consett

that arranged it more diplomatically, the dear!—desired that she should apply to Rome for the dissolution of her marriage with Christopher and that she should apply to the civil courts. She thought that probably God desired that Christopher should be freed as early as possible, Father Consett suggesting to him the less stringent course.

On her arrival at Christopher's cottage, Sylvia orders Mrs. de Bray Pape, whom she had sent to torment Christopher, to leave, and then announces: "Damn it all, I had Groby Great Tree torn down: not that tin Maintenon. But as God is my Saviour I would not tear another woman's child in the womb!" And to Valentine she adds, "It was Father Consett really (. . .) They can all, soon, call you Mrs. Tietjens. Before God I came to drive those people out (. . . .) But I wanted to see how it was you kept him." Valentine herself gains a new insight into Sylvia's difficulties, and Sylvia's face seems to her "Dark shadowed under the eyes. And sorrowful. And tremendously dignified. And *kind*."[132] Each in this scene directly encounters the other for the first time, and each also encounters her own private guilt. And just as Sylvia is forced to sense the rightness of Christopher's situation, so Valentine is able to feel secure enough in Christopher to feel compassion for Sylvia. Each is given a new strength by Christopher's new way of life.

Mark's reconciliation is especially significant in that it both closes the tetralogy and expresses his affirmation through Christopher of the same future he had recently renounced. After he has resolved for himself the questions of his father's death and the parentage of Sylvia's child, Mark has a strong sense of a divine reality. He hears, "a rushing sound," and feels, although with some doubts of his own feelings, "the presence of the Almighty walking upon the firmament." Christopher returns, appearing for the first time in the novel, and he is momentarily broken as he holds a piece of Groby Great Tree in his hand. As he leaves, Valentine suffers a moment of doubt, during which, despite the fact that both reject great wealth, she wonders how they are to live. And Mark, who had so long been silent, is moved to speak to her, and to admonish her never to be harsh with Christopher: "Never thou let thy barnie weep for thy sharp tongue to thy good-man (. . . .) A good man!" And with this final expression of faith in his brother, Mark asks Valentine to hold his hand and dies.[133] His affirmation becomes all the more striking if we recall that Christopher's relinquishing of Groby had been one of the two causes of Mark's willful silence. Thus Christopher is able to build on the ruins of his old world, a new one that evokes the confidence even of the adherents of the old.

The nature of this new world of limited heroism became an increasingly central concern for Ford during the final decade of his life. Since the Tietjens novels were pivotal to this change of focus, they contained

A NEW BEGINNING

aspects of both the old and new variants of heroism; and the Tietjens who was seen at the end of the tetralogy was a greatly changed figure from the rather conventional aristocrat who had sat in the railway carriage with Macmaster at the start of the series. Admittedly, the seeds of this change —Tietjens' internal doubts and his overt opposition to the callousness of certain members of his class—were evident in *Some Do Not*. But these small indications, as we have seen, were very much modified by a double attitude, which in itself diminished throughout the first three novels and became a device by which Ford directed our responses to his main character. It was not until he had experienced a series of trials, culminating in the slow agony of the War, that Tietjens was able to achieve a sufficient degree of self-definition to consciously sever himself from his traditional world and to assume, together with Valentine Wannop, the role of the limited hero. Tietjens was even able through the evident strength of his position to inspire a somewhat lesser sense of resolution in those around him. And while the four Tietjens novels thus became the strongest fictional embodiment of both the change and its ensuing responses, the new limited heroism remained the dominant concern in Ford's work of his final period, where it was developed imaginatively in some of the novels and somewhat more didactically in the books of "travel" and social commentary.

During this period, Ford turned more and more to an explicitly personal style of non-fiction as a medium for his most pressing ideas. As the historical and political reality of the 1930's, with its increasing political violence and its overhanging threat of another world war began to take shape, Ford's sense of protest became progressively urgent. It became obvious that the First World War had not been the final culmination of the social collapse, but simply one of the many possible breaking points. The world seemed to be getting worse rather than better; and for Ford the limited hero and his way of life appeared to offer the only alternative, all the while that the existing reality caused such an alternative to seem inadvertently futile. Because of the nature of this period, during which society seemed always on the verge of destroying itself, and in which the alternative of limited heroism grew constantly more desirable, Ford's work began to veer off in two directions. The double attitude that had marked his great work fell apart into two halves; and while he continued to advocate the solution of limited heroism, he also increasingly damned the current society. Such a split in attitude was not congenial to his talents as a novelist, for it did not allow for the complexity that had characterized his major work. And Ford himself seems during his last ten years to have lost interest in his fiction, and to have turned increasingly to forms of prose which enabled him to speak more openly and directly, and to voice more strongly his sense of disturbance. His major effort during

this decade was spent on his "travel" books; and these volumes, written just prior to the outbreak of the Second World War, reflected a certainty of impending danger, and a sense that the world had to be shown the way of the limited hero before it became too late.

NOTES

[1] Ford Madox Hueffer, *When Blood Is Their Argument, An Analysis of Prussian Culture* (New York, London, 1915), p. 311.
[2] *Ibid.*, p. 20.
[3] *Ibid.*, pp. 316–317.
[4] *Ibid.*, pp. 56–57.
[5] *Ibid.*, p. 65.
[6] *Ibid.*, p. 206.
[7] *Ibid.*, p. 55.
[8] Hueffer, "Preface" to *When Blood Is*, p. x.
[9] Hueffer, *When Blood Is*, p. 318.
[10] Ford Madox Hueffer, *Between St. Dennis and St. George, A Sketch of Three Civilizations* (London, New York, Toronto, 1915), pp. 9–11, 226.
[11] *Ibid.*, p. 245.
[12] *Ibid.*, p. 34.
[13] *Ibid.*, pp. 190–191.
[14] *Ibid.*, p. 80.
[15] Ford Madox Ford, *Return to Yesterday, Reminiscences 1894–1914* (London, 1931), p. 405.
[16] Hueffer, *Between St. Dennis*, p. 12.
[17] *Ibid.*, pp. 54–55.
[18] *Ibid.*, pp. 85–86.
[19] *Ibid.*, p. 68.
[20] *Ibid.*, pp. 77–78.
[21] *Ibid.*, pp. 194–195, 222.
[22] Ford Madox Ford, *Joseph Conrad, A Personal Remembrance* (London, 1924), p. 205.
[23] Hueffer, *Between St. Dennis*, pp. 184–185.
[24] Douglas Goldring, *South Lodge* (London, 1943), p. 145.
[25] Ford Madox Ford, "Chroniques," *transatlantic review*, I (January, 1924), 84.
[26] Ford Madox Ford, "Chroniques," *transatlantic review*, I (February, 1924), 69–70.
[27] Ford, "Chroniques," *transatlantic review*, I (January, 1924), 84.
[28] Ford Madox Ford, "Pax!," *Harper's*, CLV (September, 1927), 429.
[29] Ford Madox Ford, "And on Earth Peace," *New York Essays* (New York, 1927), p. 19.
[30] Ford Madox Ford, *It Was the Nightingale* (Philadelphia, London, 1933), pp. 24, 100–101, 63.
[31] *Ibid.*, pp. 260, 270.
[32] Ford Madox Ford, "Chroniques," *transatlantic review*, I (April, 1924), 197–198.
[33] Ford, *Conrad*, pp. 258–259.

A NEW BEGINNING

[34] Ford Madox Ford, *The Marsden Case, A Romance* (London, 1923), pp. 55, 160–161.
[35] *Ibid.*, pp. 218–219.
[36] *Ibid.*, p. 337.
[37] *Ibid.*, pp. 13, 304–305.
[38] Paul Wiley, *Novelist of Three Worlds: Ford Madox Ford* (Syracuse, 1962), p. 211.
[39] Ford, *Return to Yesterday*, pp. 416–417.
[40] Ford Madox Hueffer, *The Critical Attitude* (London, 1911), pp. 29–30.
[41] Wiley, p. 204.
[42] Ford, *Nightingale*, p. 199.
[43] E. V. Walter, "Political Sense of Ford Madox Ford," *New Republic*, CXXXIV (March 26, 1956), 17.
[44] Ford, *Nightingale*, p. 226.
[45] *Ibid.*, pp. 209–210.
[46] Wiley, p. 214.
[47] Ford, *Nightingale*, p. 222.
[48] Ford, *Return to Yesterday*, p. 359.
[49] Goldring, *South Lodge*, pp. 16–17.
[50] Ford, *Nightingale*, pp. 217–219.
[51] Robie Macauley, "Introduction" to *Parade's End* (New York, 1961), p. viii.
[52] John A. Meixner, *Ford Madox Ford's Novels: A Critical Study* (Minneapolis, 1962), pp. 203–204.
[53] J. J. Firebaugh, "Tietjens and the Tradition," *Pacific Spectator*, VI, 1 (1952), p. 30.
[54] Richard Cassell, *Ford Madox Ford: A Study of His Novels* (Baltimore, 1961), pp. 214–215.
[55] Melvin Seiden, "The Living Dead—VI, Ford Madox Ford and His Tetralogy," *London Magazine*, VI (1959), 49–50, 52.
[56] Meixner, *Ford's Novels*, pp. 221–231.
[57] Ford Madox Ford, *Some Do Not*, in *Parade's End* (New York, 1961), pp. 3–4. All subsequent references to the four volumes (*A Man Could Stand Up, The Last Post, Some Do Not,* and *No More Parades*) of the Tietjens tetralogy refer to this edition.
[58] Macauley, "Introduction" to *Parade's End*, p. vii.
[59] Ford, *Some Do Not*, pp. 6–9.
[60] *Ibid.*, p. 18.
[61] *Ibid.*, pp. 121, 127.
[62] *Ibid.*, pp. 32, 39–42.
[63] Macauley, "Introduction" to *Parade's End*, p. xii.
[64] Ford, *Some Do Not*, pp. 74–77.
[65] *Ibid.*, pp. 20–21.
[66] Macauley, "Introduction" to *Parade's End*, pp. vii–ix.
[67] Ford, *Some Do Not*, pp. 67, 86.
[68] *Ibid.*, pp. 96–98, 103, 107–108.
[69] *Ibid.*, p. 79.
[70] *Ibid.*, pp. 128–137.
[71] *Ibid.*, pp. 139–144.
[72] Walter, p. 18.
[73] Ford, *Some Do Not*, pp. 151, 156–158, 167–170, 172–174.
[74] *Ibid.*, pp. 176–177.

75 *Ibid.*, pp. 208–211.
76 *Ibid.*, pp. 214, 218, 222–223.
77 *Ibid.*, p. 229.
78 *Ibid.*, pp. 229–233.
79 *Ibid.*, p. 268.
80 *Ibid.*, pp. 237–239.
81 *Ibid.*, pp. 282–284.
82 Ford, *No More Parades*, p. 289.
83 *Ibid.*, pp. 296–297.
84 *Ibid.*, pp. 306–307.
85 Macauley, "Introduction" to *Parade's End*, p. xiv.
86 Ford, *No More Parades*, pp. 365–366.
87 *Ibid.*, pp. 309–311, 355–356, 359.
88 Ford, *Nightingale*, p. 216.
89 Ford, *No More Parades*, p. 336.
90 *Ibid.*, pp. 370, 377, 499–500.
91 *Ibid.*, pp. 300–301.
92 *Ibid.*, pp. 342–350.
93 *Ibid.*, pp. 379–380, 400.
94 *Ibid.*, pp. 414–417, 436–437.
95 *Ibid.*, p. 412.
96 *Ibid.*, p. 387.
97 *Ibid.*, p. 444.
98 *Ibid.*, pp. 444–464.
99 *Ibid.*, pp. 477–483, 489–490, 494–495, 499.
100 *Ibid.*, p. 454.
101 Ford, *A Man Could Stand Up*, p. 509.
102 *Ibid.*, pp. 514, 518.
103 *Ibid.*, pp. 518–521, 534–542.
104 *Ibid.*, pp. 569, 619.
105 *Ibid.*, pp. 550, 554.
106 *Ibid.*, p. 570.
107 *Ibid.*, pp. 607, 629, 630.
108 *Ibid.*, pp. 564–567.
109 Ford, *The Last Post*, pp. 813–814.
110 Ford Madox Ford, *The March of Literature from Confucius' Day to Our Own* (New York, 1938), p. 470.
111 Ford, *A Man Could Stand Up*, p. 633.
112 *Ibid.*, pp. 237–644, 657.
113 *Ibid.*, pp. 647, 668.
114 *Ibid.*, pp. 663, 666–667.
115 Ford, *The Last Post*, pp. 778, 820–821.
116 Ford, *A Man Could Stand Up*, pp. 673–674.
117 Macauley, "Introduction" to *Parade's End*, pp. xvii, xxi.
118 Douglas Goldring, *Trained for Genius* (New York, 1949), p. 258.
119 Ford, *The Last Post*, pp. 679, 688–690, 735.
120 *Ibid.*, pp. 703–704.
121 *Ibid.*, p. 727.
122 *Ibid.*, p. 745.
123 *Ibid.*, pp. 722–723, 831–832.
124 *Ibid.*, pp. 730, 831.

A NEW BEGINNING

[125] Arthur Mizener, "A Large Fiction," *Kenyon Review*, XII (Winter, 1951), 142–147.
[126] Meixner, *Ford's Novels*, pp. 220–221.
[127] Ford, *No More Parades*, pp. 345–348.
[128] Ford, *The Last Post*, p. 716.
[129] *Ibid.*, pp. 709–712, 718.
[130] *Ibid.*, pp. 801–802.
[131] *Ibid.*, pp. 779–781, 794, 795.
[132] *Ibid.*, pp. 806–808, 826–827.
[133] *Ibid.*, pp. 833–836.

5.

The Late Work and the Limited Hero

SEEN IN TERMS of limited heroism and the double perspective, Ford's work from 1929 to 1939, the final decade of his life, poses a new set of problems; for whereas the limited hero is presented with a forceful and even didactic affirmation in his non-fiction, the novels, strangely enough, suffer from a decline of power and a simplicity of view that sets them apart from Ford's great work. The causes of this decline can be found in the author's reaction to a world that was balanced precariously between the end of one great war and the threat of another. This world was even more frightening than the one in which Ford had grown up. The War had changed everything—and hardly for the better—but with the answer of limited heroism on which he ended the Tietjens novels, Ford had seemed almost optimistic about the possibility of individual survival. But when he quickly sensed that another cataclysm was on the way, the mood that had dominated the end of the Tietjens tetralogy began to wane, to be replaced by a new note of urgency, indeed, almost—as Ford admitted—a prophetic foreboding as frenzied nationalism and the firing squad became commonplace.

The conflicting demands made on his attention by this near despair, on the one hand, and the desire to extend the values of limited heroism, on the other, brought about a significant dichotomy in Ford's work. This manifested itself in apparent simplification and carelessness in the novels, and a directing of effort toward the more didactic works of non-fiction—especially the two "travel" books, *Provence* and *Great Trade Route*. Ford's own values throughout the 1930's remained essentially the same as those developed in the Tietjens novels, but they were colored now by a much more urgent sense of impending doom. Simply living these values and attempting persuasion by example no longer seemed to be enough. Thus the final "travel" books, though still drawn from Ford's private impressions, carried a new note of moral exhortation. And as Ford pushed his effort into these "travel" books, and into volumes of autobiography marked by the same sense of foreboding, his novels understandably suffered, and became for the most part dark and external pictures of a world undermined by rootlessness. Such pessimistic renderings could not, however, incorporate to Ford's satisfaction the answers and the sense of

urgency that he wanted to convey. The complex and relatively dispassionate portrait of cultural decay to which the novel lent itself no longer seemed, as it once had, to engage his interest. Although the substance of his thought remained constant, its tone had changed; and the need for didactic statement resulted in the dichotomy of purpose and the generic difference in quality that are so evident in Ford's final work.

Ford began his final decade with *No Enemy*, an autobiographical novel affirming the mode of life of the limited hero. Almost pastoral in tone, this was to be Ford's last serene presentation of the solution of limited heroism. The book contrasted sharply with his "travel" volumes in which this ideal was already shadowed by the menacing reality to totalitarian political power. The final books were pervaded by the juxtaposition of the "Small Producer" and the firing squad and their tonal contrast with *No Enemy* underlines the problem in Ford's work during the final decade of his life.

Even at his most didactic, however, Ford never attempted to establish a systematic social or political scheme. Nor is there any evidence to support Paul Wiley's interpretation of his late works as a new mythology. Rather, these writings can be seen, in line with the aims and techniques of his earlier works, as impressionistic evocations of the post-War world and of such alternatives as seemed personally meaningful. Such a reading is the only one that is consistent with a total picture of the author's work. The conclusions of the "travel" books were not given as objective truths, but as fragments of opinion on a particular situation. As if to emphasize that his "travel" books were simply records of personal thought, Ford wrote them in a style very similar to that in which he had rendered the thoughts of Christopher Tietjens on the battlefield. His statements in these books were no less private than the thoughts of his fictional hero, and they were no less public in what Ford hoped would be their moral relevance. He was trying to persuade his readers to adopt a new way of life, not through myth or political program, but through an impressionistic symbolism that was essentially subjective in tone. In the "travel" books the point of departure from the fiction was simply the greater urgency that Ford felt as he looked about him, an urgency that caused him to throw off his mask of fictional impartiality and declare the view point very much his own.

In the late non-fiction two seemingly conflicting methods are employed. On the one hand, there is a new tendency to exhort the reader, to argue and comment on the impressions in a sustained way that the novel cannot allow. On the other hand, Ford's distrust of the general statement, of the appended lesson, is still very much in evidence. The apparent conflict of these two strategies is avoided in the "travel" books through the device of a personal interior monologue. Thus Ford is able to retain the concreteness of impressionism, and yet intrude openly into the writ-

ing and present his views. In this way, he is able to comment and digress without seeming either too general or overly tendentious. The total effect is even closer to the stream of consciousness found in the Tietjens novels. The "travel" books can almost be regarded as an autobiography of the author during the 1930's, with the emphasis on ideas rather than events.

The nature of the post-War world strongly jolted Ford's ideal of dispassionate rendering and ruling by example, and brought about a major shift in his view of his own artistic role. The world was marked by two tendencies: a growing standardization, which left a climate of potentially-explosive apathy; and an upsurge of totalitarian nationalism, which appealed to the latent passions and hatreds of the populace. The standardization brought about a lack of involvement for many people in the small but recurrent details of their lives, and the resultant apathy left these same people susceptible to the combination of force and rhetoric with which they were swayed by ambitious dictators and cunning politicians. In order to counter this ever more forceful rhetoric, the artist as Ford now saw him would have to become a more explicit moralist, all the while that he adhered to his highly personal way of life.

In 1933 Ford published his autobiographical volume, *It Was the Nightingale*, in which he recounted his life from the end of the War through the early 1930's. One of the most significant qualities of this volume was its relatively early sensitivity to the danger posed by the rise of Hitler. At this point, the German dictator still seemed primarily a threat to the freedom of the arts; and this threat, introduced early in the book, hovers darkly over the entire narrative. As in his other autobiographical works, Ford did not strive here for accuracy of fact. In the introductory letter to Eugene Pressly, he remarked that he had used "every wile known to me as a novelist."[1] His aim was to capture accurately the mood of the period, and the mood of the post-War years is quickly established by the use of the title image. The author tells us that he has just seen a nightingale narrowly escape being eaten by a rat: "It seemed a fantastic and horrible conjunction, that of rat and nightingale. But after all, all poets are at outs with (. . .) let us say, their bankers. Having been, as you see, an editor, I dislike saying that editors are all the same as rats."[2] The nightingale signified the artist, whereas the rat stood for the hostile forces of society; and in spite of the jocular tone, it is clear that Ford felt a sense of imminent danger for the bird. But the rat was still an unspecified part of "the flood of laymen" who "will in the end submerge us all and dance on our graves," and who, a few pages later, were likened to Hitler:

> The layman hates the artist as the atrocious Mr. Hitler hates learning. Indeed the layman regards the artist as a sort of Jew. But to the measure of the light vouchsafed, my late comrades shine in their

places and may be content. The *pogroms* will come but, even as Heine, the greatest of German poets, they have lit beacons that posterity shall not willingly let die.³

Ford also sensed that Germany and Italy had designs on Europe. In 1933 the awful magnitude of Hitler's threat had not yet become fully evident, but by the time of the "travel" books of the late 1930's, Ford clearly saw the threat as extending far beyond the sphere of the solitary nightingale.

Ford's early sensitivity to the developments in Germany arose from his general dislike of the politician. Later in *It Was the Nightingale*, he likened Hitler to the one-time Prime Minister, Lloyd George, who had confined him to England after the First World War: "Once you have said that Mr. Lloyd George was responsible for all the sorrows that beset our poor civilization or that Mr. Hitler is the anti-Christ of culture you have said all that is to be said and it is monotonous to repeat even truth."⁴ Hitler was, that is to say, not an entirely new phenomenon. He was more rhetorical, more charismatic, and far more insane than the conventional politician; but he came from the same stock. Like the earlier politician, he could distort reality through the frequent use of rhetoric, and also like the politician, he could through the power at his disposal enforce the false reality which he created. But the new dictator—the Hitler or the Mussolini—differed from Lloyd George and his compatriots in two significant ways: he was likely to support his authority not only with political power, but with mass violence; and he was motivated not only by the considerations of power politics, but by a fervent and obsessive nationalism. The rhetoric on which his power rested was built upon an exaggerated sense of national destiny; and his nationalism was not only self-inflating, but led also to hatred of all those outside the select group. Ford confessed to feeling a "hatred for hatred," which he considered "the most maiming of all passions," as well as a monomania that curtailed all the normal human powers of judgement. "Prussia," he argued, "lost the late war because she completely misunderstood what was passing in the minds of her opponents," and "because she did not understand that though Christendom is vague in its boundaries yet by the tradition of centuries and the gradual growth of a conscience a little sense of chivalry has arisen in us."⁵ The ideal of chivalry, unlike nationalism, had bred an ethic of love and service. Nationalism only made men line themselves up on one side of a wall and their opponents against it. It created an "imaginary 'frontier,'" and was a "madness that the gods sent to people whom they are about to destroy."⁶ It was, finally and simply, another of the many forms of public heroism to which Ford, throughout his life, was so consistently opposed.

Against the new heroics of nationalism, Ford raised the medieval code

of chivalry. It was not a code to which a man could return on any sort of cultural scale. Had there been any danger of chivalry assuming the proportions of public heroism, Ford might well have been repulsed by it. It is important to realize that even though chivalry differed greatly from nationalism in tone and spirit—for it was marked by the ideals of humanity, service and spiritual as well as courtly love—Ford did not see chivalry as simply an alternate public ideal. Rather it became for him symbolic of an ethical tone that he wished to see reinstated in the modern world. The revised code was to become not so much a mass phenomenon as a pervasive spirit, which each person might manifest for himself in his daily life, and which he might pass on to others not by rules, but by his own example. In *The March of Literature* Ford blamed Cervantes for the loss of this spirit from the world. "The gentle ideal of chivalry," he said, "is the one medieval trait which, had it survived as an influence, might have saved our unfortunate civilization. Cervantes by his vulgar kick in the behind to its departing form covered it with a ridicule that is perpetuated by every schoolboy-minded contemporary who guffaws over the distresses of the good knight of La Mancha."[7] Cervantes' "kick in the behind" was a blow, Ford felt, from which the chivalric spirit had never recovered.

One of the major characteristics of the medieval spirit was a strong sense of religious faith and human limitation. A man's heroic acts, as Ford made clear in *Ladies Whose Bright Eyes*, were not done for his own glory, but for the glory of God. Faith was also an important factor in many of his novels, particularly in the Katherine Howard trilogy, *Mr. Apollo,* and the Tietjens tetralogy. It was, moreover, the central theme of a short story, "The Miracle," published by Ford in the *Yale Review* in 1928. In this story a highly successful professor, a scientist, confesses to his wife that a crucial war experience has given him faith in a divine providence.[8] With such a recurring concern throughout his work, it was not surprising that Ford, as he came to feel more and more the need in modern life for some standard of values, was attracted by an ideal of which individual faith was one of the principal elements.

With the decline of faith and the waning of individual involvement in everyday life, Ford sensed that an increasingly standardized mediocrity was spreading over the western world. He related how he had once been terribly dismayed, upon entering a restaurant in Avignon that he "had found admirable for thirty years," to learn that he was being "offered Norwegian anchovies with *hors d'oeuvres* and *pêche Melba* with California peaches out of a tin."[9] Beyond this growing standardization, which was simply another manifestation of the general apathy, lurked the spectre of Fascism. Ford commented on the decline of the Italian Riviera during the early years of Mussolini's government, and remarked how the Flatiron Building in New York had "captured the imagination of the

region that produced the Forum Romanum, the Colosseum, the Campanile of Venice, *aiolo* (. . .) and the uniform worn by the *facisti*."¹⁰ The new political heroism, compounded of nationalism and violence, made it all the more urgent that a way of life be found which would involve the individual and provide a counterforce to the new regimes that were daily placing their opponents against a wall.

The life of the "Small Producer," a life in which the chivalric spirit might be revived on an individual basis, seemed to Ford the only answer. "It is impossible to escape the conclusion," he wrote in 1935, in an article entitled "The Small Producer," "that we are in a world of weakening pulses. And even if it could continue on its way the problems of the machine dispossessing the worker must of necessity grow more and more crucial within, and between, nation and nation. There is only one escape: the dispossessed masses must go back to the land."¹¹ Through such a return to the land, the values that Ford advocated could become embodied in an individual style of life, rather than in a public superstructure. And for Ford himself, settled in France since 1922, the country to the south of England came increasingly to be his adopted land and to stand for those values which were most central to his thought.

A Mirror to France, one of Ford's many examinations of French civilization, appeared in 1926. Early in its pages the author stated that "The *chose donnée* . . . of this book is: that chivalric generosity, frugality, pure thought and the arts are the first requisites of a Civilization—and the only requisites of a Civilization; and then that such traces of chivalric generosity, frugality, pure thought and the arts as our pre-War, European civilization of white races could exhibit came to us from the district of Southern France on the shores of the Mediterranean."¹² The tone of *A Mirror to France* recalled those sections of *Between St. Dennis and St. George* in which Ford had advocated French culture as far superior to that of either Germany or England. And eleven years after his volume of propaganda had appeared, he was able to write of this book in his later work that "In spite of the fact that it was published as what was called propaganda, I used to like to think that it would be the book of mind by which I should be remembered if I were to be remembered." By 1926, Ford had to admit that the West had not made the choice which he had advocated during the War; it had adopted the way of France. "The late war," he wrote, "has changed the equipoise of material civilization from the Mediterranean to the Atlantic." Now, the world was dominated "by that Mass Production that is the one symbol of our two-branched Anglo-Saxon commonwealths," the production system that has resulted in "the white-tiled bathroom" being "turned out by the hundred thousand daily and provided with nickelled fixings and glass shelves."¹³

In the mediocre and violent post-War world, the role of the artist, grew for Ford increasingly urgent. Like the "Small Producer," the artist

was an individual craftsman, who was to teach by example, but as the social milieu grew progressively worse the teaching gradually took precedence over craft. In 1921 Ford described the reawakening, after the War, of his own desire to write:

> Then . . . came a serious call once more to revisit the glimpses of the moon. . . . But once one is tempted from green tranquillities, it is not easy to close one's ears to the groans of the Body-Politic. And who will deny that today the republic groans in all its numbers? Indeed, despair can seldom have been so general in a State not immediately menaced by Fire, Famine, Pestilence, or Strife in Arms!
> So there re-awakened in the Writer the passionate belief that Creative Literature—Poetry—is the sole panacea for the ills of harrassed humanity . . . . For Creative Literature is the only thing that can explain to man the nature of his fellow men . . . . But to do, and to be this, an Art must be exact, not an intoxicated, occupation and Artist must be self-less.[14]

By 1938, Ford wrote in *The March of Literature from Confucius to Modern Times* that although the artist "should altogether eschew—any impulses to put his *imaginative* pen at the service of any cause whatever," there was "no objection to an imaginative author's taking whatever part he pleases in direct political action; so long as he feels conscientiously convinced that he is a proper man to interfere in the destinies of a fellow man there is no reason that he should not—nay, there is every reason why he should—vote, write pamphlets, fight on barricades or in wars for great causes."[15] He had not given up his idea that the most effective art was that which most exactly observed and rendered the characteristics of its time, but he placed a much stronger emphasis than he had in his *transatlantic review* essay on art and politics on the idea that it was the "duty" of the artist, "like every other citizen . . . to persuade his day to improve itself."[16] It is clear that the historical conditions that were evident by the time he published his one-volume literary history caused Ford to question his previous views on the artist and society, and to modify them to the extent of saying that although art was still the best possible solution for a sick civilization, it was not in itself the only valid activity in which the artist could engage. The times were so pressing that even the artist might justifiably call himself to arms.

Ford's increasing emphasis on the moral relevance of art, as opposed to its more dispassionate rendering of reality, was reflected in the reappraisal of Dostoevsky which he set forth on the final page of *The March of Literature*. In 1938 Ford contended that this Russian novelist,

> man of letters though he was, must be considered to be the greatest single influence on the world of today. . . . It would be absurd to claim him as a realist because his literary equipment is that of the

romantics; but it would be absurd not to call him a realist, because the images he calls up are more real than life, and as visions have outlasted the lives of generations of men. The multitude of his characters is that of the crowds you will see piling into and out of vast industrial works; as a psychologist he surpasses anyone who ever delved into the human mind.

This statement, at the end of Ford's history of literature and almost at the end of his life, was his first acknowledgement of Dostoevsky's greatness. Earlier, Ford had considered him too passionate and too formless to rank among the artists of letters. But it is clearly apparent in his later statement that Ford's scale of values had shifted. He grew more interested in the psychology to be found in Dostoevsky's novels, a psychology that was often structured upon tormenting dualisms, and that often rested on the question of faith. These two elements of Dostoevskian psychology—the emphasis on character dualisms and the problem of faith—had already become a part of Ford's major novels; and Ford himself implied his debt and provided a clue to his own literary intent in the conclusion to *The March of Literature*.

Ford's intent had been most fully realized in *The Good Soldier* and the Tietjens tetralogy, in both of which the use of the double point of view had become a key device for rendering and controlling his pervasive moral concerns. During the 1930's, despite a lessening of this dualism in the late novels, certain devices which the author at least shared with Dostoevsky, such as the figure of the double, could still be discerned. Certainly, Ford might have derived his use of the double, or even his pronounced utilization of a dualistic psychology, from sources other than Dostoevsky, but the presence of these elements in Ford's major novels along with his increasing admiration for the Russian novelist, suggests a significant relationship. And the case for Dostoevsky's influence on Ford is further strengthened by the latter's comments on the future of the novel. Looking at the direction which he desired the novel to take in later years, Ford said: "We might prophecy, thus, that the 'great' work of art of the future will come from the fusion of the genius of Dostoevsky with the art of the impressionists."[17] Years earlier, in comparing Dostoevsky with Turgenev, Ford had called the author of *Crime and Punishment* "that portentious writer of enormous detective stories" and "that sad man with the native Slav genius for telling immensely long and formless tales."[18] But as his views on art began to center less on craft alone, and more on a synthesis of craft and moral concern, Ford grew to see Dostoevsky as much greater in perspective, and the Russian writer came to be a strong influence on Ford's own concept of the art of the novel.

To the end, Ford's primary allegiance remained with the arts, but as the need for a moral standard came to seem more and more imperative, he began to see art as less self-contained and as needing a more explicit moral

position on the part of the artist. By 1926, when he wrote *A Mirror to France*, even Victorian morality did not seem to him totally undesirable. It was still, as he saw it, an evasion of reality, but it had come "at a time of immense, of incredible material development," and it had acted upon this development as a "safeguard" against total corruption, so that, as Ford said, "we may as well speculate as to whether the world might not have been much worse without" it.[19] Like his views on that artist and society, Ford's re-evaluation of Victorian morality was not a radical change, but a shift in emphasis. In *The March of Literature* he could still speak of "The Victorian imaginative writers" as retreating "into worlds other than their own" and "turning their backs on their own day."[20] But the conditions of the post-War years, just because they so strongly impressed on Ford the need for a moral standard, also enabled him to see the morality of the Great Victorians with a double perspective. Although it had been a false and inadequate standard, it now seemed better than no standard at all.

The modification, which resulted in Ford's taking an explicit moral stance, were strong enough during the 1930's that for the first time his non-fiction assumed a dominant place in his work. As the violent post-War world seemed headed toward another war, his advocacy of the limited hero grew increasingly distressed. But just because his hero seemed so contrary to that of the actual world, Ford felt that the picture of this world which he could draw in his novels was no longer adequate to his intent, and turned instead to non-fiction through which he could address his readers directly. Only on this basis are the weakness of intent and carelessness of execution in his late novels explicable. For although they focused on the problems of the existing world, they were no longer informed by the double perspective so important in Ford's major fiction. Moreover, only one of the novels—*Henry for Hugh*—attempted to affirm limited heroism as an answer to these problems, and even then, contrivance and coincidence were so heavily relied on that it remained a much weaker statement of this solution than the "travel" books which quickly followed.

The other late novels were also marred by numerous faults, similar to those of the early novels, but now far more pronounced. There was little of the complexity of *The Good Soldier* or the Tietjens novels, and the author seemed to be satisfied with the creation of contrived situations and stock character types. Much of the material was taken from the popular fiction of the period. *When the Wicked Man*, for example, showed traces of the gangster novel, and *Vive Le Roy* was little more than a tangled and artificial political intrigue. This conventional material was often badly developed; and the obvious artificiality of the situations made the novels seem irrelevant to the very problems which they attempted to evoke. The lack of complex characters further reduced the sense of significance fo-

the stereotyped and distorted figures scarcely seemed to mirror anything in the realm of real or imagined experience. Thus, as Ford let go of the subtlety and technical control which had once distinguished his novels, his fiction became less and less convincing and only indirectly relevant to the problems of the period.

No Enemy, published in 1929, though supposedly fiction, was an autobiographical novel in which Ford minutely detailed his post-War adjustment. In this novel he was less concerned with creating characters than with projecting a way of life, so that the hero's discussions and recollections of the War are framed throughout by his life as a "Small Producer." The central character, Gringoire, was a poet who had gone to live on a small plot of land. His consciousness provided the novel's point of view, but he remained a point of departure rather than a fully developed person. It was his frame of mind that mattered, and he might just as well have been Ford himself. *No Enemy* was autobiographical to the extent that Gringoire's attitudes were very much Ford's, and some of his recollections were of people, such as the sculptor, Gaudier-Brzeska, with whom Ford was actually acquainted. In the introductory letter to Esther Julia Madox Ford, his daughter by Stella Bowen, the author wrote that "You shall find here adumberated what the world seemed like to me just when you were preparing to enter it (. . . . . .) a confused world which your coming rendered so much clearer and dearer."[21] Unlike Ford, however, Gringoire was throughout the War a fully committed "Small Producer." He may have been a thinly-veiled representation of Ford, but his attitude mirrored little of the tension between the old and the new that the author must have felt, and which he rendered fictionally in the character of Christopher Tietjens.

Gringoire's impressions of the War, all of which document his "reconstruction" as a "Small Producer" on which the book begins and ends, fall into two parts; the presentation of "four landscapes" and then of "certain interiors," all of which were meaningful to him during his army years. The impressions in the first section are built around the theme of sensitivity to landscape, and those in the second part around that of dedication to work. These are the two basic elements of Gringoire's "reconstruction," and *No Enemy* is his public acknowledgement of their importance. The novel is significant because it is the first in which Ford treats in detail the limited hero's post-War mode of life. The book undertakes the task which Ford had temporarily set aside when, in *The Last Post*, he had focused on the responses of the other characters rather than those of Tietjens himself. With Gringoire, however, Ford concentrates on the orientation of a limited hero, already secure in his chosen role and very much aware of those prerequisites by which it once had been attained.

As Gringoire thinks back to his war experiences, the four moments when he had noticed "four landscapes . . . for themselves" become again

the most vivid incidents of the entire four years.[22] These had been moments when he was able to feel closest to the land, and to regain the vital sense of privacy that was threatened by the soldier's life and by the War itself, which destroyed those small corners of land where seclusion might be found. All through the War, Gringoire had looked inside himself, so that when he is asked by the narrator how he has achieved such serenity, he can reply, "By trying to establish what that old fool Tolstoi called the Kingdom of God within me."[23] At the time he entered the army, Gringoire had already attained the degree of internal focus which Christopher Tietjens develops only through a long and painful trial. The War did not force any radical change in Gringoire's response, but simply strengthened his resolve to live afterwards as a "Small Producer." By thus making Gringoire's response a stable factor, Ford was able in *No Enemy* to focus on the nature of that response, rather than, as he had in *Parade's End*, on the growth of a character. *No Enemy* became, therefore, in spite of its historical context, one of Ford's most serene and optimistic books.

The "four landscapes" induced those four brief moments of privacy in which Gringoire was able to renew his sense of intimacy with the land. They were significant in that they allowed him to reaffirm himself and thereby to survive the War. The first landscape had appeared on "the day in 1915 when Kensington Gardens suddenly grew visible." It had taken the form of an internal vision, a sensing of the past and of the historicity of the land. "And Gringoire thought that old, stiff marionettes, rather homely courtiers and royalties, might step out of the tall windows onto the lawns and, holding tasseled canes to their lips, bow, pirouette and make legs, till the long chestnut wigs brushed the stiff rosebushes." As suddenly as it began, the vision had ended, and "the weight once more settled down." The sense of the past had changed to a fear that the land, rich in its traditions, would be invaded. As he recalls this incident, Gringoire asks the narrator, "I wonder if other people had, like myself, that feeling that what one feared for was the land—not the people but the menaced earth with its familiar aspect."

If the landscape of Kensington Gardens had set Gringoire's mind on the past, the second brief vision had, by way of contrast, fixed his thoughts upon the future. He had been waiting in a railroad station, and looking out upon "A friendless, foreign country, the Essex flats," when suddenly he began to imagine himself as a farmer in Kent after the War, and the image was so strong that he had even "considered his garden."[24] The third landscape vision had begun with an exultant sense of the present—a simple gratitude for life itself. Gringoire had been on a hillside, and had been dozing in "a pretty rotten dugout with a corrugated iron roof." A shell had suddenly "lifted his roof and dropped it again (. . .) It was his worst shock of the war." Immediately, there was a sense of triumph at the mere fact of being alive; and then from the top of the

THE LATE WORK AND THE LIMITED HERO

hill he had seen "an immense sea of blue swallows' backs." The sight of the birds made him feel as if we were "walking bouyantly, in the pellucid sunlight, waist-high through a sea of unsurpassed and unsurpassable azure. I felt," Gringoire recalls, "as if I were a Greek god. It was like a miracle."[25]

While the first three landscapes had involved Gringoire's senses of past, future, and present time, the fourth had bridged all three in a perception of the whole land and the entire world as something to be saved. Earlier, he had already decided that he was fighting "for the sake of the little threatened nooks of the earth . . . For, there," as the narrator remarks, "as on the 4/8'14, when the Huns crossed the Belgian frontier, 'near a place called Gemmenich,' it was mainly the idea that a field-gray tide of mud was seeking to overwhelm the small, verdure-masked homes, the long, white, thatched farms of the world that forced Gringoire into political action." And Gringoire also recalls how on 4 August in 1914 he had begun to write "endless, interminable propaganda; until the brain reeled and the fingers stiffened," and this effort, too, had been undertaken because "the field-gray tide threatened" all the "little sacred homes" of the earth.[26] All of these feelings had come together in the fourth vision. Gringoire had been waiting, at the top of a hill, for an officer for several hours. He had looked across the land:

> And after that it was just emotions. The landscape became landscape, with great shafts of light and shadows of clouds; the little white cottage with the green shutters, a little nook that should be inviolable; the haricots interesting as things that one might plant in a Kentish garden that sloped to the sea. The range of hills was no longer a strategic point or a tactical position. It was all that remained of one of the Kingdoms of the Earth; one could hardly look at the gray plains with the pollard willows marching along like aligned candle flames toward the horizon—one avoided looking at it because it was Lost Territory, held down, oppressed, as if it were ashamed.[27]

Even during the War at those times when he had not been alone Gringoire had tried to retain a feeling of intimate closeness with the land. There had been the momentary exultation, the lasting sense of mission; and in the hot July sun, he had tried to modify the battlefield itself; "that threatening and superhuman landscape," by playing cricket on it with his men. In this way the field took on a sense of familiarity; it "became (. . .) just a cricket field, and the frightening face which it usually wore no longer seemed quite so formidable."[28]

After he establishes his own landscape-involvement, Gringoire proceeds in the second part of the novel to explain his attitude toward work. He describes the people whom he has met within "certain interiors," and by recalling these people he develops the theme of a pride in work that

enables the individual to remain self-sufficient under the most adverse conditions. During the War, Gringoire had encountered a number of persons who had gained his admiration by their response to their work, but he had also come across some who were without involvement, and who seemed to him painful and degraded shells of their potential selves. He recalls, for example, how at a bathhouse he had seen an old man, brought in from the front lines, but possessed of a strong pride even in his menial task. The old man is quickly contrasted, however, to the French officers whom Gringoire had one day overheard complaining that their men had been assigned to menial work when they had come back from the trenches. For Gringoire, hearing these officers speak was "the most terrible moment of the war."[29] In direct contrast to these French officers there had been Lieutenant Morgan, who was killed in the trenches. Morgan had sounded for Gringoire "the note of tired but continuous laboring after a hard life." He had been a Canadian farmer, who through hard work had acquired some property in timber lots. He spoke frequently of returning to the lots after the War, "with the serene resignation of a man with no other imaginable destiny before him."[30] Lieutenant Morgan's attitude toward work had become a means of overall self-acceptance, a quality necessary to the independence of the limited hero.

But for Henri Gaudier-Brzeska, another of Gringoire's comrades, work was not only a means toward self-acceptance, but also a personal expression. Gaudier-Brzeska was able to experience pleasure through his work under the most trying conditions. This sculptor, Gringoire recalls, was drawn to enlist in the army by the bombing of Rheims Cathedral. Other works of art had to be saved. But he, too, was killed in battle "After ten months of fighting and two promotions for gallantry." Even from the battlefield, however, he could write letters of childlike wonder:

> I imagine a dull dawn, two lines of trenches, and in between explosion on explosion with clouds of black and yellow smoke, a ceaseless noise from the rifles, a few legs and heads flying, and me standing up among this like to Mephisto—commanding: 'Feu par salves à 250 mètres—joue—feu!'

With his ability to relish the aesthetic note of almost any situation, Gaudier-Brzeska had been to Gringoire a "Sacred Emperor" in "this low tea-shop that the world is."[31] And the sculptor's delight in recording his sensations in battle is similar to an impulse that Ford himself expressed in a letter to Conrad, written under German shellfire, and dated September 7, 1916:

> I wrote these rather hurried notes yesterday because we were being shelled to hell & I did not expect to get thro' the night. I wonder if it is just vanity that in these cataclysmic moments makes one desire to

record. I hope it is rather the annalist's wish to help the historian—or, in a humble sort of way, my desire to help you, cher maître! if you ever wanted to do anything 'in *this line*.'³²

In the cases of both Gaudier-Brzeska and Ford himself, the "desire to *record*"—the involvement of the artist—becomes a means of sustaining personal integrity, even under conditions of war. The creative impulse fosters self-definition and even sanity in a world that is often not only a "low tea-shop," but a virtual mad-house.

The theme of work-involvement is brought out most strongly by Gringoire through the figure of Rosalie Prudent. Although her husband and two sons had been killed in the War, this Belgian woman, who had been driven from her own town, had gone on providing food and lodging for Allied troops and keeping the house of "MM. the Proprietors" meticulously clean. Rosalie's work had been her means of survival; for as Gringoire says: "That was her pride. . . . There was a whole population of them: I came across a whole population of those quiet people, who considered only their duties to absent proprietors amongst the *rain* of shells." The figure of Rosalie Prudent—"so extremely centered in the work in hand, so oblivious to the very real danger, so brave and so tranquil"—had inspired a new tranquility and perseverence in Gringoire himself, and these qualities have remained a part of him, as we now see him in his post-War world. Rosalie's quiet dignity is magnified if we realize that at the time Gringoire had seen her, the Germans, with an absurd regularity, had "for the last four days . . . been shelling the church. From 6:00 p.m. until midnight, in their methodical manner, every quarter of an hour, they had dropped a 5-9 shell into the sacred ediface."³³ This methodical rain of shells upon a church that must itself have been an empty shell simply emphasized the ridiculousness of the War, and in the midst of this grotesque stillness, Rosalie had almost taken for Gringoire the place of the destroyed church as a symbol of stability.

Through his final self-definition and his life as a "Small Producer" Gringoire attempts to express those qualities of the limited hero which he has developed in the two sections of the book. He hopes to rule by example, and to convince others by the meaning that he himself derives from his life:

> For I will be dependent on the profits of no man's labour, and I will produce more food than I can eat and more thought than I can take from the world. So, to the measure of the light vouchsafed, shall some fragment of the world be dependent upon me.
>
> All this wrangling for power in newspapers, meetings, market places, and drawing rooms is a weariness—and when you have it, what is it? A handful of dried leaves that crumble under the touch. If you have a platoon you can make it smart; if you have a garden, you

may make it fine, luxuriant, producing marrows as large as barrels. Or if you write a poem, you must make it beautiful. Everything else is vanity.[34]

Gringoire's statement is as explicit a declaration of limited heroism as can be found anywhere in Ford's fiction. His personal involvement with the land and with his work is clearly evident, and underlying this involvement, which is an expression of strength, is a strong awareness of the limitations of the individual and of any answers that he may provide. To impose these answers through power on anyone else would be "vanity"; the limited hero can only act upon others by fulfilling himself. And Gringoire's final position is clearly Ford's own, stated with as much assurance and far more serenity than Ford himself would achieve in his later and more urgent didactic books, at the end of a very troubled decade.

After he finished the autobiographical *No Enemy*, Ford continued to work in the form of the novel. But the first of his late novels, *When the Wicked Man*, published in 1931, was basically an artistic failure, and its failings are typical of those in all the final novels. The plot is nervous and contrived, and there is a markedly forced attempt to convey a corrupted world that Ford himself does not fully comprehend. The characters emerge as types and the situations are melodramatic. And because Ford could find in the world of these final novels nothing to affirm, there is little of the complexity or subtlety that distinguishes his major works.

When the Wicked Man, is another of Ford's pictures of a hero corrupted by commercial society, but unlike *The Inheritors* or *Mr. Fleight*, there remains in this novel scarcely a vestige of moral choice, and what might once have been cause for a double perspective becomes here only irony. The movement of the businessman-hero, Joe Notterdam, is one from corruption to total degradation, until finally his very degradation brings about, almost against his will, a major rise in his public reputation. Notterdam also differs from Ford's earlier corrupted heroes in that he is dependent on and eventually becomes his public image. This image is based on his power as one of the heads of a large publishing firm, and although he is subject to occasional doubts within himself, he seldom allows them to be known by anyone else. Notterdam represents, in other words, the new type of public hero, one whose role is dependent on the position and rhetoric of power, rather than on any pretense of virtue. He is both a weary and cynical man, with little self-definition, and his weariness and cynicism make him incapable of any other sort of relationship with people than that based on his image of power. Notterdam's position is so completely dependent on this image that at the end of the novel, when he begins to perceive the emptiness of his life, he finds that he can no longer change roles because the public, itself eager for a hero, insists on perpetuating the one which it has made for him and in which he is

THE LATE WORK AND THE LIMITED HERO

already entrenched. Notterdam's final irony is that despite his position of power, his life is not at all his own.

Notterdam and his partner, Kratch, are each types of American businessmen, and when the book opens we see them fighting for control of company policy. The two men disagree over the kind of writing to be marketed. Notterdam wants to preserve at least a semblance of tradition, whereas Kratch wants to create "an American enterprise" and can exclaim, "To hell with Thomas Hardy. To hell with Alfred Tennyson." In the old days the two men had been roving business partners in the West, and it had not been uncommon for them to get drunk together in a town's saloon and then go out and purchase the entire operation of its newspaper. As a reminder of both his frontier background and his descent from generations of bricklayers, Kratch is still in the habit of carrying a trowel to board meetings.[35] Both Notterdam and Kratch unite in themselves the cut-throat ethic of the frontier and the more subtle power of the modern business world, but Notterdam, having been born in England, retains a small sense of tradition which he occasionally verbalizes. The novel's central crisis revolves around a contract, into which Notterdam has been duped by the mediocre novelist, Porter, and which he hesitates to break out of a sense of "his own personal honour" and "all the traditions of the house." Notterdam is further restrained by the fact that Porter comes from his own birthplace in England. Nevertheless, in spite of his feeble efforts at traditional morality, Notterdam in a very short time has his secretary send Porter a notice which declares the contract null and void.[36] This act marks the beginning of Notterdam's irreversible decline, and it leads ironically to his final public ascent. He is eventually, through his own action, caught in a pattern of which he no longer wants a part.

All the while that we follow Notterdam's progressive deterioration, it becomes increasingly clear that his personal life is almost wholly without meaning, and gives him little stability to counteract his self-inflicted fall. His home, for example, is nothing but a gaudy mixture of second-hand styles:

> The house being an imitation of a Mexican adobe patio, the dining room had to be Spanish seventeenth century in character. The great reception room was eighteenth century French; Elspeth's bedroom painful *Nouvel Art*, with glass tops to all flat surfaces, blue squares, scarlet angles, turquoise and emerald spatterings. Even the chief bathroom was a hothouse arrangement of alabaster and porphyry. Having seen it once, he had never entered it again.

On the night that Notterdam returns home after breaking the contract, his wife is "more than usually sardonic," and his children, "responding to her mood," are "more than usually indolent." Notterdam and his wife

have long ago given up any attempts at affection, and it is while they are discussing the possibility of a divorce that Mrs. Porter phones to inform them that her husband has just committed suicide.[37]

Lola Porter is a stereotyped character, a tough and bitter woman with one foot in the underworld, and Notterdam's attraction to her is one of the most poorly motivated and least convincing aspects of the book. Notterdam's wife, partly sensing his feelings for Mrs. Porter and partly because of a bad marriage that has included her own extramarital relationship with Kratch, decides to divorce him. Her husband then asks Henrietta Faukner Felise, Kratch's one-time private secretary, to marry him, but she is afraid to commit herself. They compromise by agreeing to an affair, but their "honeymoon" drive is only a grotesque and impotent parody of a romantic event. It is soon obvious that Notterdam, who has little but an external self to give, can receive from others nothing more than the external response which he himself elicits.

Ever since his repudiation of the contract, Notterdam has been plagued by guilt. But he is hardly penitent. He tells himself that "He must, when he had time, pray to God," and he begins to see his own double, "perhaps with the gift of his ancestor, Nostradamus. He had an idea that to see your double was a presage of harm!" At the climax of the novel, Notterdam and Lola Porter are together in Europe, and he is attempting to seduce her. Lola's boyfriend, an American gangster, has, however, followed them across the Atlantic, and he dashes angrily into the room. Notterdam is convinced that the intruder is his double, and so he shoots him and becomes an unwitting hero.[38] Ford's thematic use of the double in this novel adds an interesting sidelight on his omission of the dual perspective that had distinguished so many of his previous works. In a hero such as Edward Ashburnham, the potential good had often been latent in the very false responsibility that had resulted in his fall. This responsibility, although it had been misdirected and eventually became an illusion, had been an element of Ashburnham's conscious self. In the case of Joe Notterdam, however, whatever dualism is present in his character is relegated to his subconscious mind, from which it occasionally arises to become a manifestation of suppressed guilt. The potential for good is found in Notterdam only in its reverse form of guilt for realized evil; and when this guilt, in the figure of the double, appears before the publisher, he attempts to destroy it, for he can face neither his total corruption nor this intimation of a potentially different self. The remnants of a possible dualism have been pushed by Notterdam so far below the surface, that they have become a virtually separate person, and Notterdam himself emerges as a caricature of degeneration, barely in control of even his ow' destiny.

Along with the *doppelgänger* motif, another element of German fc ore is brought into the novel through a briefly suggested parallel with

Faust legend. Notterdam sees himself as Faust, Henrietta as Gretchen, and Lola as "whatever bad woman had first led Faust astray"; and he reminds himself that "Faustus too had been a medieval magician: like Nostradamus."[39] If Ford intended the Faust parallel to add dimension to the novel, he gave it a far too careless development. There is, to be sure, a contract. But if Notterdam parallels Faust, then Porter must play the role of the devil. If this is so, then the devil commits suicide, and Faust is granted nothing but guilt. Furthermore, Notterdam's business aspirations are hardly those of Faust, and his only acquaintance with learning is a vague sense of unkept tradition. The publisher has, through his awareness of his descent from Nostradamus and of the Faust legend, a small acquaintance with magic; but this slight interest in magicians and the sense of his own double are apparently the full extent of Notterdam's interest in non-material reality. The spiritual dimension is conspicuously absent from his life. From the confusions in his treatment of the Faust motif, it is not clear whether Ford meant this parallel to suggest only Notterdam's acquaintance with magic, or whether some larger significance was intended. In any case, the parallel should have either been clarified or dropped from the novel altogether. As it stands, it remains, like so much else in the novel, an undeveloped fragment.

Ironically, it is Notterdam's very guilt and loss of self-esteem that brings about his return to America as a hero. On his voyage to Europe, he had begun to question the value of his life: "During the long nights . . . he asked himself again and again what he was for and what his life had been for. He had gained neither serenity nor fame (. . . .) And now he found that he had not even self-esteem." All through Europe he had been plagued by his double, until finally he had shot Lola's underworld friend, whom he had mistaken for his other self. The fact that Notterdam sees himself as a gangster tells us something of his guilt, but the murder, which is really an act of self-aggression, only makes him more of a public hero on his return.[40] Notterdam becomes a public idol who no longer believes in himself, but who is forced by a starving public to maintain the pattern set by his own corruption. Even rhetoric is no longer necessary, for the public is eagerly willing to see only what it desires. And so Notterdam becomes both victim and hero, and significantly the two roles are for him simultaneous. The idea of the novel—the irony of a corrupted hero who unwittingly falls into a role of greater heroism—is an effective one, and it provides a trenchant commentary on both the degree of social corruption and the nature of individual power in the post-War world. But the faulty execution of *When the Wicked Man* unfortunately thins its effect. Although many of its individual scenes are strong, the plot is too contrived and the characterization is flat. The use of stereotyped gangsters and businessmen seriously undermines the effectiveness of the novel's social criticism. In *When the Wicked Man* Ford was in possession of

potentially good material, but judging from the texture of the work itself, he failed to give it a sufficient degree of artistic control.

The same fault is evident, although to a lesser extent, in the series comprised of the two novels, *The Rash Act* and *Henry for Hugh*. Here, Ford presents characters who are far more sympathetic than Joe Notterdam, but again they remain types and there is too much reliance on coincidence and contrived situation. The two novels center on the problem of identity, which is embodied in the dilemma of the two main characters, Henry Martin Aluin Smith and Hugh Monckton Allard Smith. The two men are of course different; yet because each lacks a coherent sense of himself they are essentially the same, both without identity, mirrors of each other's emptiness. Henry Martin is the resentful and expatriate son of an American candy manufacturer. Hugh Monckton, on the other hand, is an ostensibly self-confident heir to a British automobile company. Each attempts suicide, the ultimate negation of a self which neither has attained; and one, Hugh Monckton, is successful. Henry Martin is motivated by a coincidence to save himself, survives, and impulsively assumes the credentials and identity of the dead Hugh Monckton. The very fact that Henry Martin can so freely negate his former self is a sign of his tenuous identity. But as he assumes the role of his late friend, toward the end of the first and throughout the second novel, he finds a new identity in the specifics of Hugh Monckton's daily life, and particularly in other people's dependence on him. Gradually, this new identity becomes a part of him, so that finally when Henry Martin's actual self is revealed, he is able to honestly take over the responsibilities of Hugh Monckton, and to make them his own.

On the title page of *The Rash Act*, in an attempt to link suicide and the general world condition, Ford quotes the *Times Law Reports* for July 14, 1931: "The rash act, the coroner said, seems to have been inspired by a number of motives, not the least amongst which was the prevailing dissoluteness and consequent depression that are now world-wide."[41] Life, it is implied, receives from the modern world little sense of justification, and yet the negation of this life is an act not of protest, but simply part of the overall depression. The self-negation that suicide represents is countered in the two novels by the idea of giving pleasure. To be able to give pleasure to another person is really an affirmation of the self, and it is simultaneously an expression and a transcendence of one's own identity. The act of giving pleasure is symbolized throughout the two novels by the dancing boy of Antibes, through whom Ford links the sense of pleasure to the qualities of form and rhythm inherent in the dance, and thereby suggests that the transmission of pleasure and the artistic act are almost synonymous. As Henry Martin learns to give pleasure, as his consciousness, on which Ford focuses during most of the two novels, grows

increasingly aware of the desirability of such giving, he becomes an artist in spite of the fact that he never creates a tangible work of art.

Of the two major characters, Henry Martin receives the most attention, and his early experience is one of disillusion with conventional authority, personal failure, and a consequent sense of aimlessness and despair. After his attempted suicide, however, he is figuratively reborn; and through his assumption of Hugh Monckton's identity, he finally achieves a stronger identity as himself. In *The Rash Act* Henry Martin is made by Ford to carry the entire post-War loss of identity, and his symbolic role poses two serious difficulties. For one thing, Ford's expatriate American is weighted down by far too many problems to be a wholly credible character; and, moreover, just because he bears almost the entire burden of his age, his dilemmas seem far too exaggerated to be really typical. Embittered and disillusioned, Henry Martin feels himself caught between the "resolution" of the nineteenth century and the "mental confusion" of the twentieth, living in both, but with a place in neither.[42] He feels himself without roots, and still somewhat cowed by his father, the monolithic figure behind the desk of the Pisto-Brittle candy works in Springfield, Ohio. "In his thirty-odd years of acquaintanceship he had never sized his father up. He was like a wild boar—like a mountain."

As a student at Dartmouth, Henry Martin had wanted to become a writer, but his father had cancelled his funds and placed him in the candy factory, all the while bluntly announcing that he would have "to learn the business from the bottom. American fashion."[43] He had not followed his father's orders, but neither had he become the writer that he once intended to be. And his encounters with the commercial world had soured him in other ways as well. In the army, for example, he had discovered that Leopold Kuhn, the Y.M.C.A. representative who ran the canteen on an American troop ship was in fact transporting typewriters and sewing machines to Europe for his own profit. That was why the canteen never had enough supplies for the troops. "The effect of that voyage, Henry Martin was now aware, had been to cure him of all respect for the louder virtues (. . . .) Perhaps for all virtues! It—and all the enterprises connected with it—seemed to be like a vast smudge across the landscape of his life."[44]

But in spite of his disillusionment with "the louder virtues," Henry Martin has never been able to develop for himself a sufficient morality. His personal life has always been meaningless and emotionally sterile. At twenty-one, he had fallen in love with an older and already married actress, who intended to get a divorce. But Henry Martin's father had opposed the marriage, and while the son was in Europe with the American army, the father had talked the actress out of the marriage. Henry had gone to live with, and eventually married, another woman, but their

marriage had only led to divorce. Henry and his wife, Alice, had first met each other one Christmas, when Leopold Kuhn "had suggested that they should spend Christmas Day and the day after at Chartres. And take a couple of girls." Their marriage had simply been a formalization of their sexual union.[45] The contrast experiencing of personal failure has left Henry Martin with a fear that he is incapable of giving pleasure to anyone. On the night before his attempted suicide, he visits a night club. It is here that he meets Hugh Monckton, and that each becomes entangled in each other's life. At the night club, he is immediately attracted to a dark girl, and impulsively gives her his ring, because he feels that it will give her pleasure: "If you don't give pleasure you went down to the ooze of the sea-bottom. But if you did you became immortal." The dark girl later turns out to be Eudoxie, one of the women with whom Hugh Monckton has been involved, and one of the people who will help Henry Martin to gain his new sense of identity. The next morning, Henry Martin muses upon the Boy of Antibes who had danced and given pleasure:

> There was a mud inscription at Antibes, a few miles from where he then stood. It was on the wall of the Roman Theatre—to the memory of a boy dancer who had died young.
>
> 'SALTAVIT. PLACUIT. MORTUUS EST'
>
> 'He danced. He gave pleasure. He is dead.'
>
> It would be nice to have that on one's tombstone. But he never would. That would no doubt make his real epitaph—Only last night he had danced—well enough. But he could feel that he gave no pleasure to the little, depressed French *poule* who was in his arms.[46]

The act of giving pleasure, by which Henry Martin is motivated, but in which he thinks himself such a failure, becomes suggestive not only of the self-fulfillment of the artist or the "Small Producer," but also of a mode of relationship in which one can sense what John Dowell in *The Good Soldier* termed his "own worthiness to exist." In Henry Martin, the lack of such confidence is conspicuous, and it finally pushes him to the point of attempted suicide. Paul Wiley points out that in the image of a body exhibiting fulfilled purpose, the symbol of the Boy of Antibes also denotes a harmony, vital enough to reconcile the violent discords of post-War society.[47] And Henry Martin feels no such harmony, either from giving pleasure or from a sense of religious faith. "He could not," Ford tells us, "believe that an august First Cause would take cognizance of his existence. It had more important tasks (. . . .) What had he done to make notice of him worth while of the Deity? . . . . It was more likely that

THE LATE WORK AND THE LIMITED HERO

Providence let remorseless effect work out the punishment of individuals."[48] With little sense of either universal harmony or of his own worth, it is little wonder that Henry Martin, as we see him in the first novel, attempts to kill himself.

In the night club, on the night before he tries to commit suicide, Henry Martin recognizes Hugh Monckton, who had once been his officer during the War. Each regards the other as far more successful than himself, and each is contemplating suicide the following day. On the night that Henry Martin meets Hugh Monckton, the latter has just ended a relationship with the beautiful actress, Gloria Sorenson. As the two men walk home together, the Englishman asks Henry Martin what he would think of joining the Foreign Legion. Later, while reading his friend's suicide note, Henry Martin discovers that the negative attitude that had been reflected in his tone of voice had convinced Hugh Monckton "that there was only one means of escape."[49] As the two men talk in Hugh Monckton's room, Ford renders through fragments of thought their painful inability to communicate. Each is fully engrossed in his own tangle of thoughts, and all through the night Hugh Monckton clutches desperately at Henry Martin as though he were an angel of immediate comfort and final judgement. All the while that Hugh Monckton is talking of Gloria Sorenson, Henry Martin is thinking back to his own marriage with Alice; he had suspected his wife of lesbianism, of "going together" with her friend, Mrs. Percival, to whom he himself had been sexually attracted. As Henry Martin thinks back upon his life, Hugh Monckton keeps on grabbing him and trying to talk. "Henry Martin was only half listening. Not half! He was distracted, resentful and engrossed. This was a shadowy affair. He felt as if he were continually being grabbed by the shoulder. By a small boy." In this scene, Henry Martin has his first real experience of another person's need for him, and he cannot respond. Later, alone in his own room, he begins to feel guilt. He senses, as he thinks of Hugh Monckton, that he has "failed him," and that he once again has been incapable of giving pleasure. All the same, his thoughts keep turning back upon the image of the dark girl in the night club, to whom he has given his ring, and Hugh Monckton is forgotten until after he is dead.[50]

The suicide episode, which forms the climax of *The Rash Act*, utilizes far too much coincidence. Henry Martin, intending to drown himself, actually goes out in a small boat. But he is overtaken by a violent storm, the *"trombio,"* and his life instinct almost automatically assumes control of his mind. As he struggles to guide the boat, he is hit on the head by a swinging yardarm; and this accounts for the injury which later allows him to remain in bed, once he has assumed Hugh Monckton's role. Back on the beach, he discovers Hugh Monckton, who has killed himself by crashing his car. At first, Henry Martin changes credentials with his friend merely because he does not wish to become involved in the in-

quest. Hugh Monckton has left a note designating Henry Martin as executor of his property, and Henry Martin fears that he might "have to denounce his friend for suicide."[51] It is not long, however, before he realizes that he has a new identity, and that he can now discard his own unfortunate past. Although this change of roles may stretch credulity, it is Ford's way of symbolically depicting the thinness of identity in the modern world. In fact, identity, like all the other standardized parts of post-War life, has become interchangeable.

While he originally assumes Hugh Monckton's identity as a means of escape, Henry Martin soon finds that the change involves him in a whole set of responsibilities. He begins to discover the many small and particular ways in which other people are dependent on him, and this discovery allows him to build a new identity—one that will finally become his own—by feeling at last that he is able to give pleasure. His head injury enables Henry Martin to feign having been in an accident, and he finds himself under medical care in Hugh Monckton's hotel room. There, gradually, he begins his new pattern of involvement. One day, for example, he saves Jeanne Becquerel, another of the women who had been in love with Hugh Monckton, from what he believes to be an attempted suicide. And although he later discovers that while the girl had threatened suicide, she had been, when he had found her, under the effect of an opiate given her by Eudoxie, this act of salvation is nonetheless the beginning of Henry Martin's reconstruction.[52] For the first time, he is effectively concerned with the well-being of people around him, people who in turn reciprocate his attention by their concern for him. After Henry Martin has recuperated sufficiently, he moves with Eudoxie and Jeanne Becquerel, to a villa on the Mediterranean, there to assume the Provençal way of life; and his change of roles is given a final sanction when he discovers that Hugh Monckton had wanted him to suppress the news of the suicide in order to protect the Monckton business interests.[53] *The Rash Act* and *Henry for Hugh* are Ford's only late novels in which an attempted solution is rendered along with the post-War dilemma. And, symbolically, it is as if Henry Martin, by his change of identity in the first novel, has thrown off the past of his too-dominant father and the corrupt Leopold Kuhn in order to prepare himself for the role of the limited hero and a new commitment to the everyday.

But in spite of its centrality to Ford's basic concerns, the faults of *The Rash Act* are serious and manifold. Meixner isolates a major defect when he argues that "Ultimately the book seems pointless. Its literal realistic level is neither convincing nor interesting, and the psychology and motivation of its people, particularly Henry Martin, are peculiar in the extreme. And looked at symbolically, the nature of the characters and the plot in which they are involved seems to lack general relevance."[54] Basically, the difficulty stems from the too heavy symbolic burden which

Henry Martin is made to bear. His personal dilemmas are a summary of almost all the problems of his time, and they seem far too profuse to overtake any one man. Many of his actions are poorly motivated. For example, we might ask how, with all the revulsion that he felt toward Leopold Kuhn on the troop ship, Henry Martin was still able to maintain in Paris a friendship with him that was close enough to allow their going out together, and to lead, eventually, to Henry Martin's acquaintance and marriage with Alice. And, far more significantly, the change of identity and the resultant growth of involvement on which the novel ends are insufficiently justified, for it seems unlikely that Henry Martin, with all his symbolic burden, could alter his responses and his way of life with such decisive rapidity. The theme of the two novels is a pertinent one, but Ford does not succeed, here, as he had in *The Good Soldier*, the Tietjens novels, or even in *No Enemy*, in constructing a group of characters and a situation which are at the same time psychologically convincing and symbolically relevant. *The Rash Act* and *Henry for Hugh* are hardly pictures of even probable situations; and if they are fantasies, their details are not sufficiently coherent to make them credible.

Henry for Hugh is basically an extension of the change and development of identity begun in *The Rash Act*. Significantly, this change is completed only after it is reversed and Henry Martin returns to being himself, but with the stronger identity that he has gained through his interim experience. The main strength of the novel lies in its delineation of the specific responsibilities out of which Henry Martin's new identity gradually emerges. Ford establishes a central distinction between that responsibility toward which Henry Martin grows and that which had been a means, in *The Good Soldier* of Edward Ashburnham's self-evasion. Ashburnham's sense of obligation was expressed through rhetoric and based on a conventional public role, whereas Henry Martin's is expressed through particular relationships and based on a private commitment. His identity evolves through his involvement with the people who had been part of Hugh Monckton's life; and at the end he discovers that since Eudoxie and Hugh Monckton's Aunt Elizabeth have known his real identity all along, it is the involvement and not the name that is important. Aunt Elizabeth, by accepting Henry Martin as himself, is able to make him feel that he has finally given pleasure. With this new self-acceptance, he is able, at the novel's end, to marry Eudoxie and to assume the Monckton business responsibilities under his own name.

Like *The Rash Act*, *Henry for Hugh* has noticeable faults. Ford uses almost entirely a stream-of-consciousness technique. The consciousness is Henry Martin's; and although there is a steady fortification of the major theme through Ford's use of *progression d'effet*, the structure is entirely too discursive, and very little is said that could not have been expressed more cogently at the end of *The Rash Act*. There is a cluttering of minor

characters, such as the American publisher, Old-Smith, and these characters give the impression of weighing down rather than carrying forward the movement of the book.

This movement is built upon Henry Martin's reconstruction of identity, and more specifically on his realization of reciprocal ties to the other characters. He thinks to himself one day, as he contemplates his false identity, that it is not discovery by the police that he fears, but the probability that those people who believe him to be Hugh Monckton would be sorely disappointed; "Jeanne Becquerel, for instance, would be broken-hearted at losing her millionaire milord." He also realizes that as Hugh Monckton he must live up to a public image, for "he had been godlike.... He had been the only man in the world to bestride the crisis."[55] And Aunt Elizabeth tells Henry Martin that if she thought that it was Hugh Monckton who had killed himself, she "should not be here," and she adds that she "couldn't stand being the last great Auk—the last of our name (. . . .) Lonely. On the desolate beaches of the world."[56] As for Jeanne Becquerel, she wants more than anything to be able to hold on to her supposed Hugh Monckton for one year. She fears "to be taken in the hand and then thrown away like a crushed flower that has not pleased."[57] As had once been the case with Henry Martin, Jeanne Becquerel is terribly afraid of not being able to give pleasure, and Henry Martin soon learns that he is partly responsible for making her feel that she is wanted.

Eudoxie, who recognizes his false identity, further reminds him of the obligation of which he has already become aware. She tells him decisively: "You have started us on this voyage. You will have to continue it until you set us ashore (. . . .) Perhaps there will be no shore. Then you must continue it forever (. . . .) You will have to learn the navigation. You will have to document yourself (. . . .) You will have to learn renunciation."[58] Henry Martin must learn to forsake the sort of self-indulgence that was shown by his insensitivity to Hugh Monckton during their last night together, and ultimately by his own attempted suicide. As Christopher Tietjens had found when he and Valentine were reunited in *A Man Could Stand Up*, so Henry Martin now discovers that part of the development of the self entails the development of a sensitivity to the needs of others. This sensitivity is an essential part of the involvement in specific reality that is central to the limited hero's response.

The world outside the Monckton villa is not a major factor in *Henry for Hugh*, particularly since Ford's main concern is with the development of Henry Martin's inner self. But there are in the novel brief suggestions of the nature of this world. The political Left is represented by Hugh Monckton's hostile secretary, Macdonald, who is "forever spouting a sort of immature Communism." Macdonald has "a little nest of Communist-Intellectual friends (. . .) mostly American. They all proposed, whatever the nature of their other panaceas, to stand Hugh Monckton . . .

'up against a wall' (...) when the great day came!" Yet Henry Martin—and by implication, Ford—is able to recognize that Eudoxie is attracted to communism because her father, the French Consulate General in New York, "had continued to write her terrible details as to the state of things in New York. The dreadful image of the breadlines stretching from West Eleventh Street far uptown had been enough to drive her at times nearly mad." On another part of the political spectrum there is M. Lamoriciere, the real estate agent who is also a staunch Buonapartist. He gives a demonstration of his factional rallying cry, "his arms flying, his long face lit up with a sort of madness, against the moon which was now risen;" and he looks "like a mad player of Don Quixote dragging on to the stage an enraged Dulcinea del Toboso."[59]

In the depiction of these two factions, Ford's attitude toward policies as a type of immature heroism is reinforced. The Communist, Macdonald, is sullen and hostile, whereas the Buonapartist, M. Lamoriciere, resembles a small child craving attention. Two other men from the outside world intrude upon the villa and, in what seems an unnecessary and confusing subplot, raise again the question of Henry Martin's identity. Apparently Hugh Monckton's suicide had been announced all over the United States, and shares of the Monckton works had been sold in large quantities, only to be bought again by Henry Martin. Old-Smith and Crape, American publisher and movie producer respectively, believe that the whole affair has been a plot on Hugh Monckton's part, and that the body of Henry Martin, thought in America to be that of Hugh Monckton, was really a fake. Further doubts as to Henry's identity are cast by Macdonald, who thinks that Hugh Monckton is actually dead, and suspects Henry Martin of having been hired by the Monckton firm to conceal this fact from the public. Macdonald has, moreover, begun to spread his doubts around the neighboring town.[60]

But by the end of the novel, the question of real or false identity is of little importance; the two identities have become one. By dedicating himself to the specific responsibilities of Hugh Monckton's life, Henry Martin has gradually gained a new identity of his own. He has been able, through his new involvement, to erase for himself the spectre of his past, and thus to free himself for a new way of life. Toward the end of the novel, Aunt Elizabeth becomes fatally ill. Henry is very much concerned for her, and moves to her house in order to be beside the dying woman: "It was impossible to imagine a world in which Aunt Elizabeth had not existed (. . . .) But she hadn't existed then (. . . .) If there hadn't been an Aunt Elizabeth one would have had to invent one." She has become part of the tangible definition of his life. Henry Martin senses that he has given her pleasure, but realizes that "He could not appear to have such charm, wonder and humour, or such genius, or such dignity, or such princely habit, or such generosity (...) or to be such a dancer or to shed

such pleasure around him (. . . .) *Saltavit et Placuit* (. . .) if he hadn't appeared to be Hugh Monckton! (. . .) That was bitter!" But Henry Martin's major self-discovery occurs beside Aunt Elizabeth's deathbed, when she admits to having known his true identity all along. He discovers that his assumed role has actually fooled no one, and that its only real purpose has been to free him from himself. He returns completely to his own identity when he accepts, as Henry Martin, his new responsibilities with the Monckton works. Before he assumes these responsibilities, he and Eudoxie decide to marry, and to take a trip to New York by way of Italy.[61]

The legal right to take over Hugh Monckton's duties is established when Henry Martin finds that he and Hugh Monckton are actually related through a common grandfather.[62] The entire turn of events which resolves both the novel and Henry Martin's question of identity is very effective on the symbolic level, for it allows Henry Martin to renounce his past, develop the role of the limited hero, and then return to an original self that has been greatly altered by intervening experiences. But the minute we begin to view the novel as more than a symbol, there are serious difficulties. It is unlikely, for example, that Aunt Elizabeth would conceal for so long her knowledge of Henry Martin's identity, particularly since she has said that she could not go on if she thought that Hugh Monckton were dead. There is, moreover, little development of affection between Eudoxie and Henry Martin, prior to their final decision to marry. And the final discovery of family ties only seems an added coincidence, an unnecessary underlining of the link that is already there when Aunt Elizabeth, by her admission, cements the two identities. *Henry for Hugh* is important primarily for its symbolic linking of limited heroism with specific responsibility, but as a rendering of a possibly real situation, it has little, if any, credibility.

Vive Le Roy, which appeared in 1936, was Ford's last, complete novel; and although many of the author's recurrent themes are evident, it is at best a confused piece of work. On the surface, the novel is simply a tale of political intrigue. There are the usual plots and counterplots, one of the major characters disappears, and toward the end there is a revelation of hidden identity. Beneath this surface detail, two of Ford's more serious concerns—the violence done in the name of political order, and the establishment of a kingdom of "Small Producers"—can be discerned. However, these two themes are brought together, and this is where the confusion begins. In the French Civil War that forms the novel's setting, one of the groups contesting for control is a Monarchist faction. While the immediate goals of this faction are the restoration of a monarch to the throne and the prevention of Communist rule, one of its directors, M. Panthièvre, is an advocate of a kingdom of "Small Producers" along Fordian lines. Ford's sympathies seem to go toward Panthièvre, and yet

this verbal proponent of limited heroism is as much a politician, and is at least as capable of intrigue, as are his Communist opponents. The Monarchists even have their small group of violent fanatics, a band of toughs who call themselves the *Camelots du Roi*. When the king dies, Walter Le Roy, who is almost a perfect double for the monarch, is kidnapped by Panthièvre, in order that the death can be concealed from the public by using Walter as a substitute. Yet despite all this intrigue, Ford seems to view Walter's final position in favorable terms, and there is little questioning of the methods which the Monarchist faction employs. If such questioning were evident, the novel might be regarded as an ironic picture of the discrepancy between reality and the ideal of the "Small Producer." But Ford in *Vive Le Roy*, never goes deep enough to raise any doubts; and as a result the novel remains a story of intrigue, incidentally using two Fordian themes in a strange and conflicting relationship that remains badly developed and is never resolved.

As the novel begins, Walter Le Roy, a young doctor on a scholarship to Paris, agrees to carry with him on his trip abroad some concealed papers for the Communists. Walter's own politics are rather vague: "If he had been communist in leanings it had been because the whole world had seemed an atrocious muddle. The Russian Republic presented the spectacle of the only government that knew where it was going or how to get what it wanted in quiet. He desired to see a world fitted for bacteriologists."[63] Walter's attraction to Russia is quite similar to that professed by the publisher Sorrell in the 1935 edition of *Ladies Whose Bright Eyes*, when he explains that Russia seems to him one of the few places in the world where there is a sense of something beginning. Ford apparently sensed that one of the major appeals made by communism during the 1930's was that it offered a ready-made purpose in what often seemed a dying world. At the start of his trip, Walter Le Roy's strongest political feeling is a vehement dislike for the French Monarchist cause, a dislike that becomes highly ironic in the light of his finally playing the role of the masquerade-king.

During the voyage, Walter meets three people who will figure significantly in the novel. The first, Cassie Mathers, is an art student with whom Walter falls in love; the second, M. Panthièvre, is one of the leaders of the Monarchist cause; and the third, Mr. Penkethman, is an inspector for the League of Nations, who will look after Cassie once Walter has been kidnapped, and who will later reveal that Walter is his illegitimate son.[64] Paul Wiley, who reads *Vive Le Roy* as a myth of death and rebirth, sees this final disclosure by the inspector as highly significant, for it provides the lovers with the context of "a past within which they may achieve identity and thus provides the chief remedy for the ills noted by Ford as besetting modern man."[65] On the other hand, even if Penkethman admits to being Walter's father, such an admission does not in itself give the son

a context of identity. After all, Penkethman, until his accidental involvement with Walter in the novel, has been a father only in a biological sense, and then not even in name. The sudden concern that Penkethman shows for Walter is almost coincidental and contrived as Walter's happening to look like and therefore assuming the role of the late king.

The major action of the plot begins when M. Panthièvre receives the news aboard ship that the king has died. Obviously this fact, if it were revealed, would virtually destroy the Monarchist cause. But Panthièvre notices the coincidental resemblance of Walter to the king, and once they are in Paris the Monarchist leader contrives to kidnap the young doctor. As they go through the streets, Ford gives a picture of the violence of the Civil War, a violence that is significant because as a condition it is one of the major political motifs in his non-fiction of the 1930's. Panthièvre soon finds it necessary to reveal to Walter the nature of the Monarchist cause; and at least as this particular leader describes it, the aim of the group is to establish the kingdom of the "Small Producer" in Western Europe:

> 'Those who have accepted the Machine let them live by the Machine. But France has never accepted the Machine. First and last amongst the Nations she began and remained the land of the Small Producer.' ... The ideal of every Frenchman, M. de la Panthièvre droned on, was to see a France of small hamlets, each self-contained, each potentially self-supported, self-governing, united in one country that was France —but France almost without central government, almost without an army, almost without a fleet, completely without functionaries who are the detestation of all the French. Almost without roads even.

Thus far, M. Panthièvre's ideal state is very close to one that Ford himself might advocate. But the Monarchist's scheme for a kingdom of "Small Producers" is quickly marred by evidence of their readiness to compromise and play power politics. For example, in describing his scheme to Walter, Panthièvre quickly adds that he hopes to divide Western Europe "between Royal France and the Soviet Republic. With no cause for difference between them where would be the need for arms? Each great state, engrossed behind coterminous frontiers could pursue, for ever undisturbed, its Imperial destinies."[66] M. Panthièvre himself has no objection to the state-centered theories of the Soviet Union. But he believes that "what was good for one people was not of necessity good for another." Thus he feels that Monarchist France and Soviet Russia can divide Europe between themselves, and live in political amity ever after.[67]

Panthièvre is thus shown to be either extremely naive or much more interested in power politics and a strong central state than he will admit, for it is highly improbable that France, as a federation of small communities, could impose and maintain even on its half of Europe the sort of system he professes to advocate. The Monarchist leader's further affinities

with power politics are suggested by his views on the Civil War and the creation of the ideal state. He is "a man certain of himself and of the progress of his friends at home," and he is convinced that his faction will soon capture all of Paris. There will of course be violence. "Obviously one did not wish to take more of one's fellow subjects' lives than one had to. One had unfortunately to take some. But for that the Communists must take the responsibility." And Panthièvre adds that "when the forces of discontent had raised their heads in armed rebellion," the intended king, who was at the time the elected President of France, "had answered the cry of the whole nation, accepting the desperately dangerous missions of becoming at once the terrible armed protagonist and benevolent dictator of his bleeding country (. . . .) 'Dictator' was an ugly word. But it was a necessity of modern conditions. The Soviet Republic was a modern state, no doubt eminently suited for the conditions and mentality of its citizens. It was none the less a dictatorship. So with all the other countries of the world. Even Mr. Le Roy's country, philosophically regarded, was nothing else."[68]

By this time, M. Panthièvre appears less the advocate of the "Small Producer" than a skillful but rather obvious apologist for a supposedly temporary dictatorship, and one wonders whether his frequently stated acceptance of Soviet theory and practice does not stem from an unacknowledged similarity. The acceptance of the mechanism of a large state is certainly at odds with the tone and even the nature of the ideal of the "Small Producer." And along with this contradiction, the Monarchist faction is also weakened by its rhetorical apologetics for political violence and by the existence, on its fringe, of a group of right-wing terrorists, the *Camelots du Roi*. This group constitutes "the more undisciplined right wing of the government—young degenerates for the most part who were making Panthièvre's task of restoring order, difficult as it was, doubly difficult. They searched the houses of the leaders of the late government; mobbed their persons in the street; pulled down statues of republican heroes; pillaged the Jewish stores in the rue du Roi de Sicile." The group is said to enjoy the favor of the queen, and although Panthièvre is generally able to curb them, he is not always successful. When Cassie, for example, is taken to the morgue to identify a body that has been made up as Walter's so that he can be declared dead prior to his taking on the role of the king, she is attacked by members of the group and must be rescued by Penkethman. The existence of this violent fringe group, even though it is opposed by Panthièvre, would seem to further discredit the validity of his cause.[69]

But in the course of the novel, all the difficulties are neatly resolved. Walter's final assumption of the late king's position is viewed as sensible and desirable, and even Cassie is finally informed of the scheme and advised to accept it by Penkethman, who has assumed a paternal role

toward the girl. Once again as in *The Rash Act* and *Henry for Hugh*, a major character, in this case Walter Le Roy, who himself lacks a sense of identity is able to contrive a new self by assuming the role of someone who is his physical double. Outside of the physical likeness, there is little similarity between Henry Martin and Hugh Monckton or between Walter and the late French king. The sets of characters involved in the personality shifts are, in fact, often virtual opposites. In these novels, the Fordian character has become so devoid of complexity, or of multiple dimension, that what might once have been his opposing traits are now relegated to separate figures; and in order to attain even a semblance of personal integration, one character must become involved in a coincidental and rather incredible exchange of personalities with his physical double. Walter Le Roy does not gain a coherent political identity, beyond his vague communism, until he takes on the role of the late monarch into which he is pushed by M. Panthièvre. The fragmentation and simplification of *The Wicked Man* has in the three later novels become even more pronounced; and this simplification—itself perhaps an indication that the author found little to admire in his last fictional characters or in their world—encourages Ford to rely on the plot contrivances and coincidences that are responsible for some of the major weaknesses of his final novels.

By the end of *Vive Le Roy*, the Monarchist faction is seemingly given Ford's tenuous approval. M. Panthièvre, despite his rationalizations, of political violence and dictatorship, is finally seen, as is evident in his relationship to the *Camelots du Roi*, as the man who attempts even within his own faction, to establish a working political order. Toward the end of the novel, Cassie is taken by Penkethman to meet Walter and the *Caveau Rouge*, an underground Royalist cabaret. But their proposed marriage is not to take place. The scheme requires that she be temporarily removed from the city, and Penkethman explains that "Panthièvre appears to contemplate" her "return to Paris as soon as he has finally got the whiphand of the rebels. The ground, he considers, is already prepared" for Cassie's reappearance. "Provided with a title," she will be able to frequent the court as much as she likes. "These things," Penkethman adds reassuringly, "arrange themselves very smoothly."[70] And so Cassie is left at the end of the novel with a possible title and a chance to become Walter's mistress at court.

Paul Wiley sees the ending of *Vive Le Roy* as a symbolic rebirth. According to Wiley, Walter is finally given an identity and endowed with a set of coherent ideals; and he will also be allowed to return to America, where along with Cassie he will put into practice some of the Royalist precepts "in a humanitarian form of Communism" on a farm in upstate New York.[71] There is, however, no indication in the novel of Walter's fate, if and when a new king is found, and Wiley's reading of

THE LATE WORK AND THE LIMITED HERO

the novel as a whole is far more resolute than the work itself justifies. For although *Vive Le Roy* touches upon certain Fordian ideals, particularly those of the "Small Producer," Panthièvre's occasional statements of these ideals are overshadowed by the intrigues of his plot, so that Ford's attitude toward the Monarchist leader as a spokesman, despite a seeming affirmation, remains ambivalent. The novel is, then viewed in its entirety, essentially a political entertainment, full of situational contrivances, but marked by inadequate handling of its characters and ideas. It is interesting primarily as an expression of the political turbulence which Ford sensed so strongly during the 1930's; but if the novel is meant to be an ironic commentary on the impossibility of achieving the kingdom of the "Small Producer" through political means, the irony is never trenchant or consistent enough to be really clear. Both the plot, with its sense of final resolution, and the ambiguous characterizations, not only of Cassie and Walter, but also of Penkethman and Panthièvre, do little to clarify the overall point of view. However, since in the novel itself the tangled plot gets prior emphasis, it is quite possible that it took precedence during the writing as well, and that the ideas concerning the "Small Producer" were used primarily to help build allegiance to the Monarchist scheme as the motivating action of the plot. The ideological position of the novel may, in other words, be ambiguous because of an intentional subordination of the intellectual material to the exigencies of the plot. Whether or not this is the case, *Vive Le Roy* embodies, only to a greater extent, a fault that is common to all of Ford's final novels.

Looked upon as a group, Ford's late novels appear to be minor efforts. For the most part unconvincing, they substitute strained plots and one-dimensional characters for the complex dualisms which Ford has once rendered, but which he could no longer discern in the world around him. By the end of the decade, Ford had shifted his effort toward a more direct assertion of his individual answer; and just as the world of the late novels was seen with almost total disapproval, so the proposed alternative received, despite a heavy sense of political foreboding, the author's strongest possible affirmation. *No Enemy*, which appeared in 1929, was the last work of fiction in which Ford attained a successful synthesis of character, situation, and ideas. But this novel had itself bordered on nonfiction, for it was essentially a reminiscence in which the hero, Gringoire, was able to comment on his experiences after they had already occurred. Gringoire's comments had taken precedence over any rendering of the events themselves, and this precedence resulted in a book very similar in tone to Ford's own volumes of autobiography and interpretation. And throughout the remainder of his final decade, the author apparently found the most congenial medium for his ideas in his books of actual autobiography and in the intellectual autobiographies which he created in his two last volumes of "travel" and exhortation.

THE LIMITED HERO

Despite a considerable variance in critical response to Ford's late work, the difference between the novels and the works of non-fiction, in both quality and tone, has never been fully examined. Those critics who regard the fiction of the 1930's as unsuccessful, have tended to overlook its relationship to Ford's other prose of the period, and have usually attributed its lack of success to technical failings within the individual novels. These failings are certainly present, but they exist because the novels could no longer carry all that Ford wanted to say, and were in consequence only partial and sometimes careless manifestations of his later thought. In terms of his basic aesthetic, they had to render without passion a society toward which his own attitudes had become too explicitly direct for imaginative art. And in order to implement these attitudes, Ford turned more and more to works of non-fiction, such as the "travel" books, which allowed him to speak more tendentiously. His fiction, by comparison, was relegated to a secondary role, and the novels seem to have suffered as a result from a lessening of effort. Critics such as Meixner and Cassell call attention, however, not to this shift of interest, but to the readily discernible flaws of the novels themselves. Meixner, for example, finds that "the principle of *progression d'effet*, impressionism, and the frequent modulation of effect are used, and, as in each of Ford's post-War novels; the time shift. But the management of these techniques is not creative. Ford's characters fail to come alive, seem too often mere surfaces intensely driven by motivations—compulsions really—which are reduced to a dead formula."[72] Cassell also finds the late novels "Weakened by extremely complex and coincidental plots" and "facilely written by an author who is more and more reticent to approach an action directly."[73] All these observations are both valid and appropriate. Nevertheless, a more comprehensive view of Ford's late work is necessary in order to place the novels and their various failings in a clearer perspective.

One of the more interesting attempts at detailed and comprehensive evaluation is that made by Paul Wiley, who advances a provocative but somewhat questionable theory. He puts in a single category both the fiction and the non-fiction of the 1930's, and sees the entire output of this period as Ford's attempt to register his reaction to an increasingly ominous historical climate through the creation of a mythology. "By the 1930's," Wiley contends, "Ford had joined in the quest of that notable band of desert travelers, dismayed by the toppling of Christian culture and seeking root hold, that included Yeats, Eliot, Lawrence, Huxley, and had taken his own path among divergent roads." In developing his argument, Wiley calls attention to the Great Trade Route, the line that Ford drew in the "travel" books between the barbaric North and the non-industrial South; and adds that "In itself a figure of considerable charm, the Great Road likewise belongs to the time when literary visions of a

return to cultural unity could produce symbolic forms as different as the Byzantium of Yeats and the dark god community of Lawrence. To Yeats, perhaps, Ford stands closer than to Lawrence, since Ford's desire is for an urbane and harmonious culture grounded in civilized tradition and allowing for commerce between west and east."

Turning to the novels, Wiley suggests that in his late fiction Ford wished both to show the disunity of the modern world and to indicate a way out of the dilemma. Consequently, he employed two main devices from the tradition of the occult—the double and the change of identity. The *doppelgänger* motif, Wiley believes, expresses "dramatically . . . the ailment of modern self-division; the exchange or fusion of identities" represents "a conception of the self transformed or unified through awareness of tradition, the latter state probably being connected with the myth of the cycle of kingship, and so affording an answer to the problem of disrupted inheritance involved in works like *The Good Soldier* and the Tietjens sequence." In Wiley's reading of the novels, Joe Notterdam of *When the Wicked Man* comes to exemplify the Nordic barbarian, descended from the bandit ethic which existed to the north of the Trade Route, and he is further blackened by his association with Nostradamus and Faust. Notterdam's fate is embodied in the theme of the double which runs through the novel. *The Rash Act* and *Henry for Hugh* are seen by Wiley as novels of redemption: "the international encounter of Martin and Monckton pleads for the reconciling of these agents of Western culture upon a groundwork of Mediterranean tradition; yet the assumption by Martin of Monckton's responsibilities likewise introduces a mythical allusion to the reinstatement of the cycle of kingship."[74]

Wiley's perception of certain symbolic aspects of the late works is interesting and highly provocative. But when he tries to elevate these symbolic aspects to the level of myth, his argument becomes doubtful on two counts: first, it does not take into consideration the noticeable flaws in the author's handling of his late novels; and secondly, it ignores Ford's own assertion even in the "travel" books, of the private and basically impressionistic nature of his writing. On the first point it is quickly apparent that although a novel such as *When the Wicked Man* may refer to the Faust legend, this reference is never developed, and its applicability to Joe Notterdam's life remains ambiguous. The presentation of myth would necessitate a far more coherent handling of details. The second point—the relationship of myth to Ford's own intent—Wiley, in his eagerness to justify the author's late work, seems to over-read and misinterpret the books themselves. Throughout his literary career, Ford emphasized the subjectivity of his writing, the fact that he was attempting simply to render his own impression. The dispassion of his novels was not an intellectual stance, but a visual point of view which deliber-

ately avoided direct intrusion. Always underlying the selection of details to be rendered, was the unique sensibility of the particular artist. And, as we shall see, even in the "travel" books where he openly assumed the role of prophet, Ford took great pains to emphasize both verbally and structurally the private nature of even his most direct statements.

Admittedly, such a private approach does not prohibit the use of symbols, and Wiley is correct in calling attention to the symbolic value of such devices as Henry Martin's change of identity. But when Wiley attempts to link these symbols to larger public myths, such as the cycle of kingship, his argument becomes somewhat dubious. For although a symbol can still be a means of conveying private impressions, myth by its very nature imposes a cultural scheme on the work, so that the subject is no longer presented for itself, and this would be in direct contradiction to the Fordian aesthetic. However, although definitions of the term may vary considerably, myth can be assumed to have two basic characteristics: a referential value that is public, at least within a given culture, and a coherent structural pattern, usually narrative, through which the symbolism is conveyed in an expected and reconizable form. Ford's final symbolism, even in those works where it is effectively employed, is intentionally set in a loose structure—almost a stream-of-consciousness—in order to emphasize its personal nature. And the effect of the structure is underscored by Ford's own statements, as well as by the nature of the symbols themselves. They are not public symbols; even Provence of the Middle Ages becomes a subjective correlative for the author's own vision of a desirable frame of mind. Ford felt, in his late work, a strong sense of his mission as an artist. If he had intended to write a mythological framework, one would think that he would have so indicated in the works themselves. But instead, his statements move toward an almost opposite pole, and we are led to see his final efforts, particularly the "travel" books, as private attempts to convey, discursively and symbolically, his own vision of his world and of a subjectively-meaningful, alternative solution.

The two "travel" books appeared within two years of each other, *Provence from Minstrels to the Machine* in 1935 and *Great Trade Route* in 1937; and in these two books Ford openly took the role of the prophet, hopefully leading the world closer to the ideal life of the "Small Producer." In *Provence* he announced his purpose:

> This is a book of travel and moralising—on the Great Trade Route which thousands of years before our day, ran from Cathay to the Cassiterides. Along the Mediterranean shores it went and up through Provence. It bore civilization backwards and forwards along its tides (. . .) And this may turn out to be in part a book of prophecies—as to what may and mayn't happen to us according as we re-adapt, or go

even further from, the frame of mind that is Provence and the civilising influences that were carried backwards and forwards in those days.[75]

Ford was able to jest about his newly-assumed role of moralist, to the extent of saying that "It has . . . become more and more manifest to me as the years went by me that the safest road to fame and fortune is that of the moralist. . . . And if I do not set about soon to procure myself those desiderata, fame, fortune and the consequent esteem of my fellows will be forever strangers to me." But the purpose of *Provence*, despite the jesting tone which augmented the personal flavor, was a serious one. It was "none other than to induce my readers—that goodly and attractive band —either to settle in the land of Clemence Isaure, St. Martha, the Tarasque, Marius and Olive of Marseilles, MM. Gambetta, Thiers and M. Bonhoure, the winner of the Five Millions, and other fabulous monsters, or at least to model their lives along the lines of the good Provençal and his Eden-garlic-garden."

Ford declared that he wished to be regarded "simply as prophet," and that he was "going to point out to this world what will happen to it if it does not take Provence of the XIII century for its model." For the "first time," the author found himself fully "in agreement" with those people who felt "that our Civilization—if that is what you want to call it—is staggering to its end—They have stolen away from us, unperceived, Faith and Courage; the belief in a sustaining Redeemer, is a sustaining anything; the Stage is gone, the Cinema is going, the belief in the Arts, in Altruism, in the Law of Supply and Demand, in Science, and the Destiny of our Races (. . .) In the machine itself."[76] Despite his declaration of himself as a prophet and moralist, Ford still opposed the conventional, middle-class, Christian morality, which he here symbolized in the person of Cotton Mather, because it had failed to reconcile "Beauty and Righteousness." The reconciliation of these two qualities, Ford saw as "the moral of this book." But with all the moral weight which Ford loaded upon *Provence*, he took care to emphasize that it was still a book of personal impressions. He spoke in particular of the book's intentional looseness of structure:

> In the middle of some reflections, on East Forty-second Street of the spheres of influence of Mrs. Patrick Campbell coming from her Majesty's Theatre and Mrs. Aimèe Macpherson coming from California, I may introduce some directions as to the real, right and only . . . way to make bouillabaisse (. . . .) That will be because I am capable of anything in the furtherance of a just cause and not because I suffer from a senile impotence to marshall my thoughts.

The tone of the book was one of intimate conversation, or even of private thought, and there was little attempt to hold to any factual truth. Thus he

freely acknowledged that Provence was for him more a personal symbol than an historical reality: "Provence is not a country nor the home of a race, but a frame of mind . . . a place where Truth having no divine right to glamour, experiments in thought abound. And that . . . may open for the mind the road to regions of conjecture that could not otherwise be explored."[77] The region in the south of France certainly held no connotations of a frame of mind for the majority of Ford's readers. By emphasizing this aspect, Ford was both calling attention to the private nature of his symbol and indicating that its relevance for the twentieth century was more than a matter of its geography or its history.

Provence became for Ford a focal point of the Great Trade Route, a line which he drew from China, through the Near East and southern Europe, on into the southern United States. This had been the path of the old merchant-traders; and although Ford did not develop the symbolism of the Great Route until the book to which it gave the title, he began in *Provence* to establish the character of the areas along the Route as clearly non-industrial. There was in his thought a constant antithesis between these areas and the militaristic and mechanized regions to the north. Thus, he repeated the distinction that he had earlier made in *When Blood Is Their Argument* between southern Germany and its northern, or Prussian, counterpart, and he added, "I hope that the end of Mr. Hitler—and soon—may be a long stay in a cage in the Thiergarten of some small South German town."[78] Northern Germany was simply an entire area north of the Great Route, and this area, most of the modern industrial world, was the direct antithesis of Provence.

The world of 1935, as Ford saw it, was a world without leaders, and with "no light anywhere and least of all beneath the lowering skies of Thames Valley;" it was a world that was "not so much emaciated or enfeebled but just simply hopelessly puzzled—even as to the possibility of being so much as well meaning." It was a world in which the problem stemmed not so much from the War, as from a general loss of faith. One of the decisive factors in this loss of faith was the rise of science, and "the first use of Science in the mass was to put an end to infinite millions of human lives." And although Ford could set the development of medicine against the uses of science in the War, he added that the "whole affair" of the value of scientific progress was so "paradoxical" that he hardly dared to acknowledge "even as much as that." The absence of faith had left a void, which was quickly filled by "the sense of property," along with "the ill-nature and ignorance that lead to Wars," and by the vast organizations of nationalistic and industrial societies. But, Ford added, "You cannot . . . have vast organisations without Faith—and Christianity as a Faith died a few days after the 4th of August 1914 (. . .) the only sign of protest against that reign of crime and assassination having been the death, as soon as the effects of war manifested themselves, of Benedict

X." Nonetheless, despite an urgent sense of the decline of a civilization headed for a Second World War, Ford declared in *Provence* that he was "not . . . a pessimist. I don't want our civilisation to pull through, I want a civilisation of small men each labouring two small plots—his own ground and his own soul. Nothing else will serve my turn."[79] This civilization of "small men" with their "two small plots" was for Ford the social manifestation of the Provençal frame of mind.

Ford's turning toward Provence and the way of life for which it stood was part of his recognition of the need for values. But in accord with the approach of his own limited hero, Ford did not seek these values in large and total abstractions, but in a way of life that was built upon the small and ordinary details of existence. In Provence, as he saw it, each of the inhabitants was personally involved in the work and diversions of his entire small community. The life of the Provençal citizen came to symbolize the commitment to the particular that was so important a part of the limited hero's orientation; and it was, moreoever, a way of life in which a significant balance existed between the individual's involvement in his own work and his voluntary devotion to the entire community. As an example of this voluntary loyalty, Ford told the story of M. Bonhoure, the barber, who inherited a large sum of money, but who, instead of detaching himself from his people, willed the entire village bull fights every Saturday.[80] The bull fight itself was a sign of both the individual and the community involvement that pervaded Provence. The professional bull fights were local traditions, and the great matadors were "alone today . . . as beloved as the boy who in Antipolis a couple of thousand years ago danced and gave pleasure." But, Ford added, there was a tradition that before a man could buy a seat at the commercial *mise à mort*, he had to take part in the small bull fights which were held in every village on Sunday, and in which the men did nothing more deadly to the bulls "than affix rosettes beneath their horn or in each shoulder." This tradition of personal involvement was for the author of *Provence* important both as fact and symbol, for it was a tradition which he came to regard as nothing less than "the spirit that could yet save the Western World."[81]

But the bull fight was not only a demonstration of skill or a game for the village men. With its rhythm and ritual it became, like the dance, a ceremonial form of giving pleasure. Because of this shared characteristic, Ford could liken the matador to the dancing Boy of Antibes, a symbol which Ford brought from *The Rash Act* to *Provence*, and which was obviously central to his thought during the period. Dancing he regarded as "the most lovely" and "the most fugitive of all the Arts." And picking up once again the symbol of the Boy, he remarked that "of all the beautiful and mysterious emotions that go to make up the frame of mind that is Provence the most beautiful, moving, and mysterious is that of the Northern Boy of Antibes."[82] The prevalence of dancing was, moreover,

indicative of the high place held by all the arts in Provençal life. In this region, "there arose and continued the tradition that occupation with one art or the other is a proper thing for sound men."[83] The tradition of artistic excellence went back to the Provençal courts of the Middle Ages, for "The poetry of the troubadours," as Ford saw it, "was, almost more than any other manifestation of the Arts, governed by a very definable technique; its hearers—for it had in its own day almost no readers—paid almost as much attention to, and got as much pleasure from the skillful accomplishment or circumvention of a technical point of rhyme, rhythm or metre, as they got from the actual content of the work to which they listened."[84] And in *The March of Literature* Ford ranked the age of the troubadours as "one of the greatest, certainly the most sparkling, of all literary episodes that go to make up the history of our literature today." Provençal poetry had "the sound of the voices of a people whose whole life is expressed in song. It" was "in short, Greek—of the Greece of the days of Theocritus."

Ford viewed the Greece of Theocritus in much the same light as thirteenth-century Provence. It was a settlement in which art and cultivation flourished, in a last burst of light, "just before the final disappearance of the free beauty of Greece beneath the formidable claws of the grafters and scoundrels who bore the name or titles of Caesar." The "Doric settlement in Sicily," in which Theocritus lived, as "a sheltered nook in which the arts could carry on," and which "remained, here and there, as afterwards in the Dark Ages," was a haven for creative effort. "This Greek Colony in an ideal climate, and partly because it was an island, had retained the native simplicity of manners of the eighth-century Greeks, along with a bucolic leisure and wealth in commodities such as had long been unknown elsewhere in Hellas."[85] Provençal life in Ford's own time was directly descended from the thirteenth-century civilization of the troubadours, and it is characterized for Ford by frugality, personal involvement, voluntary loyalty to a small community, and a direct participation in some form of the arts—or, that is, by all those qualities that became central to the limited hero's way of life.

As is evident in his discussion of the Greek Colony of Theocritus and the Provence of the troubadours, Ford tended to single out certain areas and historical periods as symbolic of his desired patterns of existence. And he saw these areas as constantly threatened by a hostile world, either that of the Caesars or that of the war-like and, later, industrial North. Ford's idealization of thirteenth-century Provençal culture and his belief that it was threatened and finally destroyed by a hostile world were evident in his discussion in *Provence* of the Albigensian heresy, as they were later evident in *Great Trade Route* in his premonition of the Fascist threat. The Albigensians were themselves comprised of a number of anti-sacerdotal sects who lived in southern France during the thirteenth cen-

THE LATE WORK AND THE LIMITED HERO

tury. They were highly anti-clerical, and differed from the Catholic Church primarily in their Manichean concept of the dualism of good and evil. To the organized Church, this meant that they believed in two separate gods, and that evil was given a rank equal to that of good. Moved by this theological difference, which was regarded as heresy, as well as by the fact that the anti-clericalism of the Albigensians constituted a power threat, the Church under Pope Innocent III, began a crusade against the Albigensians in 1209. To Ford, this crusade was an obvious example of the invasion of an ideal society by the brutal political forces of the outside world. "The heresy of the Albigensis," he said, "is one of the most curious and suggestive forms of near-rationalism and even as is the vast hesitation of London today it was a product of a civilization that was in the throes of disappearance."

In the face of a Europe which had become "an enormous battle ground across which in the darkness charged the countless hordes," the highly civilized and reflective beings" of Provence developed their own answer: "They evolved the civilization and poetry of the Troubadours, the heresy of the Albigensis and, for as long as they could, let the legions thunder past." Between the two groups, the aristocratic troubadours and the Albigensians, who "became more and more an agricultural commonality," there developed "an uncoded feudalism that was without regulations as without fixed prices," and which achieved an ideal feudal balance of responsibility. The Albigensians, as seen by Ford, "expressly disavowed the doctrine of the divinity of Christ, advocated a strong application of laws of both physical and mental purity and professed disbelief in any personal deity. They substituted for that Article of the Creed, a theory of two first Principles, the one of good, the other of evil." Theirs was a belief "eminently suited to the temperament of a leisured and contemplative peasantry of sufficient education to regard with skepticism a faith that was adopted as a passport to success by the most dangerous and bloodthirsty of its would-be persecutors."[86] And Ford regarded Innocent III's crusade against the Albigensians as "the most of all crusades." Angrily, he pictured St. Dominic, "striding across the field of Muret and setting his feet on the faces of the dying Albigenses who there lay."[87]

Leaving aside the question of the fairness of this image, it is evident that Ford's sympathy for the Albigensians was partly due to a parallel which he saw between their beliefs and those of the post-War world:

> As it is we are in a world of Albigenses. I do not think it is exaggerating to say that the proper man today—the man of some culture and reflection believes that there are two first principles, forgets the Divine Birth of the Saviour, regards the rest of the Christian Creeds, if with affection, yet as legends having no relation with the life of the day. He believes in the necessity for personal and moral purity, like the Cathartes; in the necessity for the reduction of the population; in

the absolute sinfulness of wars and in the right to suicide (....) His religion in fact, like that of the gentle people who were destroyed at the battle of Muret is rather one of negation than of any positiveness at all. It is a product of doubt coming after immense public catastrophe in which, as he sees it, his leaders have been found wanting—of a doubt and languor that distinguish at once the populations of London as of New York.

Ford recognized that the post-War lack of faith, like the belief of the Albigensians, was the product of a vast disillusion: "For the appalled soldiery saw all the Churches of the world plunge into that hellish struggle with the enthusiasm of schoolboys at a rat hunt."[88] And in his discussion of the Albigensians, Ford, himself a Catholic, was not particularly concerned with whether their beliefs were heretical; what definitely caught his attention was the fact that in the midst of their disillusion with the politics of the Church, they had been able to develop the sort of ideal civilization that Ford himself advocated as a solution for their modern counterparts. They had found this solution, and they had been wiped out.

It is quite possible that Ford's view of the Albigensians and the crusade was colored by his symbolic intent. The matter is still open to controversy, and historical opinion of the crusade remains unsettled. And yet, Ford's view of the crusade as cruel and politically motivated appears to have some bearing in fact. The British historian, G. G. Coulton, having examined documents from the Albigensian period, finds considerable corruption among the Catholic clergy, and finds also that the crusaders were responsible for the majority of violence. Coulton writes that the steady growth of heresy in southern France during the twelfth and thirteenth centuries was due to great corruption within the established Church and to the use of heresy by the local barons as a means to gain power. In 1209 the political murder of Pierre de Castelnau, a papal legate who had been agitating against the local barons, caused Innocent III to declare official war. The crusade quickly became a nationalistic power struggle between North and South, and Coulton adds that even from the scattered documents available, "the earliest responsibility for the worst barbarities seems to rest upon the ultimately victorious North. The learned Benedictine authors of the *Histoire de Languedoc* seem, on the whole, to incline to this view."

Coulton cites as evidence the slaughter at Béziers, one of the Albigensian headquarters, in 1209, at which twenty thousand were killed without regard to sex or age. This confession was made in a report by the current papal legate himself. The Pope wrote letters to neighboring rulers, asking their aid and urging that the faithful save their own souls by examining the heretics. Coulton concludes that "this professedly religious war degenerated into perhaps the worst combination that can be conceived. We

THE LATE WORK AND THE LIMITED HERO

have here a fatal mixture of nationalism, race enmities and territorial greed, not only in the unhappy land given over to these battles and sieges, but in other States glad to fish for themselves in the troubled waters."[89] Ford's view of the Albigensians as threatened from the outside seems to have been essentially correct. If he perhaps over-idealized the spiritual as opposed to the political nature of the Albigensian motivations, he did so because this group of Manichean sects, like so much else in his "travel" books, became not so much a fact as an impressionistic symbol of a way of life that Ford desired to revive for his own post-War world.

In the final pages of *Provence* Ford restated the dominant idea of the book. The world had, he said, to return to the life-pattern of the "Small Producer." "We must," Ford emphasized, "go back to the Dark Ages (. . . .) For if we do not go back to the Provençal Dark Ages we shall go back to those of the Teutoburger Wald with the poison-gas clouds for ever above the appalled tree tops." It was unlikely, he felt, that we could ever do away with war, churches, the sense of poverty, or machines. "But all these things must—they will inevitably—be made little. They will be reduced to their proper status either because the armament firms and scientists will blot out almost the entire populations of the world, leaving here and there mere pockets of men. Or else by a change of heart in humanity!" If the world were reallocated into small communities, the scope of wars could be limited, and the small communities, each one producing only that for which it was best fitted, could freely circulate their goods among each other by a system of barter. The "putting into practice" of such a plan "must of necessity abolish wars since no country could dispense with the products of any other country." Then, Ford said, we could return to the way of life that had once existed along the Great Trade Route, with the merchants bringing and exchanging goods and stories from other civilizations. "For I think," he concluded, "that civilizations are better things to exchange than bombs containing poison gases and loathsome infections."[90] The solution advanced in *Provence* was in accord with the limited heroism that Ford had developed gradually throughout his life. The two basic goals were, first, a severe reduction and limitation of the spheres of social operation, both economic and political, and, second, an increase in the involvement of the individual in the small details of his own and his community's existence. In any evaluation of this solution, it should be kept in mind that these characteristics of Provençal life were offered by Ford not as a political program, but as a frame of mind which he hoped would underlie any such problems that might be proposed.

In *Great Trade Route* Ford showed an increasing awareness of current political events, even though the solution advanced was the same as that formulated in *Provence*, and noticeably anti-political in its tone. In the second "travel" book, published in 1937, the author attempted to give a

much stronger sense of the threat posed by the rise of the national heroisms, and at the same time to extend the geographical relevance of the frame of mind developed in *Provence*. It was undoubtedly the desire to emphasize this extension of relevance that led Ford to choose as the central symbol for this second book not the particular region of Provence, but a Trade Route that circled the entire world. Again, as he had with Provence, Ford emphasized that the Great Trade Route was "a frame of mind to which, unless we return our occidental civilization is doomed." Geographically, it was "a broad swathe of territory running from east to West for the most part on the 40th parallel N. For singular as it may seem, on the planisphere, Pekin and Washington and Samarkand and Constantinople are still exactly in line with one another." The Route began at Pekin, ran to Constantinople, turned north above Greece to reach Venice and Genoa, and skirted the Mediterranean to the mouth of the Rhone. It turned north and up the Rhone to Lyons, and then descended the Seine to Paris. It then ran north from Paris, reached the shores of the English Channel at Calais, and finally followed the coast of England to Land's End, from which it turned back toward Pekin. The Great Route was, Ford emphasized, "more . . . a swathe of equable climate than a geographical delineation, a swathe of fertile land rather than a matter of races. It is above all a belt of the world in which men tend to be distinguished by equanimity of mind, frugality, and moderation rather than by huge appetites, crowd massacres, and efficiency. It is in short the tract of land that produced Jesus—or if you prefer it, the Rabbi Hillel—rather than that which produced Calvin."[91] It was essentially a symbolic line, connecting civilizations that were distinguished for Ford from those of the barbaric and industrial North.

The Great Route was the road which the ancient and medieval merchants had followed, as they brought the culture of the Orient and the Near East to southern Europe. Their system of exchange had been one of barter, the goods of one culture being exchanged for the goods of another. "What is certain," Ford believed, "is that our civilization . . . was born on the Great Route, and, in so far as our civilization has beauties and virtues it derives them from the Merchants and their pupils." Historically, he added, after the Flood that once engulfed the world, a "Great Will" to cooperation had seemingly arisen. The traders had set out from the East, probably from Cathay, "to impose the Great Will on that tract before post-deluvian mischief could be worked." They traveled among sparse settlements of people, all of whom had settled along the Great Route because of its equable climate and plentiful food supply. The merchants had carried with them their supplies of exotic goods; "and perhaps more than anything they evangelised with the dance." For the merchant class was comprised not of young sons and criminals, but of the "gravest and most erudite dancers, who were," the "priests."[92] The merchants of

the Great Route thus represented for Ford not only the bringers of civilizing goods, but people who in themselves had a strong sense of the rhythmic basis of both art and life. They were able to elevate their trading to a priestly function just because they were not simply mercantilists, but purveyors of values, and they were protected all along the route by a commonly-understood religious taboo. They raised their work to the level of an art, and by so doing they came to represent, for Ford, values beyond the various goods which they exchanged.

Both the merchants and their Route became for Ford private symbols for the life to which he hoped the world would return. The author actually admitted that he was using the Great Route and the merchants for their symbolic value, and that he had derived his inspiration from "Holy Writ," which "with its symbols is the most reliable and inspired history of the world."[93] But Ford did not create a symbolism with anything near the public context of that in the Bible. His approach in *Great Trade Route* was as digressive and personal as that in *Provence*, and the second book was essentially an extension of the ideas, techniques, and private symbolism of the first. Much of *Great Trade Route*, even more than of *Provence*, was devoted to travel description, and the author's eagerness to assert the symbolism of the Route led him to simplify at times some of its realities. The American South, for example, seemed to him the last stronghold of a civilized American aristocracy. Ford saw the Civil War as a decisive encroachment upon the agrarian South by the industrialized North, and he viewed this War not as a battle over an increasingly impracticable system of slavery, but as "a struggle between two commercial interests." And later, Ford, speaking to the present southern Negro, told him that if he could attach himself to any white family with sufficient means to behave in a proper aristocratic manner, he would "be better off than any hundred-percent Anglo-Saxon worker in Pittsburg, Cleveland, or Detroit. But," Ford conceded, "if you cannot, by service, by name, by tradition—by blood even—hitch onto some such family (. . . .) Well, then (. . . .) Look out (. . . .) The shadow of the rope and the flicker of the flame will be for you a constantly horrible background."[94] In accord with his own intellectual Toryism, Ford saw the race problem in the South as soluble, if only there were a sufficient number of responsible aristocrats to go around. He never paused to question the degree and value of the paternal responsibility which the southern aristocracy had actually shown. As a region along the Great Trade Route, the South had to be inherently civilized.

The only southern area strongly condemned by Ford was Spain, really a nation not directly on the Great Trade Route; and the reason for his attitude was the gray austerity of the Spanish Church. Catholicism everywhere else was "distinguished by one thing (. . .) by, precisely, a sort of gaiety." But in Spain the faith burned "with a black icy flame that

consumes all life."⁹⁵ The dark, foreboding atmosphere of the Spanish Church was directly antithetical to the religious sense of joy which the dancing, merchant-priests had carried along the Great Route. Moreover, an austere Church could hardly teach its gloomy congregation how to involve themselves in life, and this involvement was for Ford a major characteristic of the "frame of mind" that had grown up along the Route. A religion which did not inspire such involvement, along with a sense of joy in life itself, was a distortion of reality, another one of many false idealisms, and one for which Ford had little use.

Always and ominously on the outside edge of the Great Route, there was the modern world. It was a world that was on the verge of cataclysmic destruction. As Ford said:

> We are today in the exact situation of the inhabitants of the world before the deluge. That cataclysm is a few hours off. It will submerge us like a wave. When it has passed there will be very few of us left. It does not matter whether God shall assail us with water, for our sins, or whether we shall, to the greater glory of Science, Murder with wheel-byproducts (. . .) nearly everyone murdering nearly everyone else (. . . .) Then round the world, re-emerging from the clouds of poison gas, will go an afflatus. Suddenly it shall be manifest to us what we must do to be saved. History will have repeated itself.

It does not seem a mere coincidence that the metaphor of a second deluge also carried suggestions of a second cataclysmic war, one that began less than three months after Ford's death. One of the reasons behind the oncoming catastrophe was that political violence and heroic rhetoric, now almost one and the same thing, had gotten completely out of hand. Ford, in *Great Trade Route,* began to repeat over and over again one disturbing motif: the tendency of post-War politics was increasingly to put all opponents "up against a wall." "The world is dying," he said, "because all across it has run the terrible mania of putting everybody but oneself up against a wall. Everybody (. . . .) The dizzy air trembles above everyone of the nations of Christendom and Heathenesse with yelled aspirations to Heaven for the blood of every inhabitant of every other nation (. . . .) But beneath that there is another note (. . . .) In every one of those nations half or part of the nation is beginning to yell for the putting up against the wall of the other half or part (. . .) and both halves or parts are trembling." The world was torn by international and civil strife, and the placing of opponents against a wall became Ford's predominant symbol for all the violence and destructive heroics that were thereby occasioned. The world was furthermore being split in two by the "two mass manias" of communism and Fascism. "Both," Ford noted, "are products of despair and both transcend all other passions. Even patriotism cannot stand against them."⁹⁶

THE LATE WORK AND THE LIMITED HERO

It became evident in *Great Trade Route*—even more than in *Provence* —that Ford's perspective of the world had changed. It was no longer the increasing standardization, the onslaught of canned goods, that most disturbed him. By 1937, Ford had come to feel, not unjustifiably, that the political hero had grown into a maniac, and that a mood of violence and impending doom pervaded the western world. The modern man, symbolized by an American "technocrat," had become a monster who could shout, "All polacks, all wallachs, all waps . . . Up against the wall with them." He could boast that "The United States will order the British Fleet to blow every Italian town off the face of the earth till there's not a beastly mouldering on a Roman or medieval ruin and not an obscene fresco on an obscene church wall in the whole of the peninsula." There was a suggestion of Nazi rantings in the technocrat's declaration that "We shall have bullets that will pierce a hundred men on end and Machines that will convert Jewish corpses into always more Power."[97] And on his voyage to America, Ford had met aboard ship a "Nazi Professor," whose statements had sounded much like those of the "technocrat:"

> 'We shall put up against a wall—and shoot—all Jews, all Catholics, all Communists, and all the (. . . .) Ahem! . . . Up against a wall (. . . .) All that Vermin!'[98]

In his view of the Soviet Union, Ford was apparently not so much disturbed by the political violence as by the tendency of that country to put "its trust in the monstrous collections of wheels that are the Machine," and to use the hammer and sickle, the tools of farming, "merely as emblems on its banner."[99]

It is clear that Ford was profoundly disturbed by the political conditions of the 1930's. He found his world wanting in a "rule of life" and in a "Great Man as director of the public conscience."[100] His lament over the loss of the "Great Man" may seem surprising, unless we remember that Ford had always acknowledged the need for a standard of values, provided that this standard and its proponents were firmly grounded in the everyday. And with the world of the 1930's shouting itself toward greater violence and possible destruction, the "Great Man" or moralizer seemed a far-removed threat, and by comparison to the political dictator, he even began to seem desirable. Ford was not advocating a return to rhetorical heroism, but to a standard that would give the individual some basis by which he might reconstruct a meaningful life. With all the evidence to the contrary, it cannot be said that Ford's late books were lacking in political awareness, at least of existing conditions. The political feasibility of his solutions is another question, and one that will have to be raised in any final evaluation of his work.

Ford saw little hope in a political answer to the problems of the world

around him. Those politicians who were not dictators still seemed to him ineffectual and ridiculous, and their ineffectiveness was all the more serious as they seemed to be losing their edge in the balance of power. The atmosphere at Geneva, the site of the League of Nations, seemed to Ford "a sort of European Middle Western Main Street filled with wooden faces (. . .) and foreigners running on ignoble errands. And one would be just outside the limits of civilization." The representatives at Geneva were "uncouth, unpleasant to the eye," and highly corrupt. They were reflections of the societies that had elected them: "We elect them because they assure us that they will help us to take the bread out of our brother's orphan's mouth and we get the rulers—and the double crossing—that we deserve."[101] Ford's only political advice in *Great Trade Route* was to "get rid of the professional politicians." He admitted, half-jestingly, that it would probably be necessary to have "a Federal Council," but he added that this group could be selected "by going up to the top of the Empire State Building or any high place above a city and letter drop a number of parachutes labelled 'President,' 'Tsar,' 'Secretary' and so on and anyone who got one would have to take the unpleasant job (. . . .) Then they would all be shut up in Monaco."[102]

With this total rejection of the politician and, by implication, of a political solution a basic problem was raised. In the *Great Trade Route* Ford again contrasted the artist, whose "job has been to move around and observe things," with the politician, who is always by virtue of his power telling people what to do.[103] The "job" of observation and of teaching by example was given to both the "Small Producer" and the artist. Ford's proposed solution was distinctly non-political; and yet its implementation in the world—the establishment of communities of "Small Producers" —would require, at least in the beginning, some sort of political machinery. Even if Provence and the Great Trade Route were frames of mind rather than geographical or historical facts, they were nonetheless frames of mind which Ford hoped would find expression throughout the world. Given the imposing structure of existing political reality, such an expression, if it were to be more than a change of individual attitude, would require political change. Unfortunately, the question of the nature of such change was one that Ford himself, in his revulsion from politics, left unanswered.

In *Great Trade Route* the return to the life of the "Small Producer" was again proposed as an end, but the means to this end were seldom, and only jokingly, discussed. For the individual the answer was simple; he had only to adopt the appropriate way of life. But if, as Ford contended, "the Small Producer must again inherit the earth and the fulness thereof," the problem became more difficult. By contesting the growing dictatorships, the "Small Producer," unless he had a collective force behind him, might himself be put "up against a wall." Ford did not noticeably concern

THE LATE WORK AND THE LIMITED HERO

himself with this problem. Instead, he continued to assert that "the Small Producer—the man supporting himself and his family from his plot of ground and by the work of his hands is the one human being whom currency, finance, tariff, the refrigerator, and the machine—those arbiters of the destinies of all other mortals—cannot very much affect. Even wars cannot root him out."[104] The goal of the "Small Producer" was to provide the necessary sustenance for himself, his family, and those around him. He was to detach himself from the acquisitive aspirations that had so long dominated society—"Self-help they used to call it in Victoria's spacious days"—and learn how to make only that which he needed and which might allow a surplus for his neighbors in case of necessity. Ideally, what he could not make or grow for himself, the "Small Producer" was to obtain through the trading of goods.

In *Great Trade Route* Ford admonished his more fortunate readers not to "forget that every penny you make by your honesty, endurance, courage, cleanliness, technical instruction has been taken from a starving child (. . . .) It might have saved a child from starvation (. . . .) But you have it. There were last year 270,000 starving children roaming one country in bands."[105] It was, Ford believed, acceptable that a man should accumulate as property that which he had "made or grown" or which he had "been given . . . by some craftsman or grower—something, above all" that he might "take into a private place apart and examine with a long leisure . . . But," he added, "impersonal property—above all the sense of, the passion for, impersonal property—is the source of all evil."[106] Thus, the "Small Producer" was to separate himself from the prevalent values of his world. Ownership was to be for him not an abstract value, but only the possession of that which he needed or which gave him direct and personal pleasure. Such a separation was an extremely effective means of personal protest and definition. But again, almost at the end of *Great Trade Route*, the author repeated his hope that one day there would be small communities, which would live side by side, "all united by a great afflatus that makes them (. . .) oh, set up statues in every market place to the poetic genius who shall first make of the potato a lively and engaging vegetable."[107]

Ford was too perceptive of his world and too sophisticated to couch his vision in any other tone than that of the delicate self-mockery which he employed. Douglas Goldring, discussing the style of the book, speaks of it as having "a certain sloppiness suggestive of buttons undone," but adds that in spite of the "lavish peppering of dots" and "the sly intimacies between the Master and his inner ring of disciples . . . one realizes," once he has read to the end of the book, "that it has been carefully and skillfully constructed round a central theme which runs through it like the backbone of a herring, to which the inner bones—the 'digressions'—all adhere."[108] Goldring simply calls attention to the personal, or impres-

sionistic approach which Ford selected for this book, and an important device of this approach is the combination of self-revelation and self-mockery—as though one were holding conversation with a group of intimate friends. But as personal as it was, the concept of the "Small Producer" still embodied Ford's alternative to both the public hero and the historical conditions of the post-War world. As a solution for the individual—for a Gringoire or a Christopher Tietjens—the idea was successful on both counts; but as a basis for an alternative society, its practicability was questionable, even though it may have had considerable significance as a collective "frame of mind."

The two "travel" books brought to an end a decade which by its social and political turmoil had raised many new problems for Ford's work. One has only to contrast the serenity of *No Enemy* with the urgency of *Provence* and *Great Trade Route*, and to perceive the dichotomy between Ford's fiction and non-fiction during this period, to sense the strong effect of the 1930's on his thought.

Before we attempt any evaluation of Ford's thought in terms of its relevance to our own socio-political climate, the nature of these last years and the shock which they gave to Ford's sensibility should be kept in mind. Furthermore, we should recognize that Ford never pretended to offer political solutions; and if the lack of such solutions seems a limitation of his writings, we should recall that it is a limitation which he set by his own clear choice.

NOTES

[1] Ford Madox Ford, *It Was the Nightingale* (Philadelphia, London, 1933), p. 6.
[2] *Ibid.*, p. 7.
[3] *Ibid.*, pp. 10, 345.
[4] *Ibid.*, pp. 260–261.
[5] *Ibid.*, pp. 345–346.
[6] *Ibid.*, p. 343.
[7] Ford Madox Ford, *The March of Literature from Confucius' Day to Our Own* (New York, 1938), p. 680.
[8] Ford Madox Ford, "Miracle," *Yale Review*, XVIII (December, 1928), 320–321.
[9] Ford Madox Ford, *New York Is Not America* (London, 1927), p. 164.
[10] Ford Madox Ford, "I Revisit the Riviera," *Harper's*, CLXVI (December, 1932), 76.
[11] Ford Madox Ford, "Small Producer," *American Mercury*, XXXV (August, 1935), 448.
[12] Ford Madox Ford, *A Mirror to France* (London, 1926), pp. 14–15.
[13] *Ibid.*, pp. 9–12.
[14] Ford Madox Hueffer, *Thus to Revisit, Some Reminiscences* (London, 1921), pp. 18–19.
[15] Ford, *March of Literature*, pp. 738–739.
[16] *Ibid.*, pp. 764–765.

THE LATE WORK AND THE LIMITED HERO

[17] *Ibid.*, p. 850.
[18] Ford Madox Hueffer, *Henry James* (London, 1913), p. 11.
[19] Ford, *Mirror*, pp. 281–283.
[20] Ford, *March of Literature*, pp. 761–765.
[21] Ford Madox Ford, *No Enemy, A Tale of Reconstruction* (New York, 1929), p. 3.
[22] *Ibid.*, p. 23.
[23] *Ibid.*, p. 17.
[24] *Ibid.*, pp. 25–26, 34–36.
[25] *Ibid.*, pp. 43–44.
[26] *Ibid.*, pp. 68–69.
[27] *Ibid.*, pp. 84–85.
[28] *Ibid.*, p. 143.
[29] *Ibid.*, pp. 194–200.
[30] *Ibid.*, p. 193.
[31] *Ibid.*, pp. 208–217.
[32] Edward Naumburg, Jr., "A Collector Looks at Ford Madox Ford," *Princeton University Library Chronicle*, IX (April, 1948), 113.
[33] Ford, *No Enemy*, pp. 254–257, 264, 268.
[34] *Ibid.*, p. 273.
[35] Ford Madox Ford, *When the Wicked Man* (New York, 1931), pp. 3–29.
[36] *Ibid.*, pp. 98–99, 121.
[37] *Ibid.*, pp. 110–111, 151.
[38] *Ibid.*, p. 342.
[39] *Ibid.*, p. 309.
[40] *Ibid.*, pp. 303–304, 351–352.
[41] Ford Madox Ford, *The Rash Act* (New York, 1933), title page.
[42] *Ibid.*, pp. 13, 29.
[43] *Ibid.*, pp. 18–19, 26.
[44] *Ibid.*, p. 53.
[45] *Ibid.*, pp. 57–66, 105–106.
[46] *Ibid.*, pp. 32–33, 84.
[47] Paul Wiley, *Novelist of Three Worlds: Ford Madox Ford* (Syracuse, 1962), p. 271.
[48] Ford, *The Rash Act*, pp. 173–174.
[49] *Ibid.*, pp. 87–89, 380.
[50] *Ibid.*, pp. 92–155, 169, 175.
[51] *Ibid.*, p. 227.
[52] *Ibid.*, pp. 259–261, 267.
[53] *Ibid.*, p. 378.
[54] John A. Meixner, *Ford Madox Ford's Novels: A Critical Study* (Minneapolis, 1962), p. 262.
[55] Ford Madox Ford, *Henry for Hugh* (Philadelphia, London, 1934), pp. 9, 21.
[56] *Ibid.*, p. 26.
[57] *Ibid.*, pp. 169–187.
[58] *Ibid.*, p. 60.
[59] *Ibid.*, pp. 89, 108–111, 160–161.
[60] *Ibid.*, pp. 205–210, 305–310.
[61] *Ibid.*, pp. 248–249, 297–299, 324–333.
[62] *Ibid.*, p. 279.
[63] Ford Madox Ford, *Vive Le Roy* (Philadelphia, London, 1936), p. 16.

64 *Ibid.*, p. 199.
65 Wiley, p. 290.
66 Ford, *Vive Le Roy*, pp. 70–71, 73.
67 *Ibid.*, p. 66.
68 *Ibid.*, pp. 19–20.
69 Ford, *Henry For Hugh*, p. 279.
70 Ford, *Vive Le Roy*, p. 340.
71 Wiley, p. 288.
72 Meixner, pp. 257–258.
73 Richard Cassell, *Ford Madox Ford: A Study of His Novels* (Baltimore, 1961), pp. 269–270.
74 Wiley, pp. 249–250, 252–253, 255, 256–257, 258–259, 262, 275.
75 Ford Madox Ford, *Provence From Minstrels to the Machine* (Philadelphia, London, 1935), pp. 13, 58.
76 *Ibid.*, pp. 19–20, 255.
77 *Ibid.*, pp. 20–21, 66–67.
78 *Ibid.*, p. 325.
79 *Ibid.*, pp. 121, 122, 307–308, 297.
80 *Ibid.*, pp. 40–46.
81 *Ibid.*, pp. 256–257.
82 *Ibid.*, pp. 49–50.
83 *Ibid.*, pp. 227–228.
84 *Ibid.*, p. 171.
85 Ford, *March of Literature*, pp. 328, 131.
86 Ford, *Provence*, pp. 123–128, 129–133.
87 *Ibid.*, pp. 175, 182–183.
88 *Ibid.*, pp. 298–300.
89 G. G. Coulton, *Inquisition and Liberty* (London, 1938), pp. 91–107.
90 Ford, *Provence*, pp. 312–313, 351, 353.
91 Ford Madox Ford, *Great Trade Route* (New York, Toronto, 1937), pp. 28–30.
92 *Ibid.*, pp. 28–29, 114, 118.
93 *Ibid.*, p. 108.
94 *Ibid.*, pp. 147, 243, 300, 318–320, 350–351.
95 *Ibid.*, pp. 388–389.
96 *Ibid.*, pp. 106–107, 303–304, 404.
97 *Ibid.*, pp. 69–71.
98 *Ibid.*, p. 41.
99 *Ibid.*, p. 205.
100 *Ibid.*, pp. 110–111.
101 *Ibid.*, pp. 84, 89–90.
102 *Ibid.*, p. 406.
103 *Ibid.*, p. 32.
104 *Ibid.*, pp. 169–170.
105 *Ibid.*, p. 400, cited by Cassell, pp. 98–99.
106 Ford Madox Ford, *Great Trade Route*, p. 205.
107 *Ibid.*, p. 389.
108 Douglas Goldring, *South Lodge* (London, 1943), pp. 216–217.

6.

A Concluding Estimate

IN ANY ATTEMPT to evaluate Ford's ideas, one of the most crucial and controversial areas is that of politics, both because Ford was writing in a world where politics was an extremely powerful reality, and because the posing of political questions helps to point out the basically circumscribed and individual nature of his proposed solution.

During the last decade of his life Ford's political thought, expressed through his arguments for the "Small Producer" must be regarded primarily as a reaction. His was a mode of thought which arose out of a basic and quite justified disgust with politics, both as an ideal and a reality. The novelist was appalled by the politics that he saw around him, and his distrust of political rhetoric prevented his conceiving an alternative that would function through a governmental structure. His proposed solutions for the most part worked around politics, and this of course meant that they avoided a reality which Ford himself found rather prevalent. Douglas Goldring suggests, however, that a major change began to occur in Ford's thought during the 1930's, and that this change, a movement away from High Toryism and toward the political Left, was in the process of fruition in a novel on which Ford was at work in 1939, just before he died. Goldring describes certain changes in the political climate prior to the outbreak of World War II which he feels were partially responsible for the change in Ford's thoughts. After 1920, Goldring contends, "there were no 'High Tories' left in England . . . only a vast commercialized class of what Ford would have considered low Conservatives."[1] Goldring's implication is, of course, that Ford, with his own temperament and ideas, would have found little that was congenial to him on the Right. After 1920, and particularly during the 1930's, Goldring continues, there was a serious moral decline within the British ruling class and on the political Right. During the 1930's, as soon as Hitler seized power and began "beating up Jews, 'intellectuals,' Communists, Socialists and Pacifists . . . the whole attitude of our governing classes toward Germany suddenly changed. Here was a valiant crusader for 'Christian civilization' against the Bolshevik 'Beast.'" And Goldring adds that "These . . . instances of the decay of patriotism and moral sense in England's upper classes, which became so painfully visible in the Armi-

stice years, have been quoted only because of the effect, traceable in his writings, which they evidently had on Ford Madox Ford."[2]

By 1935 in Geneva, Goldring continues, Ford "found himself in a kind of watch tower, rising out of the sea of corruption, from which coming events could be foreseen long in advance." And, Goldring argues, when Ford witnessed events such as the signing by Sir Samuel Hoare of an Anglo-Nazi treaty, which gave Germany the right to build as many submarines as she wished, or the unsympathetic treatment by British officials of Jewish refugees from the Continent, he could no longer "collaborate with the barbarians—even to the extent of remaining silent."[3] A change in ideas was inevitable, for "to grow to boyhood in a country governed by a Gladstone, a Disraeli, or a Salisbury, and to die when the land of your birth was at the mercy of such men as ruled over the Armistice years, was, for an artist like Ford . . . by no means a happy experience."[4]

Goldring's view of Ford's work as showing a gradual movement toward the Left may, however, be biased. For one thing, Ford was scarcely in England during the years after 1922, and Goldring himself did not know Ford personally at any time after their years together on the *English Review*. There is, moreover, in Goldring's argument, a quite probable Marxist orientation. In his discussion of Ford's political views, Goldring refers to the author's projected utopia as "an enchanting dream," and speculates that "Perhaps if he had read David Tutaeff's *The Soviet Caucasus* he would have felt that but for the interruption of the war, the sort of communism he had in view could have been established not in a thousand years but in a generation."[5]

But Tutaeff's book is strongly pro-Soviet. The caption for its frontispiece refers to Stalin as "The greatest of all Caucasians," and the author refers to the Russian governmental councils, or Soviets, as "sturdy blossoms of the peoples will." Furthermore, Tutaeff's praise of the Soviet planners' decision to "develop industry at the risk of an inflated population having to endure bad housing conditions for a number of years" is in strong contrast to the Fordian ideal, even as understood by Goldring.[6] Goldring's favorable citation of Tutaeff's book casts a very real doubt on his interpretation of Ford's later years, if for no other reason than that Tutaeff and Ford seem to have had directly opposing views on the desirability of centralized politics and heavy industry. It is likely that with his own political bias, Goldring may overstate the importance of two late Fordian documents.

According to Goldring, further evidence of a turn toward the Left is given by Ford's published stand on the Spanish Civil War and by the manuscript of his unfinished novel. The stand on the Spanish conflict does reflect a degree of political participation that was somewhat unusual for Ford in a situation where his own country was not directly threatened or

A CONCLUDING ESTIMATE

involved. Ford may have sensed, however, that the Civil War in Spain was an unofficial practice ground for the Second World War, or he may have felt, as he did with the rise of Hitler, the seriousness of the situation, and the consequently urgent need for protest. There is sufficient evidence to indicate that while there may have been a slight shift in emphasis in Ford's thought during, and especially toward the end of the 1930's, this shift was not a radical change. As in the case of the shift in Ford's views on the role of the artist, which began just before he wrote the Tietjens novels, there was in his late political views a direct continuity with his earlier thought. Ford's position on the Spanish Civil War was expressed in a pamphlet entitled *Authors Take Sides on the Spanish War*, which was published in 1937 as a collection of answers by various writers to a questionnaire. In his reply, Ford wrote:

> I am unhesitatingly for the existing Spanish government, and against Franco's attempt—on every ground of feeling and reason. In addition, on the merest commonsense, the Government of the Spanish, as of any other nation, should be settled and defined by the inhabitants of that nation. Mr. Franco seeks to establish a government resting on the arms of Moors, Germans, Italians. Its success must be contrary to world conscience.

Goldring, who cites this passage, comments that "If there is no specific condemnation of Fascism as such, in this statement, there can be little doubt that Ford's thinking was following the general trend."[7] But it is exactly the absence of specific condemnation of Fascism that is significant, for it indicates that although Ford was opposed to the rising Fascism in Europe as a whole, his stand on Spain was based not so much on opposing political systems as on the right of a people to self-determination, without interference by a usurping dictator-hero. Goldring also mentions that "At the time of his death" Ford "was engaged on a novel... which was concerned with the shift from the Right to the Left of the Intelligentsia, due to the world events which began with the Wall Street slump and culminated in Munich." This shift, claims Goldring, reflected Ford's own change, a "development" that "was logical, consistent, and in view of his Standard of Values, inevitable."[8] But Ford himself gives an indication of his own late thought, which suggests a possible misreading on Goldring's part. In a "Paris Letter," published in 1939, the author asks: "What do you think all Paris is whispering about, all around you? About apocalyptic air visitors? About Mr. Hitler? Or the social programme of the Government?" And then he answers himself: "But if Paris really thought integrally about such things France would no more be resiliant." Actually, as Ford later reveals, all Paris, true to its essential regard for the arts, is waiting to hear an address by a member of the *Académie Français*, an address which will be a eulogy of the poet, Henri Regnier.[9]

THE LIMITED HERO

Here, as late as 1939 and one year before the German occupation which he would not see, Ford's affection for France as a center of the arts and a haven from the questions of Hitler and politics is still evident. The mood of this "Letter" almost recalls Ford's reaction to the news of Serajevo, as he described it in *Return to Yesterday*, when he had been more interested in the next installment of Joyce's latest novel than in the outbreak of war. Further evidence that Ford's thought did not undergo a radical change toward the end of his life is furnished by two letters written to this writer by Mrs. Janice Biala Brüstlein, a very close companion of Ford during his final years. In her first letter, speaking of Ford's overall political attitudes, Mrs. Brüstlein writes:

> In answer to yours of June 10th with regard to Ford Madox Ford's politics—I hardly know what to say. Ford loathed politics and politicians—His idea of politics was that every human being is the equal of every other human being and everyone should equally be free from fear and want. You might say 'a chicken in every pot' and no standing up of anyone against a wall would be a good description of his political credo.
> As for his 'support' of the Loyalists during the Spanish Civil War: Every one at that time who was against Fascism was a loyalist sympathizer—The loyalists were not considered a communist front then—as they are now—
> I think a reading of his books, especially *The Great Trade Route* would be useful.

In her second letter, Mrs. Brüstlein very kindly describes the manuscript of the unfinished novel cited by Goldring, although she does not wish to place the document itself in public circulation. With regard to the manuscript, she writes, "there are only about 22 pages of the novel and it is not sufficiently developed to be of much help to you. It was to treat of the turning of the intellectuals to the left—without in any way expressing Ford's own political convictions, such as they were.... I can only assure you that this MSS wouldn't add much to your store of knowledge about Ford's socio-political ideas."[10]

As she was closely acquainted with Ford during his final years whereas Goldring was not, Mrs. Brüstlein's views deserve stronger consideration. Her letters support the impression gained from Ford's writings themselves that Ford did not, even in his late period, write with a predominantly political emphasis. Although he was disturbed by political events, and consequently gave them greater attention than he might have in his earlier works, Ford's primary aim was still to set up a limited hero with a private "frame of mind" as an alternative to these events. Whether or not this alternative had any pragmatic validity is a very real question, but one that must, in the final sense, be answered differently by each reader. We

can say momentarily that since the character of an age or a society was determined for Ford not by political solutions, but by the moral attitudes of individual men and by the prevalent types of heroism, his solution, centering upon the limited hero, was the most valid one possible in his terms. And on the level of analytical criticism, that is all that we can ask.

The question of the relevance of limited heroism in a political context must still be raised; for although this response did not, as Ford saw it, require, at the outset, a modification of the political structure, the decentralization and reduction of power blocs was nonetheless a factor in the total scheme, and political change was thereby involved. Moreover, the very question of the limited hero's survival would necessitate some sort of truce with the political order. Ford was clearly aware of this order, for it became the main antagonist in both his "travel" books. By the time of *Great Trade Route*, the symbol of the wall against which people were placed to be shot was a central motif. Its recurrence, apart from reflecting the climate of the 1930's, also reflected Ford's dislike of the political hero throughout his work. The politician was descended from the Great Victorians; but all the while that he employed their rhetoric, he added a far more dangerous factor of power, until finally he was able to place his opponents against the very wall which Ford so understandably despised. This same element of power was noticeably absent from the alternative that Ford proposed. In the light of his revulsion from politics, this absence was perhaps to be expected; yet the limited hero was still forced to establish himself in a world where political control was a constant reality. And without some means of power at his disposal, such a hero's future would at best be dubious. In a final view, Ford's inability to come to terms with so pervasive a force gives his concept of the limited hero a note of ironic futility, for the chances of its actual realization seem very small indeed.

Yet on another level, if the concept of limited heroism is seen as symbolic of a type of personal response that Ford hoped to revive, it can still direct attention to a sphere of involvement that must underlie even the most intricate of political solutions. This sphere, that of individual commitment to the particular, remained all through the years, and the shifts of emphasis were a constant factor in Ford's thought. Whether the author was criticizing the Great Victorians or the politicians, or whether he was advocating the response of the artist or the "Small Producer," the necessity for involvement in a private reality, in the work of art, the cultivation of the land, or in human relationships, was a theme that ran continuously throughout his work. And beneath this narrowing of focus, there lay a basic recognition of human limitations. It was wrong for a man to involve himself in large truths or public systems, for he had no way of ascertaining their validity, and their over-simplifications and dis-

tortions of reality only blinded him to the more tangible truths of his daily existence. The specific truth of a person's need to be loved had greater meaning for Ford than any heroic mode of response. And the truth of an artist's observations was more true than any moral which he might impose upon them. In all of Ford's work there was an emphasis on that which could be encompassed in the particular, and a rejection of the public hero for his involvement, whether real or rhetorical, in the distortions of the abstract. And because of this explicit recognition of human limitations and of the desirability of private over mass response, the concept of limited heroism was at least a symbolically meaningful protest against inflated politics that had become far too ominously real.

Despite the fact that Ford spoke of governmental units of "Small Producers," his ideas were by nature essentially "apolitical." As formulations of a necessary "frame of mind," both his solutions and his analyses of the dilemma retained a strongly internal focus. And the same internalization evident in his views on society, could be seen as well in his literary criticism. In his discussions of the novel, for example, Ford always assumed that the work of fiction rendered a private impression of reality rather than any social truth or transcendental ideal. The work of art simply objectified as fully as possible a particular convergence of time, place, and incident as perceived by the artist; it did not impose on this convergence any moral imperative or abstract truth, but implied only that significance which the artist could convey through his arrangement of detail. Similarly, in Ford's social critiques and his advocacy of limited heroism, the responsibility for change was very much a matter of personal commitment rather than general solution. The imposition of a political system always seemed to Ford far too dangerous; for like the imposition of external truth upon the work of art, it distorted the specific reality and clouded a full grasp of the issues that were involved. This distortion lay behind the evasion and corruption which seemed to be the legacy of the conventional hero. In Ford's eyes his hero had become so tangled in his own abstractions that he had let his society collapse around him; and as it fell, his descendants had utilized his rhetoric as a veil to cover their own immersion in power and social decay. Under the Great Victorian and the politician who followed him, the language of heroism had become a veil over reality, and it seemed to Ford increasingly necessary to move back to the non-rhetorical and the particular in order to make things clear again.

The responses of the traditional hero and the various manifestations, both personal and social, of his decline, were the themes that most preoccupied Ford in his novels up to and including *The Good Soldier*. The point of view in these novels remained predominantly critical; and whereas Ford was able to show in some of these early heroes, such as George Moffat or Don Collar Kelleg, a latent superiority to their preda-

A CONCLUDING ESTIMATE

tory world, he also made it clear that the inability of these very figures to act decisively in a specific situation was to a large extent responsible for the nature of this world. These idealistic heroes had simply not been able to cope with the reality of their personal relationships or the collapse of their society. And as this society had become increasingly devoid of values, they themselves had frequently become corrupt or cynical, or even both; and their older values had withered to a rhetoric that merely disguised their close involvement with the newer world. In *The Good Soldier*, Ford had culminated his picture of the post-Victorian breakdown with the presentation of Edward Ashburnham, a hero whose sense of false responsibility had first evaded and finally veiled a vicious spiral of personal corruption. And yet by partially shifting the focus of the novel to the self-conscious and openly bewildered narrator, John Dowell, and by showing in detail both the adverse conditions which plagued Ashburnham and his inner struggle in trying to cope with them. Ford was able to change his condemnation to tragedy, and to render, with the double perspective that characterized his greatest work, the sense of anguish and uncertainty that marked the final breakdown of the pre-War world.

In the Tietjens novels, actually written during the latter part of the 1920's, Ford shifted his attention to the seeming climax of that breakdown, the First World War; and he indicated how the War, itself a reflection of the civilian collapse, had by its very sense of finality forced the hero, Christopher Tietjens, to choose for himself a totally new way of life. Because the War was so closely linked by Ford to the problems at home, Christopher's personal answer, if it was to have any lasting value, had to be made on civilian terms. It had to be an answer that, although stemming from his war experience, would confront and reshape his civilian life. These conditions were met by the limited heroism into which Tietjens grew as the series progressed. The *Parade's End* tetralogy was, in fact, the first work in which Ford gave extensive fictional development to the concept of limited heroism. And the novels were controlled in their movement toward this new response by Ford's variation of the double perspective. During the first novel, Tietjens still appeared to be an ideal culmination of the traditional aristocrat, with all virtues and faults which his position implied; but by the final book, he had become the first of Ford's new alternative figures, and limited heroism was for him an established way of life.

The concept of limited heroism became the dominant motif of Ford's work for the remainder of his life. As his work moved into its final period, the conditions of the surrounding world grew so adverse that Ford was compelled by a growing sense of danger to adopt a new and rather foreign tone of didacticism. His major effort was placed not in his novels, which were no longer adequate to his total viewpoint, but in his works of non-fiction, where he could address his readers directly on the

necessity of assuming the limited hero's "frame of mind." The "frame of mind" was marked by the specific involvement and the sense of limitations which seemed to Ford the only answer to the overblown schemes of the new political heroes. And as Ford looked increasingly to his final "travel" books as expressions of this later thought, the double attitude which had once distinguished his major novels virtually disappeared from his works. The world, heading toward a second great war, could hardly be seen as embodying its own potential for good. This potential was consequently transferred by Ford to his non-fiction, where it became a suggested possibility rather than an aspect of what actually was.

Throughout his lifetime, Ford was faced with the problem of finding alternatives to a recurrently collapsing world. Because the social reality was so disheartening, he found himself conceiving such alternatives on individual terms—whether those of the artist or the "Small Producer"—and his tendency to think in these terms may well have been the factor that caused him to view the failures of the Victorians as individual ones, and therefore to condemn them so personally for not having come to grips with their world. And while he viewed the Victorian failure as one of individuals, and especially of the rhetorical public hero, Ford also saw his alternative as a private matter, centered around the self-sufficiency of the limited hero. The author thus tended to view his world through the circumscribed perspective of the individual, and his work showed both the strengths and weaknesses of this position.

It may be said that Ford's advocacy of the "Small Producer" and the Provençal way of life grew to seem increasingly hopeless in a world marked by inept politicians and dictators who pushed their opponents "up against a wall." In a sense, his ideas, read in the light of all the history that has occurred since his death in June, 1939, have an ironically empty ring. The sense of urgency which resulted in the weakness of Ford's final novels and their subordination to his "travel" books—a weakness and subordination that can scarcely at such a late stage in his life be attributed to literary apprenticeship—is in itself an indication of the irony that shadowed his final work. For he hardly had time to advance his position before it was lost in the welter of a second war. And yet, Ford's late writings show that he was aware of the political realities of the 1930's and that he was becoming progressively concerned over their recurring manifestations. He chose, however, not to seek a solution in the very area of which these manifestations were a part. Therein, he thought, lay certain failure. Within the terms that Ford openly set for himself, his work shows a persistent attempt to grapple with the problems of his world. This world and its alternatives were rendered as he saw them, and this, too, was in accord with his view of the artist's role. The relevance of Ford's approach may be limited, but his plea for the limited hero is true

A CONCLUDING ESTIMATE

to its own terms; and for the reader it at least recalls awareness of a private sphere that ought hopefully to underlie any public solution.

But it is really through its anguished sense of the bewilderment and attempted solutions which accompanied the historical crisis that Ford's work makes its strongest appeal. There is never a suggestion, even in the didactic "travel" books, that the proposed solution would be easy. And the dualistic psychology that characterized all his best work, although a means of indicating complexity of character, was also a way of indicating the intense dislocations to which his heroes were subject in the period between the Victorian collapse and the Second World War. It was a dislocation partly of their own making; and sometimes, as in the case of Christopher Tietjens or the hypothetical "Small Producer," there was also a solution. But when Ford's work is seen in retrospect, the factors that remain strongest are Dowell's aware but paralyzed bewilderment in *The Good Soldier;* Tietjens' struggle to achieve his final role and his isolation once this role is achieved from a world that is falling apart around him; and the urgency of the "travel" books, the juxtaposition of the "Small Producer" and the ominous looming of the firing squad. The solution is never easy. It is a late and needed personal assertion in the face of a world crisis so great that it can render ineffectual the old heroic norms and leave the former heroes—themselves partly to blame—inert and unresolved. The response of limited heroism offers a possible and limited resolution; but it is a resolution cradled in crisis, and in the final analysis, it is perhaps Ford's acute sense of this crisis that is most emotionally striking and intellectually significant.

NOTES

[1] Douglas Goldring, *South Lodge* (London, 1943), p. 210.
[2] *Ibid.*, pp. 211–212.
[3] *Ibid.*, pp. 215, 221.
[4] *Ibid.*, pp. 203–205.
[5] *Ibid.*, p. 218.
[6] David Tutaeff, *The Soviet Caucasus* (London, 1942), pp. 77, 90.
[7] Goldring, *Genius*, pp. 270–271.
[8] *Ibid.*, p. 271.
[9] Ford Madox Ford, "Paris Letter," *Kenyon Review*, I (Winter, 1939), 22–24.
[10] Two letters to this writer from Mrs. Janice Biala Brüstlein, dated June 14, 1961, and November 30, 1962.

A Working Bibliography

1. BOOKS BY FORD:

Hueffer, Ford Madox. *The Brown Owl, A Fairy Story*. London, 1892.
———. *The Feather*. London, 1892.
———. *The Shifting of the Fire*. London, 1892.
Reviewed: *Athenaeum*, C (Nov. 19, 1892), 100.
Haig, Fenil, pseud. *The Question at the Well, With Sundry Other Verses for Notes of Music*. London, 1893. (In the copy located in the Princeton University Library there is an envelope in the handwriting of the author, addressed to Thomas Hutchinson, the former owner of the book. Hutchinson has initialed a note opposite the half-title to the effect that Fenil Haig is a pen name of F. M. Hueffer.)
Hueffer, Ford Madox. *The Queen Who Flew, A Fairy Tale*. London, 1894.
———. *Ford Madox Brown, A Record of His Life and Work*. London, New York, and Bombay, 1896.
Reviewed: *Athenaeum*, 3618, 3620 (Feb. 27, March 18, 1897), 284–285, 352–354; *Critic*, XXX (Feb. 6, 1897), 93; *Edinburgh Review*, CXXCV (April, 1897), 501–503; *Living Age*, CCXIII (June 12, 1897), 714–715; *Nation*, LXIV (Feb. 11, 1897), 110–112; *Spectator*, LXXVIII (Feb. 13, 1897), 245–246.
———. *The Cinque Ports, A Historical and Descriptive Record*. Edinburgh and London, 1900.
Reviewed: *Athenaeum*, 3816, II (Dec. 15, 1900), 798–799; *Blackwood's*, CLXVIII (Nov., 1900), 711–718; *Magazine of Art*, XXVI (Dec., 1901), 70–71.
———. *Poems for Pictures and for Notes of Music*. London, 1900.
——— and Joseph Conrad. *The Inheritors, An Extravagant Story*. New York and London, 1901.
———. *Rossetti, A Critical Essay on His Art*. London and New York, 1902.
Reviewed: *Nation*, LXXV (Aug. 14, 1902), 136.
——— and Joseph Conrad. *Romance*. London, 1903, New York, 1904. Published in Paris in 1926 under the title *L'Aventure*, trans. Marc Chadourne.
Reviewed: *Athenaeum*, 3967, II (Nov. 17, 1903), 610; *Dial*, XXXVII (June 16, 1904), 37; *Outlook*, LXXVII (June 18, 1903), 424–425.
———. *The Face of the Night, A Second Series of Poems for Pictures*. London, 1904.
———. *The Benefactor, A Tale of a Small Circle*. London, 1905.
———. *Hans Holbein the Younger, A Critical Monograph*. London and New York, 1905.
Reviewed: *Dial*, XLI (Nov. 1, 1906), 285; *Independent*, LXI (Oct. 4,

A WORKING BIBLIOGRAPHY

1906), 818; N.Y. *Times Book Review*, XI (May 19, 1906), 329; *Outlook*, LXXXIII (July 21, 1906), 670.

―――. *The Soul of London, A Survey of a Modern City.* London, 1905.
Reviewed: *Bookman* (London), XXVIII (May, 1905), 60-61.

―――. *Christiana's Fairy Book.* London, 1906.

―――. *The Fifth Queen: And How She Came to Court.* London, 1906.
Reviewed: *Bookman* (London), XXX (April, 1906), 37.

―――. *The Heart of the Country, A Survey of a Modern Land.* London, 1906.
Reviewed: *Bookman* (London), XXX (June, 1906), 111.

―――. *An English Girl, A Romance.* London, 1907.

―――. *England and the English, An Interpretation.* New York, 1907.

―――. *The Pre-Raphaelite Brotherhood, A Critical Monograph.* London, 1907.

―――. *Privy Seal: His Last Venture.* London, 1907.

―――. *The Spirit of the People, An Analysis of the English Mind.* London, 1907.
Reviewed: *Bookman* (London), XXXIV (June, 1908), 110.

―――. *The Fifth Queen Crowned, A Romance.* London, 1908.
Reviewed: *Bookman* (London), XXXIV (May, 1908), 77.

―――. *Mr. Apollo, A Just Possible Story.* London, 1908.

―――. *The 'Half Moon,' A Romance of the Old World and the New.* London, 1909.
Reviewed: *Bookman* (London), XXXVI (June, 1909), 134-135; *ALA Booklist*, VI (Sept., 1909), 27; *Athenaeum*, 4253, I (May 1, 1909), 525; *Bookman*, XXIX (Aug., 1909), 648; *Nation*, LXXXIX (Sept. 23, 1909), 278; N.Y. *Times Book Review*, XIV (July 24, 1909), 451; *Review of Reviews*, XL (Aug., 1909), 253; *Saturday Review*, CVII (May 15, 1909), 633; *Spectator*, CII (May 29, 1909), 864.

―――. *A Call; The Tale of Two Passions.* London, 1910.

―――. *The Portrait.* London, 1910.

―――. *Songs from London.* London, 1910.

―――. *Ancient Lights and Certain New Reflections, Being the Memories of a Young Man.* London, 1911.
Reviewed: *Bookman* (London), XL (May, 1911), 90-91; *ALA Booklist*, VII (June, 1911), 424; *Athenaeum*, 4360, I (May 20, 1911), 567; *Dial*, L (May 1, 1911), 345; *Independent*, LXXI (July 6, 1911), 44; *Nation*, XCII (June 8, 1911), 581; N.Y. *Times Book Review*, XVI (April 30, 1911), 260; *New York Times*, XVI (May 7, 1911), 277; *New York Times*, XVI (June 11, 1911), 373; *North American Review*, CXCIV (Sept., 1911), 468; *Review of Reviews*, XLIV (Aug., 1911), 254; *Saturday Review*, CXI (May 6, 1911), 555.

―――. *The Critical Attitude.* London, 1911.
Reviewed: *Bookman* (London), XLI (Jan., 1912), 218.

―――. *High Germany, Eleven Sets of Verse.* London, 1911.

―――. *Ladies Whose Bright Eyes, A Romance.* London, 1911.
Reviewed: *Athenaeum*, 4373, II (Aug. 19, 1911), 211; *Books*, N.Y. *Herald Tribune* (May 26, 1935), 6; *Bookman* (London), XLI (Oct., 1911), 59-60; Boston *Transcript* (May 15, 1935), 2; *Christian Science Monitor* (June 4, 1935), 16; *Nation*, CXL (June 26, 1935), 752; N.Y. *Times Book Review*, XVII (May 12, 1912), 288; *New York Times* (May 19, 1935), 7; *Pratt Institute Quarterly* (Autumn, 1935), 37;

Saturday Review, CXII (Sept. 16, 1911), 371; *Saturday Review of Literature*, XII (May 18, 1935), 7.

————. *Memories and Impressions, A Study in Atmospheres.* New York and London, 1911.

Chaucer, Daniel, pseud. *The Simple Life Limited.* London, 1911. (In the Princeton University Library copy there is a letter which Edward Naumburg, Jr., claims is from Ford to Violet Hunt, and which is dated April 9, 1911, from Giessen. It is signed Daniel Chaucer.)

————. *The New Humpty-Dumpty.* London and New York, 1912.

Hueffer, Ford Madox. *The Monstrous Regiment of Women.* Place unknown. Published by the Women's Freedom League, 1912.

————. *Henry James, A Critical Study.* London, 1913.

Review: *ALA Booklist*, XIII (Dec., 1916), 112; *Athenaeum*, *4499*, I (Jan. 17, 1914), 88; *Bookman* (London), XLV (March, 1914), 302–307; *Bookman*, XLIV (Nov., 1916), 298; Boston *Transcript* (Oct. 21, 1916), 8; *Dial*, LXI (Nov. 2, 1916), 345; N.Y. *Times Book Review*, XXI (Oct. 1, 1916), 385; *Saturday Review*, CXVII (Jan. 13, 1914), 22.

————. *Mr. Fleight.* London, 1913.

————. *The Panel, A Sheer Comedy.* Indianapolis, 1913.

————. *Ring for Nancy.* Indianapolis, 1913.

Reviewed: *Nation*, XCVII (Nov. 27, 1913), 509; N.Y. *Sun* (Oct. 25, 1913), 3.

————. *The Young Lovell, A Romance.* London, 1913.

————. *Collected Poems.* London, 1914. (This collection includes *High Germany, Songs from London, From Inland, The Face of the Night, Poems for Pictures,* and *Little Plays.*)

————. *Antwerp.* London, 1915.

————. *Between St. Dennis and St. George, A Sketch of Three Civilizations.* London, New York and Toronto, 1915.

Reviewed: *Bookman* (London), XLIX (Oct., 1915), 26.

————. *The Good Soldier, A Tale of Passion.* London and New York, 1915.

Reviewed: *Athenaeum*, 4563, I (April 10, 1915), 334; Boston *Transcript* (March 17, 1915), 24; *Independent*, LXXXI (March 22, 1915), 432; *Nation*, C (April 29, 1915), 470; *New Republic*, III (June 12, 1915), 155; N.Y. *Times Book Review*, XX (March 7, 1915), 86; *Saturday Review*, CXIX (June 19, 1915), supp. 4; *Springfield Republican* (March 25, 1915), 5.

————. *When Blood Is Their Argument, An Analysis of Prussian Culture.* New York and London, 1915.

Reviewed: *ALA Booklist*, XII (Nov., 1915), 83; Boston *Transcript* (July 24, 1915), 210; *Spectator*, CXIV (April 17, 1915), 546; Springfield *Republican* (June 3, 1915), 5.

————. *Collected Poems of Ford Madox Hueffer.* London, 1916.

———— and Violet Hunt. *Zeppelin Nights, A London Entertainment.* London and New York, 1916.

Reviewed: *Bookman* (London), VII (Oct., 1916), 10.

————. *On Heaven and Poems Written on Active Service.* London and New York, 1918.

Reviewed: *ALA Booklist*, XV (Dec., 1918), 97; *Dial*, LXV (Nov. 16, 1918), 417; *Nation*, CVII (Nov. 30, 1918), 660; N.Y. *Times Book*

A WORKING BIBLIOGRAPHY

Review, XXIII (Dec. 1, 1918), 525; *Outlook*, CXXI (Jan. 8, 1919), 55; *Review of Reviews*, LVIII (Nov., 1918), 555; *Saturday Review*, CXXV (May 11, 1918), 413; *TLS* (April 18, 1918), 187.
——. *A House*. London, 1921.
——. *Thus to Revisit, Some Reminiscences*. London, 1921.
Reviewed: *Booklist*, XVIII (Oct., 1921), 11; Boston *Transcript* (July 27, 1921), 6; *Dial*, LXXI (Dec., 1921), 5; *Nation*, CXIII (Nov. 30, 1921), 624; *Nation and Athenaeum*, XXIX (May 28, 1921), 328; *New Statesman*, XVII (June 11, 1921), 282; N.Y. *Times Book Review* (July 17, 1921), 16; *North American Review*, CCXIV (Nov., 1921), 697; *Spectator*, CXXVII (Sept. 17, 1921), 368; *TLS* (May 12, 1921), 310.
Ford, Ford Madox. *The Marsden Case, A Romance*. London, 1923.
——. *Mister Bosphorus and the Muses, Or a Short History of Poetry in Britain, Variety Entertainment in Four Acts.* . . . London, 1923.
——. *Women and Men*. Paris, 1923.
——. *Joseph Conrad, A Personal Remembrance*. London, 1924.
Reviewed: *Literary Review* (Dec. 20, 1924), 2; *Nation*, CXX (Jan. 14, 1925), 45; *Nation and Athenaeum*, XXXVI (Dec. 6, 1924), 366; *New Statesman*, XXIV (Dec. 6, 1924), supp. xvi; N.Y. *Times Book Review* (Dec. 7, 1924), 3; N.Y. *World* (Dec. 7, 1924), 8e; *Spectator*, CXXXIII (Nov. 15, 1924), 742; *TLS* (Nov. 13, 1924), 727.
—— and Joseph Conrad. *The Nature of a Crime*. London, 1924.
——. *Some Do Not*. London, 1924.
——. *No More Parades*. London, 1925.
Reviewed: *Atlantic's Bookshelf* (May, 1926); *Books*, N.Y. *Herald Tribune* (Nov. 22, 1925), 3; *Cleveland Open Shelf* (Nov., 1926), 122; *Independent*, CXV (Dec. 5, 1925), 650; *Literary Review* (Dec. 5, 1925), 4; *Nation*, CXXII (March 10, 1926), 260; *Nation and Athenaeum*, XXXVIII (Oct. 31, 1925), 186; *New Statesman*, XXV (Oct. 10, 1925), 727; *New York Times* (Nov. 8, 1925), 9 and (Dec. 6, 1925), 2; N.Y. *World* (Nov. 22, 1925), 7; *Saturday Review*, CXL (Oct. 10, 1925), 410; *Springfield Republican* (March 28, 1926), 7; *TLS* (Oct. 1, 1925), 636.
——. *A Man Could Stand Up*. London, 1926.
Reviewed: *Books*, N.Y. *Herald Tribune* (Oct. 17, 1926), 5; Boston *Transcript* (Dec. 8, 1926), 3; *Independent*, CXVII (Nov. 6, 1926), 536; *Literary Review* (Nov. 6, 1926), 3; *Living Age*, CCCXXXI (Dec. 15, 1926), 560; *Nation and Athenaeum*, XL (Oct. 23, 1926), 116; *New Republic*, XLIX (Dec. 22, 1926), 143; *New Statesman* XXVIII (Oct. 23, 1926), 48; *New York Times* (Oct. 27, 1926), 7; N.Y. *World* (Oct. 31, 1926), 11; *Saturday Review*, CXLII (Nov. 13, 1926), 592; *Saturday Review of Literature*, III (Dec. 4, 1926), 365, and III (Dec. 18, 1926), 445; *Spectator*, CXXXVII (Oct. 16, 1926), 652; *TLS* (Oct. 14, 1926), 694.
——. *A Mirror to France*. London, 1926.
Reviewed: *Booklist*, XXIII (Dec., 1926), 126; *Bookman*, LXIV (Oct., 1926), xxx; *Cleveland Open Shelf* (Nov., 1926), 120; *Independent*, CXVII (Aug. 28, 1926), 246; *Literary Review*, (Oct. 9, 1926), 14; *Nation*, CXXIII (Sept. 8, 1926), 225; *Nation and Athenaeum*, XXXIX (June 12, 1926), supp. 298; *New Republic*, XLVIII (Oct. 13, 1926), 228; *New Statesman*, XXVII (June 19, 1926), 274; *New York Times*

223

(Aug. 29, 1926), 3; *Saturday Review of Literature*, III (Sept. 4, 1926), 83; *Springfield Republican* (Sept. 22, 1926), 8; *TLS* (May 20, 1926), 333; *Yale Review*, XVI (Jan., 1927), 396.

———. *New Poems*. New York, 1927.

———. *New York Essays*. New York, 1927.

———. *New York Is Not America*. London, 1927.

Reviewed: *Booklist*, XXIV (March, 1928), 244; *Books*, N.Y. *Herald Tribune* (Jan. 22, 1928), 7; *Cleveland Open Shelf* (April, 1928), 50; *Dial*, LXXXIV (Feb., 1928), 161; *Nation and Athenaeum*, XLI (Aug. 6, 1927), 613; *New Statesman*, XXX (Nov. 5, 1927), 120; N.Y. *Evening Post* (Dec. 4, 1927), 12; *New York Times* (Jan. 15, 1928), 2; *Pittsburgh Monthly Bulletin*, XXXIII (March, 1928), 173; *Saturday Review of Literature*, IV (Feb. 18, 1928), 607; *Spectator*, CXXXIX (Sept. 10, 1927), 396; *TLS* (Sept. 8, 1927), 603.

———. *Last Post*. London, 1928.

Reviewed: *Booklist*, XXIV (May, 1928), 322; *Books*, N.Y. *Herald Tribune* (Jan. 15, 1928), 3; *Boston Transcript* (Feb. 8, 1928), 4; *Dial*, LXXXIV (March, 1928), 251; *Independent*, CXX (Feb. 4, 1928), 117; *Nation*, CXXVI (Feb. 15, 1928), 191; *Nation and Athenaeum*, XLII (Feb. 18, 1928), 752; *New Republic*, LIII (Jan. 25, 1928), 279; *New Statesman*, XXX (Feb. 4, 1928), 533; N.Y. *Evening Post* (Jan. 21, 1928), 14; *New York Times* (Jan. 15, 1928), 9; *North American Review* (March, 1928), 225; *Pittsburgh Monthly Bulletin*, XXXIII (April, 1928), 193; *Saturday Review*, CXLV (Feb. 18, 1928), 199; *Spectator*, CXL (Feb. 4, 1928), 168; *Springfield Republican* (March 18, 1928), 7; *TLS* (Jan. 19, 1928), 47, and (Jan. 26, 1928), 60.

———. *A Little Less Than Gods, A Romance*. London, 1928.

Reviewed: *Books*, N.Y. *Herald Tribune* (Nov. 4, 1928), 5; N.Y. *Evening Post* (Nov. 3, 1928), 9; *New York Times* (Oct. 28, 1928), 7; *North American Review* (Dec., 1929), 226; *Outlook*, CL (Dec. 5, 1928), 1290; *Saturday Review*, CXLVI (Nov. 25, 1928), 692; *Saturday Review of Literature*, V (Nov. 24, 1928), 398; *Spectator*, CXLI (Dec. 8, 1928), 896; *TLS* (Nov. 1, 1928), 802.

———. *No Enemy, A Tale of Reconstruction*. New York, 1929.

Reviewed: *Books*, N.Y. *Herald Tribune* (Dec. 29, 1929), 5; *Boston Transcript* (Dec. 18, 1929), 2; N.Y. *Evening Post* (Dec. 21, 1929), 12; N.Y. *World* (Nov. 17, 1929), 11; *Outlook*, CLIII (Nov. 13, 1929), 427.

———. *The English Novel from the Earliest Days to the Death of Joseph Conrad*. Philadelphia and London, 1929.

Reviewed: *Booklist*, XXV (June, 1929), 351; *Nation*, CXXVIII (April 17, 1929), supp. 482; N.Y. *Evening Post* (April 6, 1929), 11; *Outlook*, CLI (March 27, 1929), 513; *Saturday Review of Literature*, V (April 13, 1929), 889.

———. *I Saw Thrones*. London, 1931.

———. *Return to Yesterday, Reminiscences 1894–1914*. London, 1931.

Reviewed: *Booklist*, XXVIII (March, 1932), 306; *Books*, N.Y. *Herald Tribune* (Jan. 17, 1932), 1; *Boston Transcript* (March 12, 1932), 1; *Catholic World*, CXXXV (May, 1932), 250; *Chicago Daily Tribune* (Jan. 16, 1932), 10; *Commonweal*, XVI (May 25, 1932), 111; *Forum*, LXXXVII (March, 1932), viii; *Nation*, CXXXIV (April 6, 1932), 403; *New Republic*, LXX (March 23, 1932), 160; *New Statesman and Nation*, II (Nov. 14, 1931), 615; *New York Times* (Jan. 24, 1932), 2;

A WORKING BIBLIOGRAPHY

Outlook, CLX (Jan. 27, 1932), 121; *Pittsburgh Monthly Bulletin,* XXXVII (June, 1932), 42; *Pratt Institute Quarterly* (Spring, 1932), 33; *Saturday Review of Literature,* VIII (March 5, 1932), 569; *Spectator,* CXLVII (Nov. 21, 1931), 685; *TLS* (Nov. 12, 1931), 890.

———. *When the Wicked Man.* New York, 1931.

Reviewed: *Bookman,* LXXIII (April, 1931), 187; *Books,* N.Y. *Herald Tribune* (May 31, 1931), 7; Chicago *Daily Tribune* (May 23, 1931), 8; *Forum,* LXXXVI (July, 1931), xii; *Nation,* CXXXIII (July 29, 1931), 114; *New Republic,* LXVII (July 8, 1931), 213; *New York Times* (May 24, 1931), 4; *Outlook,* CLVIII (June 3, 1931), 150; *Saturday Review of Literature,* VII (June 27, 1931), 925.

———. *It Was the Nightingale.* Philadelphia and London, 1933.

Reviewed: *American Review,* II (Nov., 1933), 101; *Booklist,* XXX (Dec., 1933), 118; *Books,* N.Y. *Herald Tribune* (Oct. 22, 1933), 7; Boston *Transcript* (Dec. 3, 1933), 1; *Nation,* CXXXVII (Nov. 8, 1933), 544; *New York Times* (Nov. 12, 1933), 2; *North American Review,* CCXXXVI (Nov., 1933), ii; *Saturday Review of Literature,* X (Oct. 21, 1933), 199.

———. *The Rash Act.* New York, 1933.

Reviewed: *Booklist,* XXIX (June, 1933), 310; *Books,* N.Y. *Herald Tribune* (Feb. 26, 1933), 4; Boston *Transcript* (March 18, 1933), 1; *Nation,* CXXXVII (Aug. 2, 1933), 138; *New Outlook,* CLXI (March, 1933), 58; *New Republic,* LXXIV (March 29, 1933), 192; *New Statesman and Nation,* VI (Sept. 16, 1933), 238; *New York Times* (March 12, 1933), 16; *Spectator,* CLI (Sept. 8, 1933), 321; *Springfield Republican* (March 26, 1933), 7; *TLS* (Sept. 14, 1933), 608.

———. *Henry for Hugh.* Philadelphia and London, 1934.

Reviewed: *Books,* N.Y. *Herald Tribune* (Oct. 12, 1934), 12; Boston *Transcript* (Jan. 2, 1935), 3; *New York Times* (Oct. 21, 1934), 6; *North American Review,* CCXXXVIII (Dec., 1934), 574; *Saturday Review of Literature,* XI (Oct. 13, 1934), 205.

———. *Provence from Minstrels to the Machine.* Philadelphia and London, 1935.

Reviewed: *American Review,* V (Sept., 1935), 488; *Booklist,* XXXI (April, 1935), 262; *Books,* N.Y. *Herald Tribune* (March 24, 1935), 1, and (April 7, 1935), 32; *Catholic World,* CXLI (Aug., 1935), 636; *Cleveland Open Shelf* (March, 1935), 7; *Commonweal,* XXI (April 12, 1935), 688; *Nation,* CXL (May 8, 1935), 533; *New Republic,* LXXXIII (May 29, 1935), 82; *New York Times* (March 24, 1935), 9; *Pratt Institute Quarterly* (Summer, 1935), 29; *Saturday Review of Literature,* XI (April 13, 1935), 621; *Yale Review,* XXIV (Summer, 1935), 831.

———. *Collected Poems.* New York, 1936.

Reviewed: *Books,* N.Y. *Herald Tribune* (Nov. 1, 1936), 5; Boston *Transcript* (Oct. 31, 1936), 6; *Commonweal,* XXV (Nov. 13, 1936), 84.

———. *Vive Le Roy.* Philadelphia and London, 1936.

Reviewed: *Books,* N.Y. *Herald Tribune* (April 18, 1936), 16; Boston *Transcript* (May 23, 1936), 4; Chicago *Daily Tribune* (April 11, 1936), 12; *Nation,* CXLII (May 20, 1936), 657; *New Republic,* LXXXVII (June 3, 1936), 112; N.Y. *Herald Tribune* (April 9, 1936), 21; *New*

York Times (April 19, 1936), 20; Pratt Institute Quarterly (Autumn, 1936), 39; Time, XXVII (April 13, 1936), 91.

———. Great Trade Route. New York and Toronto, 1937.
Reviewed: Booklist, XXXIII (April, 1937), 240; Books, N.Y. Herald Tribune (Feb. 21, 1937), 5; Boston Transcript (Jan. 16, 1937), 3; Chicago Daily Tribune (Feb. 20, 1937), 8; Christian Science Monitor (June 23, 1937), 10; Commonweal, XXVI (April 20, 1937), 28; Forum, XCVII (April, 1937), v; Nation, CXLIV (March 27, 1937), 358; New Republic, XC (May 5, 1937) 385; New York Times (Feb. 21, 1937), 2; Saturday Review of Literature, XVI (Aug. 28, 1937), 19; Spectator, CLVIII (Jan. 22, 1937), 134; TLS (Jan. 16, 1937), 38.

———. Portraits from Life. Boston and New York, 1937.
Reviewed: Booklist, XXXIII (May, 1937), 267; Books, N.Y. Herald Tribune (March 28, 1937), 5; Boston Transcript (April 17, 1937), 1; Catholic World, CXLV (May, 1937), 250; Christian Science Monitor (April 28, 1937), 11; Commonweal, XXV (April 2, 1937), 650; Nation, CXLIV (March 27, 1937), 358; New Republic, XCI (May 19, 1937), 54; New York Times (April 4, 1937), 3; Pratt Institute Quarterly (Autumn, 1937), 22; Saturday Review of Literature, XV (April 3, 1937), 14; Springfield Republican (April 4, 1937), 7; Time, XXIX (March 29, 1937), 76; Wisconsin Library Bulletin, XXXIII (June, 1937), 111.

———. The March of Literature from Confucius' Day to Our Own. New York, 1938.
Reviewed: Booklist, XXXV (Nov. 15, 1938), 95; Books, N.Y. Herald Tribune (Oct. 23, 1938), 7; Boston Transcript (Oct. 29, 1938), 2; Christian Science Monitor (Nov. 23, 1938), 11; Cleveland Open Shelf (Nov., 1938), 19; Commonweal, XXIX (Nov. 4, 1938), 50; Forum, C (Nov., 1938), iv; New Republic, XCVI (Oct. 26, 1938), 339; New York Times (Oct. 9, 1938), 2; New Yorker, XIV (Oct. 1, 1938), 79; Saturday Review of Literature, XVIII (Oct. 8, 1938), 12, and (Oct. 22, 1938), 9; Springfield Republican (Oct. 16, 1938), 7; Time, XXXII (Oct. 17, 1938), 79.

———. Mightier Than the Sword; Memories and Criticisms of Henry James, Joseph Conrad, Thomas Hardy, H. G. Wells, Stephen Crane, D. H. Lawrence, John Galsworthy, Ivan Turgenev, W. H. Hudson, Theodore Dreiser, and Algernon Charles Swinburne. London, 1938.

———. Parade's End. New York, 1950 (the Tietjens tetralogy, with an introduction by Robie Macauley).
Reviewed: Atlantic, CLXXXVI (Oct., 1950), 84; Chicago Sunday Tribune (Sept. 17, 1950), 5; College English, XII (Nov., 1950), 125; Kenyon Review, XIII (Winter, 1951), 142–147; Library Journal (Sept. 1, 1950), 1406; N.Y. Herald Tribune Weekly Book Review (Oct. 1, 1950), 4; N.Y. Times Book Review (Sept. 17, 1950), 1, 22; Saturday Review of Literature (Oct. 21, 1950), 16; Sewanee Review, LIX (Jan.-Mar., 1951), 154–161; Yale Review, XL (Autumn, 1950), 189.

2. WRITINGS IN PERIODICALS BY FORD:

Hueffer, Ford Madox. "Dante Gabriel Rossetti and His Family Letters," Living Age, CCIX (April 4, 1896), 53–59.

———. "Millais and Rossetti Exhibitions," Fortnightly Review, LXIX (February, 1898), 189–196.

A WORKING BIBLIOGRAPHY

———. "Sir Edward Burne-Jones," *Contemporary Review*, LXXIV (August, 1898), 181–195; also *Living Age*, CCXIX (October 8, 1898), 110–121.

———. "In Adversity," *Living Age*, CCXX (February 18, 1899), 468 (poem).

———. "For the Bookplate of a Married Couple," *Living Age*, CCXXVI (August 18, 1900), 427 (poem).

———. "Gipsy and the Cuckoo," *Living Age*, CCXXVI (September 29, 1900), 808 (poem).

———. "Lullaby," *Living Age*, CCXXVII (October 6, 1900), 14 (poem).

———. "Mother," *Fortnightly Review*, LXXV (April, 1901), 741–746.

———. "To Christina at Nightfall," *Athenaeum 1901*, II (October 26, 1901), 588 (poem).

———. "To a Tudor Tune," *Living Age*, CCXXXII (January 4, 1902), 64; also *Current Literature*, XXXII (May, 1902), 576 (poem).

———. "At the End of a Phase," *Living Age*, CCXXXIII (April 12, 1902), 128 (poem).

———. "Difference," *Cornhill*, XXCVIII (August, 1903), 276–288.

———. "Old Conflict," *Living Age*, CCXL (February 6, 1904), 354–363.

———. "Collected Poems of Christina Rossetti," *Fortnightly Review*, XXCI (March, 1904), 393–405; also *Living Age*, CCXLI (April 16, 1904), 158–167.

———. "Every Man: A Sequence," *Living Age*, CCXLVI (July 1, 1905), 2 (poem).

———. "Philosophy of a Lover and a Gentleman," *Living Age*, CCXLVI (September 9, 1905), 642 (poem).

———. "Dr. Richard Garnett: In Memoriam," *Bookman* (London), XXX (June, 1906), 89–91.

———. "Mid Winter Night," *Living Age*, CCXLIX (June 9, 1906), 578 (poem).

———. "After All," *McClure's*, XXVIII (February, 1907), 28 (poem).

———. "Individualist," *Living Age*, CCLVII (June 20, 1908), 760–762.

———. "Fascination of London," *Putnam's Magazine*, VI (May, 1909), 213–215.

———. "Call: A Tale of Passion," *English Review*, III (August—November, 1909), 93–134, 283–314, 460–476, 629–652.

———. "Modern Poetry," *Living Age*, CCLXIV (January 15, 1910), 176–184.

———. "Old Circle," *Harper's*, CXX (February, 1910), 364–372.

———. "Pre-Raphaelite Reminiscences," *Harper's*, CXX (April, 1910), 762–768.

———. "Group of Pre-Raphaelite Poets," *Harper's*, CXXI (October, 1910), 778–785.

———. "William Holman Hunt," *Fortnightly Review*, XCIV (October, 1910), 657–665; also *Living Age*, CCLXVII (November 12, 1910), 387–393.

———. "Christina Rossetti," *Fortnightly Review*, XCV (March, 1911), 422–429.

———. "Master's and Music," *Harper's*, CXXII (March, 1911), 617–626.

———. "Reisenberg," *English Review*, VIII (April, 1911), 24–25.

———. "Pace That Kills," *Atlantic*, CVII (May, 1911), 670–673.

———. "In High Germany," *Fortnightly Review*, XCVI (December, 1911), 1069-1071 (poem).
———. "Joseph Conrad," *English Review*, X (December, 1911), 68-83.
———. "Investiture of the American Cardinals," *Collier's*, XLVIII (December 16, 1911), 10-12.
———. "Fun of Genius," *English Review*, XIII (December, 1912), 52-63.
———. "De Morgan's When Ghost Meets Ghost," *Living Age*, CCXXC (March 28, 1914), 818-821.
———. "Trois Hours de Permission," *Living Age*, CCXCI (November 4, 1916), 310-312.
———. "What the Orderly Day Saw," *Poetry*, IX (March, 1917), 293-294 (poem).
———. "One Last Prayer," *English Review*, XXVI (April, 1918), 289 (poem).
———. "Sanctuary" and "Silver Music," *Poetry*, XII (April, 1918), 19-20 (poems).
———. "Iron Music," *Literary Digest*, LIX (October 5, 1918), 37 (poem).
———. "Old Houses of Flanders," *Literary Digest*, LIX (October 5, 1918), 37 (poem).
———. "Ypres Salient," *Literary Digest*, LIX (October 5, 1918), 37 (poem).
———. "Claire de lune," *Current Opinion*, LXV (November, 1918), 329-330.
———. "English Country," *New Statesman*, XIII (August 23—September 6, 1919), 518-519, 542-543, 565-566.
———. "Henri Gaudier, The Story of a Low Tea-Shop," *English Review*, XXIX (October, 1919), 297-304.
———. "After the Rain," *Living Age*, CCCIII (October 18, 1919), 187 (poem).
———. "Thus to Revist," *English Review*, XXXI-XXXII (July—September, 1920, November—December, 1920, February—April, 1921), 5-13, 107-117, 209-217, 395-404, 506-514, 116-121, 216-222, 311-319; also in *Dial*, LXIX-LXX (July—September, 1920, January, 1921), 52-60, 132-141, 239-246, 14-23.
———. "House," *Poetry*, XVII (March, 1921), 291-310 (poem).
Ford, Ford Madox. "Haughty and Proud Generation," *Yale Review*, XI (July, 1922), 703-717.
Hueffer, Ford Madox. "Rhymes for a Child," *Spectator*, CXXIX (September 16, 1922), 367.
Ford, Ford Madox. "Rhymes for a Child: Seven Sleepers," *Living Age*, CCXV (November 4, 1922), 304.
Hueffer, Ford Madox. "Ulysses and the Handling of Indecencies," *English Review*, XXXV (December, 1922), 538-548.
Ford, Ford Madox. "Seven Shepherds," *Poetry*, XXII (June, 1923), 122 (poem).
———. "Mister Bosphorus and the Muses," *Poet Lore*, XXXIV (December, 1923), 532-613.
———. "Stevie," *Literary Review*, IV (July 12, 1924), 881-882.
———. "Young America Abroad," *Saturday Review of Literature*, I (September 20, 1924), 21-22.
———. "From a Paris Quay," *Literary Review*, V (December 13, 1924), 1-2.

A WORKING BIBLIOGRAPHY

———. "Poeta Nascitur," *Poetry*, XXIX (March, 1927), 326–333.
———. "Traveler's Tales," *Harper's*, CLIV (April, 1927), 546–553.
———. "Lordly Dish," *Harper's*, CLV (June, 1927), 55–63.
———. "Pax!," *Nineteenth Century and After*, CII (August, 1927), 145–157; also *Harper's*, CLV (September, 1927), 422–430.
———. "Mascot," *London Mercury*, XVII (December, 1927), 133–146.
———. "Tiger, Tiger," *Bookman*, LXVI (January, 1928) 495–498.
———. "Romantic Detective," *Yale Review*, XVII (April, 1928), 517–537.
———. "O Hygeia," *Harper's*, CLVI (May, 1928), 768–776.
———. "On Conrad's Vocabulary," *Bookman*, LXVII (June, 1928), 405–408.
———. "Miracle," *Yale Review*, XVIII (December, 1928), 320–331.
———. "English Novel," *Bookman*, LXVIII–LXIX (December, 1928—March, 1929), 369–375, 538–547, 672–682, 69–79.
———. "Working with Conrad," *Yale Review*, XVIII (June, 1929), 699–715.
———. "René Béhaine," *Saturday Review of Literature*, VI (October 12, 1929), 260.
———. "Miracle," *English Review*, LI (August, 1930), 243–252.
———. "Three Americans and a Pole," *Scribner's*, XC (October, 1931), 379–386.
———. "Stage in American Literature," *Bookman*, LXXIV (December, 1931), 371–376.
———. "Buckshee: Compagnie Transatlantique," "Fleuve Profonde," "Chez Nos Amis," "L'Interprete au Careau Rouge," "Champetre Ripostes," "Vers L'Oubli," *Poetry*, XXXIX (February—March, 1932), 233–245, 317–323 (poems).
———. "I Revisit the Riviera," *Harper's*, CLXVI (December, 1932), 65–76.
———. "For Poorer Travelers," *Harper's*, CLXVI (April, 1933), 620–630.
———. "Contrasts," *Atlantic Monthly*, CLI (May, 1933), 559–569.
———. "John Galsworthy and George Moore," *English Review*, LVII (August, 1933), 130–142.
———. "Pre-Raphaelite Epitaph," *Saturday Review of Literature*, X (January 20, 1934), 417–419.
———. "Techniques," *Southern Review*, I, 1 (July, 1935), 20–35.
———. "Hands Off the Arts," *American Mercury*, XXXIV (April, 1935), 402–408.
———. "Conrad and the Sea," *American Mercury*, XXXV (June, 1935), 169–176.
———. "Dicennial," *London Mercury*, XXXII (July, 1935), 223–231.
———. "Small Producer," *American Mercury*, XXXV (August, 1935), 445–450.
———. "Master," *American Mercury*, XXXVI (November, 1935), 315–327.
———. "The Master," *London Mercury*, XXXIII (November, 1935), 46–52.
———. "Stephen Crane," *American Mercury*, XXXVII (January, 1936), 36–45.
———. "W. H. Hudson," *American Mercury*, XXXVII (March, 1936), 306–317.
———. "Galsworthy," *American Mercury*, XXXVII (April, 1936), 448–459.

————. "H. G. Wells," *American Mercury*, XXXVIII (May, 1936), 48–58.
————. "D. H. Lawrence," *American Mercury*, XXXVIII (June, 1936), 167–179.
————. "Thomas Hardy," *American Mercury*, XXXVIII (August, 1936), 438–448. Reply to reader's query, XXXIX (November, 1936), xx, xxii.
————. "Latin Quarter," *London Mercury*, XXXIV (September, 1936), 391–396 (poem).
————. "Turgenev, the Beautiful Genius," *American Mercury*, XXXIX (September, 1936), 41–50.
————. "London Revisited," *London Mercury*, XXXV (December, 1936), 177–184.
————. "Swinburne," *American Mercury*, XL (January, 1937), 104–115.
————. "Theodore Dreiser," *American Mercury*, XL (April, 1937), 488–496.
————. "Flame in Stone," *Poetry*, L (June, 1937), 158–161.
————. "Sad State of Publishing," *Forum and Century*, XCVIII (August–September, 1937), 83–86, 126–128.
————. "Food," *Forum and Century*, XCIX (April, 1938), 241–247.
————. "Paris Letter," *Kenyon Review*, I (Winter, 1939), 18–31.
————. "Memories of Oscar Wilde," *Saturday Review of Literature*, XX (May 27, 1939), 3–4.
————. "Travel Notes," *Saturday Review of Literature*, XX (June 10, 1939), 13–14.

3. BOOKS WITH CONTRIBUTIONS BY FORD:

Exhibition of the Works of Ford Madox Brown Held at the Grafton Galleries, 8 Grafton Street, London, W. London, 1897 (the introduction is signed by Ford Madox Hueffer, and the notes to some of the pictures are signed with his initials.

Martindale, E., trans. *Stories From De Maupassant*. London, 1903 (Preface by F. M. Hueffer).

Hutchings, W. W. *London Town Past and Present*. London, 1909 ("The Future in London," by F. M. Hueffer, II, 1094–1110).

Hunt, Violet, and Mrs. Alfred Hunt. *The Governess*. London, 1912 (According to Naumburg, this book written by Violet Hunt and her mother has an introduction by Hueffer. Naumberg cites Douglas Goldring's *South Lodge* for his contention that Violet Hunt's Preface to *Thornicraft's Model* acknowledges this introduction).

Hunt, Violet. *The Desirable Alien at Home in Germany*. London, 1913 (Preface and two additional chapters by F. M. Hueffer).

Transatlantic Stories. London, 1926 (selections from the *transatlantic review*, with an introduction by F. M. Ford).

Asch, Nathan. *Love in Chartres*. London, 1927 (an introduction by F. M. Ford).

Rhys, Jean. *The Left Bank and Other Stories*. New York and London, 1927 (Preface by F. M. Ford).

Conrad, Joseph. *The Sisters*. New York, 1928 (an introduction by F. M. Ford).

Chadourne, Marc. *Vasco*, trans. Eric Sutton. New York, 1928 (Preface by F. M. Ford).

A WORKING BIBLIOGRAPHY

Acland, Peregrine. *All Else is Folly; A Tale of War and Passion.* New York, 1929 (Preface by F. M. Ford).
Conrad, Joseph. *A Conrad Memorial Library.* New York, 1929 (an edition limited to 501 copies, taken from the collection of George T. Keating; an introduction by F. M. Ford to *The Inheritors*, pp. 74-83).
Defoe, Daniel. *The Life and Strange Surprising Adventures of Robinson Crusoe of York, Mariner.* San Francisco, 1930 (Limited Editions Club edition, an introduction by F. M. Ford).
Imagist Anthology 1930. New York, 1930 (contains an introduction by F. M. Ford entitled "Those Were the Days," pp. 13-21 as well as two poems, "Winter-Night Song," pp. 167-169, and "Two Songs," pp. 171-173).
Hemingway, Ernest. *A Farewell to Arms.* New York, 1932 (Modern Library edition, with an introduction by F. M. Ford).
Pound, Ezra. *The Cantos of Ezra Pound.* New York, 1933 (contains testimonials by Ernest Hemingway, T. S. Eliot, Hugh Walpole, Archibald MacLeish, James Joyce, as well as by F. M. Ford, pp. 13-16).
Schreiber, Georges, ed. *Portraits and Self Portraits.* Boston, 1936 (autobiographical sketch by F. M. Ford, pp. 30-40).
Béhaine, René. *The Survivors,* trans. E. Crankshaw. Boston and New York, 1938 (Preface by F. M. Ford).
Authors Take Sides on the Spanish War. London, 1937 (statement by F. M. Ford).

4. TRANSLATIONS BY FORD:

Loti, Pierre. *The Trail of the Barbarians, being "L'Outrage des Barbares,"* trans. F. M. Hueffer. London, 1917.
Carco, Francis. *Perversity,* trans. F. M. Ford. Chicago, 1928 (translation disavowed by Ford, now ascribed to Jean Rhys).

5. PERIODICALS EDITED BY FORD:

English Review, I, 1 to IV, 3 (December, 1908—February, 1910).
transatlantic review, I, 1 to II, 6 (January—December, 1924).

6. BOOKS ABOUT FORD:

Aldington, Richard. *Life for Life's Sake.* New York, 1941, pp. 149-159.
Bowen, Stella. *Drawn From Life.* London, 1940.
Cassell, Richard A. *Ford Madox Ford: A Study of His Novels.* Baltimore, 1962.
Ellis, Seth Howard. *The Contributions of Ford Madox Ford to Twentieth Century Narrative Technique.* Dissertation, University of Southern California, Los Angeles, 1958.
Goldring, Douglas. *Odd Man Out.* London, 1935.
———. *South Lodge.* London, 1943.
———. *The Last Pre-Raphaelite; A Record of the Life and Writings of Ford Madox Ford.* London, 1948.
Reviewed: *Spectator* (May 28, 1948), p. 654.

———. *Trained For Genius, The Life and Writings of Ford Madox Ford.* New York, 1949 (American edition of *The Last Pre-Raphaelite*). Reviewed: *Booklist*, XLV (July 1, 1949), 375; *Christian Science Monitor* (June 20, 1949), 14; *College English*, XI (October, 1949), 57; *Commonweal*, L (June 17, 1949), 249; *Kenyon Review*, XI (Autumn, 1949), 696–699; *Kirkus*, XVII (April 15, 1949), 220; *Nation*, CLXIX (July 30, 1949), 110; *New Republic*, CXX (May 30, 1949), 18; *N.Y. Herald Tribune Weekly Book Review* (May 22, 1949), 1; *New York Times* (June 12, 1949), 10; *New Yorker*, XXV (May 28, 1949), 98; San Francisco *Chronicle* (June 3, 1949), 14; *Saturday Review of Literature*, XXXII (June 25, 1949), 11; *Springfield Republican* (June 26, 1949), 6; *TLS* (December 18, 1948), 708.

Gose, Elliot Bickley, Jr. *Passion and the Tradition: A Critical Appraisal of Ford Madox Ford.* Dissertation, Cornell University, Ithaca, 1954.

Greene, Graham. *The Lost Childhood.* London, 1951, pp. 89–91.

Harvey, David Dow. *Ford Madox Ford, 1873-1939: A Bibliography.* Princeton, 1963.

Herndon, Richard James. *The Collaboration of Joseph Conrad with Ford Madox Ford.* Dissertation, Stanford University, 1957.

Hind, C. Lewis. *More Authors and I.* London, 1922, pp. 152–158.

Hunt, Violet. *The Flurried Years.* London, 1926; Published as *I Have This to Say.* New York, 1926.

Kenner, Hugh, *The Poetry of Ezra Pound.* London, 1953, 174–175, 264–272, 307–308.

———. *Gnomon Essays on Contemporary Literature.* New York, 1958, pp. 144–170.

Lid, R. W. *Time in the Novels of Ford Madox Ford.* Dissertation, University of Michigan, Ann Arbor, 1958.

———. *Ford Madox Ford: The Essence of His Art.* Berkeley and Los Angeles, 1964.

Ludwig, Richard. *Letters of Ford Madox Ford.* Princeton, 1965.

MacShane, Frank. *The Life and Work of Ford Madox Ford.* New York, 1965.

Meixner, John Albert. *Ford Madox Ford's Novels: A Critical Study.* Minneapolis, 1962.

Ohmann, Carol. *Ford Madox Ford: From Apprentice to Craftsman.* Middletown, Conn., 1964.

Pegis, Anton George. *The Technique of Ford Madox Ford: His Theory and Practice.* Dissertation, University of Denver, 1956.

Pound, Ezra. *Pavannes and Divisions.* New York, 1918, pp. 101, 107, 111, 129–137.

Putnam, Samuel. *Paris Was Our Mistress: Memoirs of a Lost and Found Generation.* New York, 1947, pp. 118–127.

Sturgeon, Mary C. *Studies of Contemporary Poets.* New York, 1916, pp. 122–135; revised and enlarged edition published London, 1920.

Wells, Herbert George. *Experiment in Autobiography.* New York, 1934, pp. 525–526, 527, 530–531.

Wiley, Paul. *Novelist of Three Worlds: Ford Madox Ford.* Syracuse, 1962.

Young, Kenneth. *Ford Madox Ford*, no. 74 in series entitled "Writers and Their Work." London and New York, 1956.

Zabel, Morton Dauwen. *Craft and Character.* New York, 1957, pp. 253–263.

A WORKING BIBLIOGRAPHY

7. WRITINGS ABOUT FORD IN PERIODICALS:

Aiken, Conrad. "Fiction of Rhythm," *Dial*, LXV (November 16, 1918), 417–418.
Allen, Walter. "The Tietjens Books," *New Statesman and Nation*, XXXI (April 20, 1946), 285.
Bartlett, P. A. "Letters of Ford Madox Ford," *Saturday Review of Literature*, XXIV (August 2, 1941), 3–4, 14.
Bishop, J. P. "Poems of Ford Madox Ford," *Poetry*, L (September, 1937), 336–341.
Blackmur, R. P. "The King Over the Water: Notes on the Novels of Ford Madox Hueffer," *Princeton University Library Chronicle* (April, 1948), 123–127.
Bornhauser, Fred. "Ford As Art Critic," *Shenandoah*, IV (Spring, 1953), 51–59.
Bronner, M. "Ford Maddox Hueffer—Impressionist," *Bookman*, XLIV (October, 1916), 170–175.
Brower, J. "Ford Madox Ford: A Memoir," *Saturday Review of Literature*, XX (July 8, 1939), 8.
Crankshaw, Edward. "Ford Madox Ford," *National Review*, CXXXI (August, 1948), 160–167.
Dreiser, Theodore. "The Saddest Story," *New Republic*, III (June 12, 1915), 155–156.
Espey, J. J. "Epigraph to T. S. Eliot's Burbank with a Baedeker: Bleistein with a Cigar," *American Literature*, XXIX (January, 1958), 483–484 (influence study).
Firebaugh, J. J. "Tietjens and the Tradition," *Pacific Spectator*, VI, 1 (1952), 23–32.
Gerber, Helmut E. "Ford Madox Ford," *English Fiction in Transition*, I (Fall-Winter, 1957), 2, 20–22; I (Fall-Winter, 1957), 39–48; I (Spring-Summer, 1958), 2–19.
Goldring, Douglas. "Ford Madox Ford," *New Statesman and Nation*, XVIII (November 11, 1939), 679–680.
Goldring, Douglas. "Portrait of an Editor," *English Review*, LIII (December, 1931), 820–829.
Gordon, John D. "What's in a Name? Authors and Their Pseudonyms," *Bulletin of the New York Public Library*, LX (1956), 107–128 (contains material on some of Ford's pseudonymous books from the Berg Collection).
Gorman, Herbert. "Ford Madox Ford: A Portrait in Impressions," *Bookman*, LXVII (March, 1928), 56–60.
———. "Ford Madox Ford: The Personal Side," *Princeton University Library Chronicle*, IX (April, 1948), 119–122.
Gose, Elliot B., Jr. "The Strange Irregular Rhythm: An Analysis of *The Good Soldier*," *PMLA*, LXXII (June, 1957), 494–509.
———. "Reality to Romance: A Study of Ford's *Parade's End*," *College English*, XVII (May, 1956), 445–450.
Greene, Graham. "Dark Backward: A Footnote," *London Mercury*, XXXII (October, 1935), 562–565.
———. "Ford Madox Ford," *Spectator*, CLXIII (July 7, 1939), 11.
Gris, J. "Portrait," *Saturday Review of Literature*, III (December 11, 1926), 419.

Hafley, James. "The Moral Structure of 'The Good Soldier,' " *Modern Fiction Studies*, V (Summer, 1959), 121–128.
Harris, Markham. "A Memory of Ford Madox Ford," *Prairie Schooner*, XXIX (Winter, 1955), 252–263.
Hicks, Granville. "Ford Madox Ford—A Neglected Contemporary," *Bookman*, LXXII (December, 1930), 364–370.
Hynes, Samuel. "The Epistomology of *The Good Soldier*," *Sewanee Review*, LXIX (Spring, 1961), 225–235.
Kenner, Hugh. "Remember That I Have Remembered," *Hudson Review*, III, 4 (Winter, 1951), 609 ff.
Lid, R. W. "Tietjens in Disguise," *Kenyon Review*, XXII (Spring, 1960), 265–274.
Ludwig, Richard M. "The Reputation of Ford Madox Ford," *PMLA*, LXXVI (December, 1961), 544–551.
McFadyean, Andrew. "Ford Madox Ford," *TLS* (January 8, 1949), 25.
Macauley, Robie. "The Dean in Exile: Notes On Ford Madox Ford as Teacher," *Shenandoah*, IV (Spring, 1953), 43–48.
———. "The Good Ford," *Kenyon Review*, XI (1949), 269–288.
———. "Observations on Technique: Some Notes on a Lecture Given by FMF at Olivet College in June, 1938," *Shenandoah*, IV (Spring, 1953), 49–50.
Macshane, Frank. "Ford Madox Ford," *Spectator* (May 14, 1954), p. 582.
———. "Pattern of Ford Madox Ford," *New Republic*, CXXXII (April 4, 1955), 16–17.
Meixner, John A. "The Saddest Story," *Kenyon Review*, XXII (Spring, 1960), 234–264.
Mizener, Arthur. "A Large Fiction," *Kenyon Review*, XII (Winter, 1951), 142–147.
Naumburg, Edward, Jr. "A Collector Looks at Ford Madox Ford," *Princeton University Library Chronicle*, IX (April, 1948), 105–118.
———. "A Catalogue of a Ford Madox Ford Collection," *Princeton University Library Chronicle*, IX (April, 1948), 134–165.
New Directions, Number Seven (1942), pp. 441–494. (This issue contains "Homage to Ford Madox Ford—A Symposium," with articles by Richard Aldington, Sherwood Anderson, William Rose Benet, John Peale Bishop, Joseph Brewer, Carl Van Doren, Paul Engle, Granville Hicks, Christopher Morley, Katherine Anne Porter, Ezra Pound, etc., along with a short check list by Edward Naumburg, Jr.).
Newsweek Staff. "Ford Revisited," *Newsweek*, XXXVIII (September 17, 1951), 94.
Obituary. Ford's obituary appeared in the following publications: *Newsweek*, XIV (July 3, 1939), 33; *Nineteenth Century and After*, CXXVI (August, 1939), 178–181; *Poetry*, LIV (August, 1939), 290; *Publisher's Weekly*, CXXXVI (July 1, 1939), 24; *Time*, XXXIV (July 3, 1939), 47; *Wilson Library Bulletin*, XIV (September, 1939) 6.
Prince, L. M. "Writings of Ford Madox Hueffer," *Poet Lore*, XXXI (September, 1920), 432–453.
———. "Ford Madox Ford," *University of California Chronicle*, XXVII (October, 1925), 346–365.
Rascoe, B. "Contemporary Reminiscences," *Arts and Decoration*, XXIV (February, 1926), 57, and XXVI (December, 1926), 1955.

Redman, Ben Ray. "Ford Madox Ford in His True Colors," *Saturday Review of Literature*, XXXXII (June 25, 1949), 11.
Schorer, Mark. "The Good Novelist in *The Good Soldier*," *Princeton University Library Chronicle*, IX (April, 1948), 128-133; also appeared in *Horizon*, XX (August, 1949), 132-138, slightly revised.
Scott-James, R. A. "Ford Madox Ford When He Was Hueffer," *South Atlantic Quarterly*, LVII (Spring, 1958), 236-253.
Seiden, Melvin. "The Living Dead—VI. Ford Madox Ford and His Tetralogy," *London Magazine*, VI (1959), 45-55.
Time Staff. "Uncle Toby on Kanchenjunga," *Time*, LVI (September 25, 1950), 102.
Walter, E. V. "Political Sense of Ford Madox Ford," *New Republic*, CXXXIV (March 26, 1956), 17-19.
Washburne, C. C. "Sophistication," *Nineteenth Century and After*, XCV (October, 1925), 605-613.
Whitmore, J. B. "Ford Madox Ford," *TLS* (February 5, 1949), p. 93.
Zabel, Morton Dauwen. "Ford Madox Ford," *Nation*, CLXIX (July 30, 1949), 110-111.

society. These nominal aristocrats, in turn, gave way to the politicians, who were equally cynical and without values, but who were also a far greater threat to society by virtue of the power at their disposal. Finally, during the nineteen-thirties the emerging political dictators gave this power a new and especially violent expression.

Misdirected and evasive heroism became one of the dominant motifs in Ford's work, but it was a motif that was given complexity by the author's dual response to the public hero and his proposal of an alternative. This complexity required that Ford develop a technique which would register his double attitude, and which would render the simultaneous dignity and ineffectiveness of his major characters. Concentration on these public heroes, along with the use of the double perspective, and the gradual movement toward the alternative of private heroism became the distinctive features of Ford's work. This study is an examination of the development (and the techniques through which it evolved) of the limited hero and reveals a unity and pattern in all of Ford's work that has not yet been perceived. All of which helps clarify his special place in the world of late nineteenth and twentieth-century letters.

Norman Leer received his Ph.D. in English from Indiana University. He has contributed to numerous scholarly journals on a variety of subjects, taught in the State University of New York at Stony Brook, and is presently a member of the English Department in Beloit College.

Ever since 1950, when the Tietjens tetralogy under the title of *Parade's End* received its first one-volume publication, there has been a marked upsurge of interest in the writings of Ford Madox Ford. In England, Graham Greene is directing a project to reissue all of Ford's works, and Ford scholarship has been given fresh impetus by the recent publication of important critical works. Such an increased interest in Ford indicates that he is now being taken seriously in his own right, and is no longer dismissed as the writer who collaborated with Joseph Conrad. The growth of Ford scholarship is testimony to his uniqueness as a writer, and at the same time a sign that the provocative nature of his ideas is gaining greater recognition.

Ford was acutely conscious of the collapse of the Victorian world as well as of the violent and unstable years which followed. He viewed the Victorian period and its aftermath in terms of figures, such as Ruskin or Carlyle, whom he saw as public heroes and whom he blamed for their tendency toward verbal abstractions at the expense of effectiveness in countering the breakdown of their world. Partly because of his preoccupation with the failure of the Great Victorians, Ford came to see not only the Victorian era but the world during his lifetime in terms of the heroic figure. In his eyes, the Victorian idealists were supplanted—in the years before World War I—by leaders who were without values and who themselves reflected the corruption of their